GETTING (MORE OF)
WHAT YOU WANT

GETTING (MORE OF) WHAT YOU WANT

How the Secrets of
Economics and Psychology
Can Help You Negotiate
Anything, in Business
and in Life

MARGARET A. NEALE
AND
THOMAS Z. LYS

BASIC BOOKS
A Member of the Perseus Books Group
New York

Books published by Basic Books are available at special discounts for bulk purchases in the United States by corporations, institutions, and other organizations. For more information, please contact the Special Markets Department at the Perseus Books Group, 2300 Chestnut Street, Suite 200, Philadelphia, PA 19103, or call (800) 810-4145, ext. 5000, or e-mail special .markets@perseusbooks.com.

Designed by Milenda Lee

A CIP catalog record for this book is available from the Library of Congress.
ISBN: 978-0-465-05072-7 (hardcover)
ISBN: 978-0-465-04063-6 (e-book)
10 9 8 7

To Franziska and Al, our parents—both passed and present—and the four-legged family members, all of whom have made our lives so much more than we could have ever imagined.

CONTENTS

PART TWO—THE NEGOTIATION

PREFACE

I n early 1996, when we were both teaching at the Kellogg Graduate School of Management at Northwestern University, one of our students approached Thomas for help in responding to a business opportunity.[1] A physician had offered the student, a product manager for a large pharmaceutical company, the opportunity to purchase a patent the company had been using for the last ten years in the production of one of its most profitable medical test kits. In the past, the physician had received annual royalties based on successfully produced kits. And each royalty cycle, the physician and the company disagreed over the exact number of successful kits that had been produced. Ostensibly tired of these annual disputes, the physician was offering to sell the patent to the corporation for the remainder of its seven-year life. His asking price was $3,500,000.

Before responding to the physician's offer, our student wanted Thomas to check his analysis of the most his corporation should be willing to pay based on their estimate of the expected value of the royalty payments for the next seven years. The analysis was quite involved, and revealed that the maximum amount the corporation could pay for the patent was $4,100,000. At that price, there was no difference to the company between owning the patent and continuing to lease it from the doctor.

Margaret walked in as the student was summarizing his analysis: he could accept the physician's offer and realize an immediate profit of $600,000 ($4,100,000 – $3,500,000). Or, if he were to negotiate, he could likely secure an even better deal by not accepting the doctor's first offer: "If I could get him to agree to $3,000,000 or so, I would realize a $1,000,000 benefit for my company," said the product manager. "This will make me look so good—my next promotion is virtually assured."

"Just a second," said Margaret, who had been reviewing the details of the offer. "You're not ready to negotiate." The student was surprised—and was even more so when Thomas commented: "She's right."

Our student was way ahead of himself. In his mind, he was already enjoying the $1,000,000 benefit of this prospective deal. Because he was so taken with the potential benefit and what that could mean for his future with the company, he had come up with a number and then leaped to an obvious, but woefully incomplete, answer.

In the student's analysis, the deal looked like a sure win of at least $600,000 for the company—but from the doctor's perspective, the offer made no sense. Given the facts, he simply was asking for too little. "A deal should make sense to both sides—and this one doesn't," said Margaret, continuing, "and why, after ten years of leasing the patent to you, has he now decided he should sell?" Maybe, we suggested, the numbers alone didn't tell the full story.

Thomas stepped up to the white board where he and the student had done their calculations. Except this time, they looked at the deal from the doctor's perspective. That analysis showed that the expected present value of the payments to the physician for the next seven years under the current arrangement was approximately $5,000,000. "Why is he willing to make an opening bid of $3,500,000, when the 'status quo' is worth approximately $5,000,000 to him?" asked Margaret. Seeing where we were going, our student made a last-ditch effort to save his promotion: "Maybe the doctor can't do present values, or—"

"Or maybe he knows something you don't know," said Margaret.

Our student had fallen into a classic negotiation trap. He had focused on the analysis from his own perspective, ignoring the doctor's side. Caught up in the prospect of closing the deal, he became convinced by his initial, favorable computations and failed to do any due diligence.

Three psychological factors contributed to his behavior: the power of a familiar story, the confusion of accuracy and precision, and the inherent attraction of reaching an agreement. First, the company and the physician had a decade-long relationship, and our student was only too familiar with the patent and the difficulties that had arisen from the contract. It was easy for him to believe that the doctor had decided to sell the patent simply as a matter of convenience.

Second, our student had computed a value for the patent (to several decimal points) that made sense to him and promised a quick deal and a great return. Although his numbers were precise, he had done precious little to test their accuracy.

Finally, once people are negotiating—as they had already begun to do since the doctor had made the first offer—getting to "yes" often feels like success, even if accepting the deal were not in all parties' best interest. For example, negotiators are more likely to choose an outcome that is worse for them if that outcome is labeled "agreement" than if it is labeled "option A."[2] All of those factors made it easy for our student to take the next obvious step: Get the deal done and move on!

Driven by these psychological factors, the student might have rushed to close a deal with the physician—but after considering our advice, he decided to conduct some further analysis. After consulting with us, the company decided not to pursue the doctor's offer. In less than a year, the company was using a new patent (not developed by the doctor) that was superior to the original one. The original patent had become essentially worthless.[3] Systematically integrating psychological principles into economic calculations led to a superior outcome for both our student and his organization: He avoided wasting $3,500,000 and likely losing out on acquiring the new patent to boot. With our help, he took a more disciplined approach to calculating the economic value of the deal for both parties, while also acknowledging the psychological pressure to reach a deal—all of which ultimately led him to temper his initially bullish analysis. By integrating economic and psychological perspectives in this way, both our student and his company were able to get more of what they wanted: not only did they avoid losing $3,500,000 on a soon to be obsolete patent but it also allowed them to secure the rights to the new technology.

The negotiation perspective we present in this book dates back to 1994. That summer, the dean of the Kellogg School challenged us and our fellow faculty members to come up with interdisciplinary business approaches that prepared managers for the real world. Managerial decisions, the dean observed, do not fall neatly into the discipline-based silos of accounting, finance, organizational behavior, or marketing. Rather, successful managers must integrate knowledge of multiple fields.

The dean's challenge resonated with our own experience. Combining the insights from economics and psychology in our research had helped us understand the mistakes that organizational leaders often make and gave us insight into what they might do differently. In response, we developed a new course that incorporated systematic psychological responses with economic principles of decision making. The dean's challenge—and our course—foreshadowed a trend of linking behavioral and economic insights in business education—a trend that took off over the next decade.

Back in 1994, however, most of our colleagues thought our proposal to combine the psychology of organizations and economics into one course was crazy. Ironically, after hearing our proposal, the dean thought so as well. What possible benefit, he and many of our peers wondered, could come from abandoning the tenets of economic rationality—where reasonable, disciplined human beings made choices that maximized their utility—and try to incorporate the impulses that distract undisciplined individuals from doing what was best for them? Nevertheless (and indeed as psychological theories would predict), our colleagues' and the dean's skepticism only reinforced our resolve to make our experiment work, and we forged ahead.

As we developed a model for our integrated course, our combined backgrounds proved to be a major asset. They allowed us to develop a far more sophisticated model than each of us would have been able to create individually. Thomas's academic foundation is in classical economics and is based in the belief that people act rationally. From his point of view, people know exactly what they want in negotiations and other decision-making situations, and they engage in behaviors that help them achieve it. There is a direct connection between actions and outcomes as predicted by rational actors—*homo oeconomicus*—and everything else, psychology, irrationality, and the like fade to irrelevance and thus can, or even should, be ignored.

In contrast, Margaret's training focused on factors that get in the way of negotiators' ability to translate their wants into outcomes. In her view of negotiation, the parties' desires and demands often change, even in the absence of new information. Situational characteristics such as the parties' emotions, the powerful impact of past actions, and the idea of saving face predictably influence their behavior. In Margaret's world, negotiators often make choices that thwart their best interests.

As we worked together, we quickly learned to respect the insights that each discipline brings to the study and practice of decision-making generally and negotiation specifically. The economic perspective offers a benchmark by which we can judge our performance; while social psychology helps us understand, intervene, and incorporate the predictable—but not always rational—ways in which we and our counterparts behave: ways that can hamper our efforts to get more of what we want.

Much to our delight (and relief), the integrated class that we created at Kellogg proved to be a big success; Thomas even won the prestigious "best professor" designation in 1996. In large part, our success resulted from our ability to explain managerial successes and failures not as a result of luck but rather the systematic—and therefore, predictable—ways in which humans process and integrate information.

Unfortunately, we were able to offer our integrated course only twice, because Margaret soon left Kellogg for the Stanford Graduate School of Business. Yet the brief experience had convinced us of the value of our approach. In the years since, behavioral economics has hit its stride, moving from the fringes of its two parent disciplines to mainstream theory and empirical research, along the way having a considerable impact on public policy and producing best-selling books, including *Freakonomics, Predictably Irrational, Nudge,* and *Thinking Fast and Slow.* Behavioral economics has provided a new way of understanding the systematic failures of many individuals as they save for retirement, choose to become organ donors, or select among health plans. Behavioral economics is so useful because it integrates economics and psychology—something that we have been advocating in business for some two decades.

Despite its popularity, however, this kind of integrated thinking has not yet made its way to the field of negotiation. We hope this book will help to correct this oversight, and update the practice of negotiation for a new, more scientific age.

The standard approach to negotiation has long been based in large measure on the book *Getting to Yes* and its direct descendants. At first, *Getting to Yes* seems to be a perfect title for a book on negotiating. It implies that agreement is the outcome to which every negotiator should aspire: agreement = success. And the way to arrive at an agreement is to create value for your counterpart as well as yourself—the famous win-win solution. This leads to a clear recipe for success: Create as much value as you can, and you will get an agreement that will make you richer, wiser, happier, and maybe even a bit healthier. More specifically, *Getting to Yes* assumes that the more value you create, the more value you can claim and the less conflict will exist between you and your counterpart. After all, dividing up a larger pie will make everyone happier.

If all of this sounds too good to be true, it is. The *Getting to Yes* recipe, while relatively simple and palatable, cannot ensure negotiation success. As with any recipe, there is a specific set of ingredients and one ideal outcome. A recipe, however, sometimes limits the cook's capacity to innovate. The *Getting to Yes* framework ignores a critical point: Regardless of how much value you create in a negotiation, what's important is the amount of value you ultimately get. Ironically, viewing value creation as your primary focus will handicap your ability to claim value.

This is our first big point of departure from the *Getting to Yes* perspective: Good agreements are those that make you better off—that get you more of what you want. Agreements for the sake of agreeing are not so great, unless of course agreement is all you care about. But then, if that were the case, you wouldn't need to negotiate. You'd just need to accept your counterpart's first offer.

In this book we will show you how to think about, prepare, and implement strategies that will help you claim more value in your negotiations. The gold standard in negotiations is not how much value you and your counterparts create, but how much value available in the negotiation you are able to claim.

The second big difference between our book and those like *Getting to Yes* is that our advice and approach are based on decades of research on negotiation. Although stories and anecdotes alone may be entertaining, what is critical is knowing what, on average, works—and what doesn't. Leveraging the results of decades of empirical research, we have painstakingly analyzed different strategies to ascertain which are most effective—when. Anecdotes and isolated experiences cannot allow us to accurately measure performance; empirical research can. We use the results of these studies to help you make better choices in your negotiations and increase your odds of success.

The third critical contribution our book makes is showing that, by integrating insights from economics and psychology, you can better articulate what you want in each negotiation and influence your counterpart to accept outcomes that are in your interest. By understanding your counterpart, you can be more strategic in the information you share and more successful in the outcomes you attain. You will also get a better handle on what information you should share and what you should keep to yourself.

And you will be able to create value without handicapping your ability to get more of what you want.

Our unique integration of economics and psychology has yielded impressive results from the very beginning. The first time we taught our integrated negotiation course, we had much more to say about how to be a better negotiator, including predicting what negotiators would do that would make them worse off. This allowed us to develop strategies and create interventions that improved our students' performance in their negotiations.

Consider how you would respond when a buyer accepts your asking price for your used car. Are you pleased? Economic theory would suggest that you should be; after all, as the owner of the car you know more about it than anyone else, so your determination of its value—your asking price—is bound to be the most extreme. Yet more often than not you feel bad—you should have asked for more! Paradoxically, if the buyer had negotiated and you had agreed to less than your asking price, you would be more pleased with this deal. From an economic perspective, such a response makes no sense. You value money—and yet you are happier with less. From a psychological perspective, however, your response is predictable: People have expectations about how social interactions including negotiations should unfold. You make a first offer that you think is extreme. By accepting, your counterpart is making it clear that your offer wasn't as extreme as you had thought—and you are disappointed because you believe you could have asked for even more. Thus, a buyer acting strategically should not accept your first offer; rather she should negotiate—getting you to agree to less and making (both of) you happier. She used her knowledge of your expectations to get the car for less; while you are pleased because you got more than you expected, even though it was less than your first offer. Now that is a winning combination!

And that is just one example. Our method of thinking about negotiations can help you get more of what you want in your interactions with colleagues, superiors, spouses, friends, enemies and strangers. Here are a few examples of other situations in which our model of negotiation has been put to the test—and helped us get more of what we want, time after time.

THE DRY CLEANER. Margaret stopped by her favorite dry cleaner to pick up her laundry. The owner apologetically told Margaret he had lost a bedspread

she'd left to be cleaned. He offered to compensate her for the loss, and
asked what a reasonable amount would be. Margaret had a better solution.
Rather than taking the owner's money for the discounted value of the bedspread ($150), she said he could pay the price of a new bedspread ($250) in
service, rather than in cash. That way, both Margaret and the drycleaner
were better off. The cost to the drycleaner was also much less than the benefit to Margaret. She got $250 worth of dry cleaning while the dry cleaner
incurred costs of only $125—which was $25 less than the dollar amount he
would have paid; plus he retained Margaret's good will and continued
business. Not only had Margaret created additional value—she had also
claimed more of it in a way that made both parties better off.

THE NEPHEW. Thomas's nephew was living with him. He had not realized
how challenging a seventeen-year-old could be. He was especially surprised by the number of hours his nephew slept on the weekend—and was
uncertain whether this represented a real need for sleep or just a way to get
out of the chores that Thomas had assigned him. Early in his stay, Thomas's nephew wanted permission to drive Thomas's SUV on Saturday nights.
Rather than simply saying yes or no, Thomas had a slightly different proposal. Because Thomas wanted him to help out with chores—specifically
cutting grass in the pastures that surround the house—he proposed that
the nephew could use the car on Saturdays if he were willing to mow two
of the pastures each Saturday. Thomas knew that his nephew liked to sleep
in on Saturdays but he also had a love of large, noisy machines. Although
mowing the pastures was not particularly attractive, when Thomas yoked
the chore with the opportunity to drive the tractor and permission to use
the SUV, the package trumped his nephew's desire to sleep. This deal lasted
until the first snow.

THE FRIEND. A friend of Margaret's was bragging about the "smoking" deal
he'd just gotten on a new truck. As he described what he did—negotiating
the price of the new truck, then negotiating the trade-in of his old truck,
and then negotiating the extended warranty—Margaret knew that he
could likely have done much better. By combining all three issues (the
truck, the trade-in, and the warranty) into one negotiation rather than
three separate negotiations, he could have folded three issues of differing
value into the same negotiation—allowing him to gain more leverage
and obtain an even lower aggregate price. But because he was Margaret's

friend—and was so happy with his new truck and the deal that he got—she thought better of pointing out his missed opportunity!

THE DEAN. This fourth and final example is complex, but also revealing of the various factors that can complicate a negotiation. Quite awhile ago, the director of executive education at Kellogg asked Margaret to serve as the academic director for a custom executive program for a large law firm. Such a position would require significant extra work, but she agreed to take on the role after coming to what she thought was an agreement on the extra compensation. Later she learned that the director understood their agreement quite differently. Rather than arguing with him, Margaret decided that the benefits she would receive from running the program were not worth the conflict, so she offered to step down as director to allow another faculty member to take her place.

The director insisted that he wanted her as the program director, but just not at the price she thought they had agreed on. To overcome this impasse, he asked Margaret's boss, the school's dean, to pressure Margaret to accept his version of the compensation package. When called into the dean's office—an experience much like being called into the principal's office—Margaret realized that the dean also wanted her to take this position because of the importance of the program for the larger executive education initiative at Kellogg and the pressing deadline to present the program to the client. The dean gave Margaret a piece of paper and said, "Write down what you think you should get for designing and running the program. Whatever you write down, I will honor. In fact, I will instruct our accountant to pay whatever the note says."

At this point Margaret found herself in a position not uncommon in salary negotiations; two options immediately came to mind. She could write down the number that she thought they had agreed to in the first place. Or, if she approached the situation from a purely economic perspective, she might, now knowing how badly she was wanted, write down a much larger number. As it turns out, however, neither of these would have been the optimal solution.

By the time Margaret faced this decision, she had been studying negotiation for over fifteen years, and so she knew the problems that accompanied the most obvious two options. If she wrote down a large number, the dean might well have interpreted her behavior as a sign of greed—as taking advantage of the looming deadline and his strong desire to have her manage the program. His offer to let her name her price represented only the first move in a much larger interaction, in which the dean constantly updated his idea of Margaret's essential character, the extent of her self-interest, and her commitment to the institution. Although she might get the higher amount in the short run, in the long run, taking advantage of this situation would reveal to the dean a what-is-in-it-for-me-today orientation.

On the other hand, if Margaret had written down the original number she had expected as compensation—a number that, after all, she had once thought was a reasonable deal—she would be passing up the chance to extract more value from the interaction. The new circumstances—the dean's offer to let her choose her own compensation, and the director's willingness to use the dean to make sure she directed the program—immediately struck her as a chance to get more of what she wanted. In this case, it wasn't just about the money. She now had an opportunity to signal her good faith and offer the dean an opening to do the same.

And so, when the dean asked for her number, Margaret handed the paper back to him, saying, "You decide my compensation for designing and conducting this program; I will accept whatever you think is appropriate." The dean looked up surprised, and then smiled. Taking back the paper, he wrote down a figure and passed the paper back to her. His number actually exceeded the amount Margaret thought she had originally agreed to. The result: She organized and conducted the program, was well paid, and earned the admiration of her dean.

Margaret got more of what she wanted. She learned something about her dean. When given the opportunity to choose between taking advantage of her and acting generously, he chose the latter. That knowledge was at least as valuable as the money she got paid, particularly as she expected their relationship to continue for many years. And, just as important, her willingness to give the dean control over the situation by accepting his proposal sight-unseen made it perfectly clear to him that she expected he would value her long-term interests. So, in the end, she got the complete package: more money, a more favorable evaluation from the dean, and the reputation of someone who put the institution's interests above her own—a patriot.

For this strategy to be successful, of course, there must be a future in which the dean and Margaret expect to return to the negotiating table. Our advice would change drastically had this dispute taken place among parties unlikely to ever face each other again. In that case, the economist's solution of writing down the largest number likely to be accepted might prove the dominant solution. Of course, such a situation would make the dean's initial offer unlikely in the first place and would also increase the likelihood that—contrary to what he said—he would reject an offer that he deemed too large. There is a big difference in the information that you can glean from the interaction if you demand X dollars (and get paid that amount) versus what you can learn if your counterpart offers you that same X dollars. Finding out the true nature of your long-term partner is priceless!

Good negotiation outcomes require more than wishful thinking or luck—but knowing how to negotiate better is only one of the ingredients for success. It also takes discipline to get more of what you want. Discipline is a factor that is often overlooked in the development, care, and feeding of negotiators because it is not something one can learn from a book (or many books!).

To be disciplined requires practice—but to be effective you need to couple discipline with knowledge. You need to know when to walk away and have the discipline to follow through—even when it would be easier just to say "yes." It also takes discipline to gather information: to figure out what your counterpart wants, what information you should share—and how to share it (or not). It takes discipline, too, to think creatively about potential solutions that let your counterpart agree but that also make you better off than settling for a compromise. And it takes discipline to ask, and to engage your counterparts in the social exchange that is negotiation.

This is a book for people who seek out negotiations and for people who avoid negotiations—and for those who wonder if they could have gotten a better deal when they did. Our approach provides a roadmap for effective negotiating: to make you more knowledgeable about what it is you want in a negotiation and how to develop and implement a plan to achieve better outcomes, regardless of the metric that defines those outcomes. The value that you are interested in claiming is not limited to greater wealth. Perhaps what you want is a better reputation, a more predictable environment, more influence in your team or organizational decisions, more security in your job, or a hundred other dimensions of unique value to you. What you want can be as different as the situations you face. But in each and every situation, our integration of economic and psychological perspectives can help you get more of what you want.

In the chapters that follow, we share not only our own stories but also those of clients, students, and organizations, although we have changed names and identifying details to preserve anonymity. We have chosen each vignette specifically to embody the strategies and tactics that our research (and that of our colleagues around the world) has proved effective.

When you apply our approach to your negotiations, you will be able to answer the questions that arise at the various points in a negotiation.

- When should you negotiate? (Chapter 1)
- How do you know what a good deal is? (Chapter 2)
- At what point should you walk away? (Chapter 2)
- What are the trades you need to consider when you think about claiming value and creating value? (Chapters 3 and 4)
- What should you know (or attempt to discover) about your counterpart? (Chapter 5)
- What information will help you claim value—and what information will hurt? (Chapter 6)
- When should you make the first offer? (Chapter 7)
- How can you fill in gaps in your knowledge about your counterpart? (Chapter 8)
- What strategies can you use to encourage your counterpart to make concessions? (Chapters 9, 10, and 11)
- How should your strategies change when your counterpart is a team or when you are confronting multiple counterparts? (Chapter 12)
- When should you think about switching from negotiations to auctions? (Chapter 13)
- How should you end your negotiation? (Chapter 14)

This book is divided into two parts. The sequence of these parts corresponds to the order in which you would need them as you consider and implement a negotiation. The first part is effectively a boot camp. It contains the basics of negotiation, starting with how to decide whether to negotiate and moving on to the basic structures of most negotiations. Although the more experienced reader may wish to skim these chapters, they provide a framework on which we build in the main part of the book—so they are worth a look even for the most experienced reader. We focus on the strategic underpinnings of the information exchange neces-

sary for successful negotiations and the ways in which planning and preparation can facilitate getting more of what you want.

In the second part, we focus on the factors that push us and our
counterparts to behave in ways that complicate our negotiations. Are you
better off making or receiving the first offer? How should you respond to a
threat? What are the challenges that are unique to negotiating when you
are in a team? What should you do in negotiations that become emotional?
How can you mitigate the downside of not having power? In the final
chapter, we wrap up with a discussion of what you need to keep in mind
after you get to an agreement—especially how to reduce the chances that
you have left value on the table and how to reduce the chances that the deal
will get foiled in the last moments. In negotiations, as in so much else,
what may seem like the end is actually just another beginning—and just
another chance to get more of what you want.

PART ONE
THE BASICS

WHY AREN'T YOU NEGOTIATING?

The Choice to Negotiate

L ast summer, Margaret was sitting in her office when she received an email from her dean about a recent change in how her teaching credits would be computed. The provost (the dean's boss) wanted to create consistency across the university between the number of student contact hours in a course and the amount of course credit a faculty member received. And so from now on, the credit for all short courses would be reduced from 0.6 to 0.5 credits per course. Margaret was required to teach 3 units of courses per year as her regular teaching load. This seemingly innocuous memo meant that instead of teaching five courses, she would now have to teach six.

That got Margaret's attention. She immediately requested a meeting with the dean. She prepared questions and a couple of proposals beforehand, and at the meeting, she asked the dean to go into more detail about the reason for the change. He said he was simply complying with the provost's requirement for a common way of equating teacher course credit and student contact hours.

This gave Margaret the opening she needed. She had information that the dean did not have. The sessions in her short courses invariably went longer than their allotted time—creating a problem for students who expected each class to end on time. At first, she had seen this as a cost associated with teaching experiential courses. This had just been a problem for her students and, to a lesser extent, for Margaret. But after she received the dean's memo, she saw that she now had an opportunity. She was teaching more credits' worth of course time than her schedule reflected.

Margaret presented this information to the dean and then suggested another—better—solution. She proposed that the dean increase the scheduled class time (to reflect what was really happening) rather than reducing her teaching credit per course. The dean readily agreed to this proposal, and her course load went back to five courses.

There are over a hundred faculty members in the Stanford Business School—yet no one but Margaret saw this email as an opportunity to negotiate, as a problem to be solved. Why was she the only one? What is it about the situation that led her colleagues to give in despite all their complaining in the hallways? One explanation is that they did not see this exchange as the start of a negotiation. They did not think about creating a better outcome. After all, this was a decision handed down from the provost's office.

If you are like Margaret's colleagues, you probably think that negotiating is appropriate in only a limited set of situations. You negotiate only when a lot of money is involved, but you don't realize that the more common activities of daily life often give you chances to get more of what you want. For instance, you might be willing to negotiate over a car or a home purchase or when a contractual relationship is at stake, as in a new job. Yet even in these situations, some people just accept what is offered. Certainly, few people realize that shopping at a department store is an opportunity to negotiate. This was exactly the mindset of Margaret's colleagues. They might haggle over compensation but not over a small change in allocating course credits—no matter what the consequences.

To take an even more mundane example, consider meetings. Almost everyone attends meetings, whether at work or in your community. You are asked to attend the meeting. Why? The most common reason is that you have resources—both tangible and intangible—and the person who called the meeting wants access to them. Maybe those resources are your time, your expertise, your political capital, financial contributions, or your support. Why do you attend? Because others have resources to which you want access. They may have expertise, attention, or control of resources that you want. The formal agenda may be to prepare a presentation for a senior manager or to organize a volunteer effort, but the context of these meetings is about negotiating—which of your scarce resources will you contribute and what do you hope to gain by working with your counterparts.

Sometimes the idea of negotiating over relatively mundane issues may be uncomfortable, particularly when the situation involves friends or family. However, your discomfort likely stems from looking at negotiation as a conflict with winners and losers—a conflict in which anything you gain comes at the expense of someone else. Of course this causes discomfort, because most people consider this way of looking at things to be incompatible with close relationships.

But what if you thought about negotiating as solving a problem? Instead of thinking about negotiation as a zero sum game where I get more and you get less, think about negotiation as *a situation in which two or more people decide what each will give and receive through a process of mutual influence and persuasion, by proposing solutions and agreeing on a common course of action.*

This broader definition of negotiation—as a response to disputed or scarce resources—lets you see opportunities to negotiate where once you saw none. And this perspective may ease another concern—the fear that if you negotiate, others will think you are greedy, demanding, or unpleasant. Who wants to be known as someone who always demands more or wants special treatment?

If all you do is demand more when you face resource scarcity, then your concerns are well-founded. But that is exactly our point. Seeing that negotiation is a way of finding solutions that are better for you (and to which your counterparts can agree) will help transform your negotiations from simple demands for more into exchanges in which you can solve your counterparts' problems, as well as your own.

The first challenge is deciding when to accept the status quo and when to negotiate—and how to tell the difference. Let's start with the easy one first: when should you *not* negotiate?

WHEN *NOT* NEGOTIATING MAY BE THE RIGHT CHOICE

Negotiating takes time—you need to think, gather information, and strategize. So, the easy answer is not to negotiate when the costs of negotiating exceed the potential benefits. If you are selling your car, and are in no particular hurry, you might prefer to set the price and wait for a buyer rather than waste time haggling with people who might never get to that level. Or just think about how long it would take to shop if everyone in the checkout line attempted to negotiate the price of every item.

You also might avoid negotiating because you consider the issue at stake too important to risk having your counterpart walk away. A good example is Thomas and Margaret's search for their first academic positions. Thomas interviewed with a large number of schools and received nine offers, while Margaret interviewed with fewer schools and received only one. Thomas negotiated his salary, while Margaret did not. Margaret feared that any attempt to negotiate with her first employer, the University of Arizona, might make the university back out, so she signed the offer and sent it back by express mail.

Why was Thomas so willing to incur the risk of rejection while Margaret was not? The biggest difference was that Thomas had eight other options while Margaret had none. As an extreme example, consider a situation in which an armed stranger tells you, "Your money or your life!" Even Thomas would not consider this a first offer in a negotiation. Rather than countering, "How about half my money and I get to keep my life?" Thomas would hand over his money. Beginning in Chapter 2, we explore how having—and not having—alternatives changes how, what, and whether you should negotiate.

Just as you might not negotiate because the stakes are too great, you might also forgo negotiation because the benefits are too small. Take the grocery store example. You might choose not to negotiate because even a generous assessment of the potential benefit would be dwarfed by the cost of your time, the ill will of those behind you in line, and, perhaps, your own stress at acting like this in public.

The final reason for avoiding negotiations is lack of sufficient preparation. If you lack the time, inclination, or resources to plan, you may be better off avoiding negotiations. Sometimes, however, when a chance to negotiate takes you by surprise, it's a sign that you have not thought far enough ahead. Sometimes students have confessed that, when talking to an employer, in what they thought was an early stage of the process, they were caught completely flat-footed when the recruiter asked: "So what would it take to get you here?" Perhaps the question was unexpected *at that moment*, but it was clearly something any job candidate should expect. Most likely, the candidates did not want to think about the answer because it would make them embrace rather than avoid the opportunity to negotiate.

One of the main factors that distinguish successful negotiators is the quality of their prenegotiation planning. The better prepared you are, the more control you will have; you will be much more capable of predicting what your counterpart wants and coming up with creative solutions. In short, preparation can turn a negotiation into a winning situation in which you and your counterpart search for a solution that makes you both better off—and allows your counterpart to say yes. (If you need to get more insight into how to prepare for a negotiation right now, you might want to jump ahead to Chapter 5.)

CHOOSING TO NEGOTIATE

How *do* people choose to negotiate—and how *should* they choose? The answers to these two questions do not always align. Consider two sisters who reach for the last orange in the fruit bowl. They both want it, but only one can have it, so they argue over who deserves it. If they are like most siblings, the solution is straightforward. They compromise. One sister cuts the orange into two pieces, and the other one gets to choose her half. Both sisters get a quick solution, although each only gets half of what she wanted.

If each sister had taken the time to uncover why the other wanted the orange, however, a very different solution might have presented itself. After they split the orange, one sister takes her half and squeezes the juice to make a smoothie while the other sister peels the zest for her icing. They both could have gotten more of what they wanted if they had taken the time to find out what the other one wanted.

Sometimes, choosing the easiest compromise can actually make you worse off. This is a classic—and often disastrous—shortcut, and it's by no means the only one. When trying to assess whether you want to initiate negotiations, you may find yourself relying on another common shortcut: the search for confirming evidence.

Our own psychology can be our greatest enemy. Humans dislike uncertainty because predictability increases our sense of control. Everything you have observed, been taught, and learned from experience creates a series of personal theories about how the world works, why things happen, and why people behave the way they do. When you encounter information in your environment that supports these theories, you feel good. When information appears to refute your personal theories, however, it can be deeply upsetting.

To avoid having their theories about the world shattered, people develop a "confirmation bias." This is the tendency to interpret information in a way that confirms their preexisting theories.

Confirmation bias is a huge problem; indeed, it prevents many people from negotiating in the first place. For example, if you don't believe that negotiating is even an option, your confirmation bias will keep you from even trying to negotiate—even if negotiating were, in reality, a completely legitimate choice. Many people believe that negotiation creates conflict and that conflict is to be avoided unless the benefit is significant. This reluctance to negotiate, combined with natural confirmation bias, leads people to miss valuable negotiating opportunities.

Of course, the search for confirming evidence works both ways. If you love to negotiate, you may overestimate the benefits and underestimate the costs. Objectively, you might not want to incur the reputational costs of becoming one of those people who's always trying to get more. If your confirmation bias leads you to negotiate too often, you'll probably want to think long and hard before initiating new negotiations.

Confirmation bias is not the only psychological mechanism that prevents people from negotiating; gender plays a role, too. Ample evidence suggests that women are less likely than men to initiate negotiations. This is perhaps best illustrated by Linda Babcock and Sara Laschever in *Women Don't Ask: Negotiation and the Gender Divide.*[1] The authors found that in a survey of Carnegie-Mellon MBA students, male graduates received starting salaries 7.6 percent higher than those of their female counterparts. At first glance, most of us will reach a conclusion—perhaps resulting from confirmation bias—that the study confirms what we already know: that on average women are paid less than men for equal work.[2] But that outcome could be achieved in two different ways. Companies could actively discriminate against women. Or women and men could behave differently once they get an offer.

It seems likely that both tendencies are to blame. When the participants in this survey were asked whether they attempted to negotiate a higher salary, only 7 percent of the women said they had, compared to 57 percent of the men. What may be surprising is that the authors found no differences in the success rates of the male and female MBA graduates who attempted to negotiate their starting salaries. Those who did negotiate (mostly men) successfully increased their starting salaries by 7.4 percent on average: almost precisely the difference between the men's and women's starting salaries. Clearly, had male and female MBA graduates attempted to negotiate higher salaries in equal numbers, that 7.6 percent difference in starting salaries would have been dramatically reduced.

Women tend to pass up other, less obvious opportunities to negotiate. In the 2006 U.S. Open, a new instant-replay system allowed the players to challenge line calls. Challenges by both male and female players were upheld approximately a third of the time. However, in an equal number of U.S. Open matches, the men challenged seventy-three calls, compared to only twenty-eight by women.[3] Although it is conceivable that referees might be more accurate in judging women's tennis than men's, another hypothesis is difficult to ignore: that women—even the most highly skilled, professional tennis players—are less willing to ask for more when this means asking for reconsideration of a referee's call. Calling into question a referee's call creates a conflict, and women may see such behavior as inconsistent with their sense of good sportsmanship.

Being female is obviously not the only factor that prevents people from negotiating. Ninety-three percent of women did not ask for a higher salary, but there were also plenty of men who did not ask either. Regardless of your gender, you may fear that asking for a different package will make you look greedy or demanding. So you might accept the first offer you're given; after all, those who did negotiate only got an additional 7.4 percent, and that benefit may not be worth the potential reputational cost (or risk of having your offer rescinded, as uncommon as that may be).

Yet that small difference in starting salary can grow into a significant difference over time. To give you an idea of just how big, suppose that two equally qualified thirty-year old applicants Chris and Fraser receive identical salary offers from the same company for $100,000 per year. Chris negotiates a 7.4 percent salary increase to $107,400, while Fraser accepts the initial offer of $100,000. Both stay at the company for thirty-five years, receiving identical 5 percent annual raises each year.

If Chris retires at sixty-five, Fraser would have to work for an additional eight years to be as wealthy as Chris at retirement. Consider that for a minute. The *only* distinction between the compensation that Chris receives and the compensation that Fraser receives is that initial 7.4 percent increase that Chris negotiated.

And this is a conservative estimate. That eight-year figure reflects a scenario in which the company gave Chris and Fraser exactly the same percentage increase each year. But what if the company treated them differently, precisely *because* Chris commanded a higher salary than Fraser? A simple metric for one's value to an organization is how much one is paid, so the company will consider Chris more valuable. More valuable employees get better raises. Changing Chris's raise to 6 percent a year compared to Fraser's 5 percent would mean that, by the end of thirty years, Chris is earning

$100,000 more per year than Fraser. This will require Fraser to work an additional *four decades* after Chris retires. Now are you reconsidering the benefits of negotiating?

This example highlights the cost of Fraser's one-time decision not to negotiate, a decision that may have seemed inconsequential when Fraser made it. But Fraser will be feeling the effects of that decision for decades. While we do not propose that you negotiate every social exchange, you should consider the long-term cost of *not* negotiating.

It's not outrageous to suppose—as in this example—that your employer's assessment of you may be influenced by how much you are being paid! In a recent study, researchers served two glasses of the same wine, but told participants that one cost $45 and the other $5. The subjects not only reported enjoying the $45 glass of wine more, but the part of the brain that experiences pleasure became significantly more active when drinking it as compared to the brain activity when drinking the $5 glass of wine. These researchers documented both that price implied quality and the fact that the higher (perceived) price of the wine changed the nature of the individual's experience on a biological level.[4] Clearly, your boss's assessment of your performance should be far more complex than your assessment of wine quality, but this experiment suggests that you—and your boss—may judge your value more highly the more expensive you are!

What do the tennis example, the wine tasting, and your willingness to negotiate all have in common? Your outcomes are affected by your expectations. You expect the expensive wine to be more enjoyable than the modest wine, and that expectation changes how you experience it. Similarly, being concerned that others might perceive you as too demanding, greedy, or unpleasant can result in your censoring your behavior—whether that is challenging a referee's call or initiating a negotiation.

Your environment and your experience combine to set your expectations. Different cultures have different norms about when it's appropriate to negotiate. Americans tend to view primarily nonroutine, expensive interactions as negotiable while people from the Middle East extend their boundaries to include all sorts of transactions, big (organizational mergers) and small (market purchases). These are examples of cultures that are country or region specific. But in these situations the behavior of people much closer to you—such as family members, mentors, and role models—also sets your expectations. If your mom or dad were willing to negotiate, even in places where it wasn't typical, such as a fancy department store, you would see a shopping excursion in a much different light than if your parents viewed asking for a better deal as unacceptable or inappropriate.

Based on whatever mix of these factors you have experienced and observed, you probably have a pretty firm idea of what to expect in a negotiation. Yet because those expectations can motivate or handicap your performance, it's crucial to understand how they work—and how you can use them to your advantage.

THE POWER OF EXPECTATIONS

Expectations are powerful because they are the goals you set for yourself. If you set your expectations too low, you will not do as well as you could. If your expectations are extreme, you may not meet them—and you will likely feel disappointed. What is important here is performance. The goal of setting a goal is not to achieve the goal but to improve performance. Setting expectations sets the standard to which you aspire. One of the biggest changes that you could make to get more of what you want is to set higher expectations, even if you don't achieve them. Setting higher expectations will change your behavior—and can lead to better performance.

Expectations are so powerful, in fact, that the expectations of others— even if we are ignorant of them—can affect how we perform. One famous study demonstrated what came to be known as the Pygmalion Effect: elementary school teachers unconsciously behaved in ways that encouraged or discouraged the success of their students.[5] More recently, researchers have investigated another psychological phenomenon called stereotyped threat: the concern people feel about confirming a negative stereotype about the group to which they belong, producing anxiety, lowered expectations, and reduced performance.[6]

An example of how stereotypes affect performance can be seen in the common stereotype that white athletes are successful because they are smart (sports intelligence) while black athletes are successful because they are athletic (natural sports ability). When white and black athletes played golf after being told that performance reflected their sports intelligence, black athletes underperformed white athletes. When told that performance reflected natural athletic ability, white athletes underperformed.

If you play golf, you may not be persuaded; there are lots of things that can put you off your game. You probably do not feel the same way about math, however. Consider Asian females, who fall under two conflicting stereotypes: "Asians are good at math" and "females are bad at math." To test this, researchers primed two different groups of Asian females to one of the two stereotypes: bad or good in math. When the students had to specify their gender, thereby invoking the I-am-bad-at-math threat, they scored significantly worse on the math test than did their female counterparts who, by identifying their ethnicity, invoked the I-am-good-at-math stereotype which did not generate threat.[7] Merely identifying their gender was enough to create a stereotyped threat and inhibit the Asian women's ability.

Expectations, whether they are set by ourselves or by others, can drive behavior. Think about this: before making pay decisions managers learned that they might have to explain why they gave the raises they did. They assigned lower raises to women than to equally performing men.[8] These managers seemed to change their allocations based on what they expected: men would ask for more—but not all men. Some were satisfied with the raises they received. So to keep as many men out of their offices asking for more, they may have given them higher initial raises. In contrast, managers expected that women would simply accept the raises without question. So they preemptively gave the men more. It is little wonder, then, with this cycle of diminished expectations both from employers and their female employees that women make substantially less than men in equivalent positions with equivalent qualifications.

Changing this cycle requires a starting point—namely, changing your expectations about what is possible in a negotiation. After all, if you don't expect to achieve much if you do ask, it is not surprising that you don't ask or you ask for substantially less. The more uncertain you are about the correctness of negotiating, the more likely you are to accept less than you might have received if you had made the attempt.

A study at one of the country's top business schools revealed just how vital a role expectations play in determining compensation. The study revealed that female MBA graduates of Harvard Business School (HBS) accepted starting salaries some 6 percent lower than their male counterparts, after controlling for the industries they entered, pre-MBA salaries, functional areas of expertise, and cities of employment. Even worse, female HBS MBAs accepted yearly bonuses approximately 19 percent lower than their male counterparts. The main determinant of their salaries and bonuses, it seems, was their expectations. The more ambiguous their expectations, the bigger the discrepancy between male and female graduates. But when expectations were equated by providing information about current salaries and bonuses, the negotiating behaviors and the resulting outcomes were the same for both men and women. Similar expectations lead to similar results.[9]

Another study demonstrated just how powerful expectations—especially negative expectations—are in affecting the ability to negotiate. In this study, equal numbers of male and female participants were divided into two random groups. The first group was told that negotiators achieve bad outcomes when they rely on a selfish, assertive, or bullying negotiating style, hyper-rational analysis of the other's preferences, and limited displays of emotion—all stereotypes of male behavior. The second group was told that they would produce bad results if they expressed their interests only in response to direct questions, relied on their intuition or listening skills to move the negotiation forward, or displayed emotion—all negative female stereotypes.[10]

After being primed with those suggestions, participants listed their expectations about how they would perform in the negotiation. When exposed to the negative male stereotype, male negotiators expected to perform significantly worse than their female counterparts. When exposed to the negative female stereotype, female participants expected to perform significantly worse than their male counterparts.

Not surprisingly, these expectations strongly correlated to the participants' actual performance in the negotiations. Male negotiators outperformed female negotiators when both were exposed to negative female stereotypes, and female negotiators outperformed males when both were exposed to negative male stereotypes.

The lesson of these studies is clear; if you want to change the way you negotiate, experience wine, determine an acceptable compensation package for a position, or perform on math tests, it is critical that you set appropriate expectations for each scenario. Doing so will give you a decided advantage in getting more of what you want—be it a higher salary, a more satisfying glass of wine, or a better test score.

SUMMARY

Every day, you have opportunities to negotiate. Most people miss these chances to get more of what they want because they have a narrow understanding of when it is appropriate to negotiate. To take advantage of these opportunities, you need to broaden your horizon of what is and is not negotiable.

Situations of resource scarcity and social conflict are especially good opportunities for negotiation. When confronting such scenarios, assess whether you could negotiate to get more of what you want.

The key takeaways of this chapter are:

- The benefits of negotiation can be applied to a wide variety of social conflicts, even though these conflicts may not initially resemble typical negotiation opportunities.
- It is important to assess each potential negotiation carefully. Even though there are many opportunities to negotiate that could make you better off, consider the costs that you may incur if you try to negotiate.
- Even when you see an opportunity to negotiate, your discomfort with negotiation may result in your overweighting the costs and underweighting the benefits of negotiating. Beware of confirmation bias: if you feel uncomfortable with negotiation, you will generally be blind to the opportunities around you. Discount that discomfort accordingly.
- Expectations drive behaviors. If you set high expectations for your negotiating, you will do better. You may not reach the standard that you set, but remember that the primary goal of a negotiation is to achieve a better deal, not reach your own benchmarks. Setting higher expectations results in better performance, even if you don't actually achieve all your expectations.

CHAPTER TWO

CREATING COMMON GROUND

The Infrastructure of Negotiation

All negotiations are exchanges, but not all exchanges are negotiations. Exchanges and negotiations allow you to trade your current status, position, or solution for a new one. In an exchange, you swap your current status quo for a new one that you prefer, but neither party tries to alter the preset terms of the exchange. For example, in a typical exchange, the seller sets the price and the buyer agrees. In contrast, one party may make a first offer, which is only a starting point in a negotiation. Moreover, while you may simply accept the offer—in which case we would consider it an exchange—you may reject it by making a counteroffer, thus starting the negotiation.

In most exchanges, value is created for both you and your counterpart. (The exceptions are involuntary, coercive exchanges, such as a robbery—something we will not address in this book!) For example, you buy a loaf of bread for $5; this purchase creates value since you care more about the bread than you do about the $5, while the baker values the $5 more than the bread. Thus, value is created because you each received something that you value more in exchange for something that you value less.

To establish how much value is created in an exchange, we need to know each party's reservation price; that is, the most the buyer is willing to pay and the least the seller is willing to accept. For example, assume that you value the bread at $6.50 (that is, you would be just indifferent between paying $6.50 for the loaf of bread and keeping your money). Similarly, the baker is unwilling to sell the bread for less than $2.50. An exchange would then create \$4.00 of value, \$1.50 to you (\$6.50 – \$5.00) and \$2.50 (\$5.00 – \$2.50) to the baker.

Now add a negotiation component to this exchange. The baker has set a price of \$5. You want the bread, but believe you could do better, hoping to get it for \$2—your aspiration price—and so you counter the baker's offer at \$2. If a deal is eventually struck, the agreement will be somewhere between the baker's offer of \$5 and your counteroffer of \$2. Suppose the baker reduces her price to \$3. Relative to the original exchange, no additional value was created in this negotiation, but you claimed an additional \$2 in value that the baker lost when she agreed to reduce her price. This is value claiming. Your negotiating resulted in your getting the bread for \$3 rather than for the initial offer of \$5.

Of course, all of this is based on an important assumption—you and the baker value dollars equally. What if you and the baker do not value dollars equally? Assume she values each dollar more than you—maybe you derive pleasure from the experience of eating fresh-baked bread, while the baker is concerned that her start-up bakery be a success. If she values dollars more than you, more value is created for the exchange at the higher the price. Going from a price of \$3 to a price of \$5 is worth more to the baker than the cost to you of paying the additional \$2. Yet because there is only a single issue—the cost of the bread—there is no incentive for you to pay more, even though you value the incremental dollars less than the baker.

This situation would change if there were an additional issue that were valuable to you and that the baker could accommodate. Perhaps it is the fresh-baked aspect. If you were willing to pay \$3 for a loaf of bread, what would you be willing to pay for a loaf of bread that just came out of the oven? If the baker valued dollars more than you and you valued the aroma and taste of just-out-of-the-oven bread more than it cost her to customize your bread, then you could offer to pay more—say, \$5—if she were willing to bake a loaf of bread for you right now. In this case, she would get what she valued more: the dollars; and you would get what you valued more: the experience of eating fresh-baked bread. This is value creation through negotiation. The benefit of the fresh-baked bread is worth more to you than the additional \$2 you agreed to pay for it. For the baker, the cost of custom baking the bread is less than the \$2 she gets for her just-out-of-the-oven bread. You and the baker each got what you value more: she—the dollars; you—the freshly baked bread.

To move from the value created by an exchange to realizing the value that can be created within a negotiation requires you to interact thoughtfully and strategically with your negotiation partners. One way to claim more value is to create more value within the negotiation; by creating more value, you may be able to claim more. But be careful. One does not guarantee the other. In fact, if you were not thoughtful, you might claim less even when more value is created because the information you reveal when creating value can make it easier for your counterpart to claim more. Your counterparts can use this additional information to their advantage (see Chapter 4).

How much value is created or claimed depends on the negotiation. What you want is a good deal, one that not only meets your goal but is also better than your alternatives, exceeds your reservation price, and is as close to your aspiration as you can get. In the next section, we consider a systematic approach to establishing what you want to achieve; then, we will determine the contribution of each of these parameters to your overall success in a negotiation.

IDENTIFY YOUR GOAL

Negotiators can have different goals, even multiple goals. For example, when you negotiate the purchase of a new car, you typically focus on paying as low a price as possible. In other negotiations, your goal may be to beat your counterpart or to reach an agreement as quickly as possible. In yet other negotiations, you may want to improve your relationship with your counterparts even if that comes at some cost to your short-term interests.

It may seem obvious that negotiators should have their goals clearly in mind before commencing a negotiation, but many don't abide by this most basic rule. Many negotiators start the process before identifying precisely what they wish to achieve, much less how to achieve it. Moreover, unless you have a very clear understanding of what the goal is, you run the danger of becoming confused in the excitement of the negotiation. Indeed, negotiators often lose sight of their original goal and either focus only on getting more than their counterpart or resort to a quick agreement to avoid an uncomfortable situation.

As mentioned in the preface, negotiators have an affinity for reaching agreements, yet agreements do not always equal success.[1] Indeed, a successful negotiation is one in which you get more of what you want—not one in which you just arrive at an agreement. If your assessment of a good deal shifts to one where you simply reach an agreement with your counterpart, you have not only redefined success, but also put yourself in a position where you may end up with less of what you want. Once your counterpart recognizes that you merely want to reach an agreement, he will have a great advantage, primarily because it will allow him to claim a larger amount of any surplus created in exchange for your highly valued outcome: an agreement. We strongly advise you to guard against such a shift during the negotiation.

To avoid losing sight of your original goal and simply negotiating to reach an agreement, you need to know what a good deal is—and what it is not. This means that you must understand and value the issues that you consider important. You must establish your reservation prices and your aspiration. And you must do so in a manner that keeps you from losing focus on those goals, reservation prices, and aspirations.

ESTABLISH THE PARAMETERS OF YOUR NEGOTIATION

To begin to define the parameters of the negotiation, you need to determine the worst possible outcome you are willing to accept. This is your reservation price. It is the point where you are indifferent between saying yes and taking your alternative. Obviously, to determine where that tipping point is, you must also assess your alternatives; what will happen if this negotiation ends in an impasse.

The most obvious (and common) alternative is the status quo—what your situation was like before you started the negotiation. However, your alternatives can also be other deals with other negotiators. Collectively, your alternatives represent your *safety net*, or what you will get if you walk away from the present negotiation, and rationally, you should not agree to an outcome that is worth less than your alternatives.

Obviously, the better your alternatives, the more willing you will be to walk away from the negotiation and hence the more—on average—you will be able to claim if agreement is reached. Therefore, one of your most immediate sources of power is the value of your alternatives. In essence, alternatives force your counterpart to "pay" you at least the value of your alternatives to stay in the negotiation. Thus, the single most important aspect of your preparation before entering into any negotiation is to establish your alternative: What are your options if no agreement is reached?

Of course, your counterpart will also have alternatives that empower her to walk away, potentially forcing you to "pay" *her* to stay in the negotiation. Indeed, research shows that the negotiator with the better alternative—on average—claims more of the value in the negotiation.[2]

Recall the case of Margaret and Thomas's reaction to their first academic job offers, discussed in Chapter 1: Thomas had nine offers, while Margaret had only one. Clearly Thomas was in a much more powerful position because of his alternatives! Indeed, he used his power to negotiate while Margaret signed her offer letter as quickly as possible.

The quality of your alternatives also has an impact on how you behave and how you are perceived by your counterpart. Good alternatives change the intensity of your negotiating behavior. Negotiators with great alternatives often come across as aggressive and competitive, while negotiators with poor alternatives come across as cooperative, warm, and friendly.[3] Thus, analyzing your counterparts' behavior can help you triangulate their alternatives. For example, if your counterpart behaves more aggressively than you expect, that may indicate that his alternatives are better than you had thought.

THE POWER OF ALTERNATIVES

A good alternative (or alternatives) can dramatically alter your behavior in a negotiation. Consider the following:

In 2000, BusinessWeek released its semiannual survey of MBA programs, ranking Stanford's Graduate School of Business a shockingly low eleventh, an all-time low. This surprisingly low ranking stemmed from recruiters rating Stanford's MBAs very poorly, citing their arrogance in interviews. Allegedly, when Stanford MBAs actually showed up for interviews, they would often come dressed casually, more appropriate for a game of golf than a job interview. Two years later, Stanford's GSB was ranked fourth overall. What accounted for this meteoric rise?

When asked that very question, the dean indicated that in the ensuing two years, he had instituted career management classes focused on conveying the importance of each student representing Stanford. Superficially, the classes seemed to work, as recruiters rated Stanford's MBAs dramatically higher in 2002.

Consider another explanation. In 2000, dotcom mania gripped Silicon Valley, with the average Stanford MBA receiving more than six job offers. The class of 2002 was not nearly so lucky; with the economy in a tailspin, the average MBA received less than one job offer. It seems possible that the difference arose not from these career management classes, but rather from the number and quality of their alternatives; with worse alternatives, the students had less leverage in their interviews, which likely caused them to present themselves more respectfully. You decide!

Alternatives can also change people's behavior even when they are irrelevant to the situation at hand. Think about how a good-cop/bad-cop strategy works. Because people assess value through comparisons, the good cop makes the bad cop seem worse, and the bad cop makes the good cop's offers seem more attractive. However, there is a third alternative: don't take either offer. Therefore, from a rational perspective, the offer by the bad cop is whatever it is, and its value is not dependent on the offer of the good cop and vice versa.[4]

Once you have identified your alternatives, you can set your reservation price. The reservation price is the highest price a rational buyer will pay, or the lowest price a rational seller will accept. It is your true bottom line. At the reservation price, you are indifferent between your accepting counterpart's offer or walking away and accepting your alternative; the better your alternatives, the more extreme your reservation price.

Naturally, the lower bound of sellers' reservation prices is set by their alternatives, while the upper bound of buyers' reservation prices is set by theirs. However, some sellers lower their reservation prices (or buyers raise theirs) as the negotiation drags on, because they factor in the effort that has already gone into the negotiation. This is a mistake known as a sunk-cost fallacy. Alternatives do not change because a negotiation is taking longer than expected, so reservation prices should not change either.

Reservation prices represent the last bastion, your resistance to the siren call of agreement. So think of your reservation price as a red line—a standard that you have the discipline not to violate. Imagine that you are considering purchasing a theater ticket from a scalper. You have considered your alternatives and decided that you are willing to pay no more than $30 for the ticket, but the scalper wants $60. After some haggling, the scalper has come down to $31 dollars: $1 more than your reservation price. You believe that this is the lowest that he will accept for the tickets. How should you respond?

Most people will accept his offer, violating their reservation price. To do so, they create excuses as to why the $31 ticket was actually a good deal, despite violating their reservation price of $30. "I got him to concede $29 dollars on his initial ticket price," for example, or "just a dollar more than what I was willing to pay, and my time is worth at least that much, and I have heard this is really a great show . . ." These are not explanations; these are excuses. You already knew the value of your time before you started the interaction, and you also knew how good the show was. And by that logic, you should be willing to pay even more had the scalper first demanded $90 dollars for the ticket. You learned nothing new after setting your reservation price; you merely violated the boundary of your reservation price so that you could say yes.

But are you really going to walk away for only one dollar? From a psychological perspective, it seems silly. What is one dollar, more or less? After all, you surely value the time you spent negotiating at more than one dollar. If you have an alternative from which you could extract as much pleasure as the play and which costs exactly $30, then the reservation price of $30 could have some real sticking power.

Yet it's not merely a question of the dollar. Violating your reservation price creates a slippery slope. If you were willing to accept $31, you should also be willing to accept $32 (only one more dollar), $33 . . . $35. And if you accept $35, you are likely to accept $40. Where is the point at which you would walk away? Perhaps that point is $60, the original asking price of the ticket. But then, why bother negotiating at all?

This is a question of discipline: If you accurately set your reservation price at $30, then you should say no to the offer of $31. Of course, it's possible that your reservation price was not accurate, that $30 was an underestimation of your reservation price, or that you failed to assess your alternatives. But if not—if you learned nothing new in the course of the negotiation *that you could not have known* prior to the negotiation—then your reservation price should not change. Your reservation price is a standard against which you judge the lower bounds of the acceptability of a proposal; it is not something you modify to justify accepting a proposal.[5]

Note that we are not suggesting that you *never* adjust your reservation price. If, in the course of the negotiation, you discover something that you could not have known when you calculated your reservation price, then there is room for revision. However, exercise caution when you consider revising; be sure to do so only because of new information, and not simply as a way to justify getting an agreement.

The closer you get to the reservation price, the harder it becomes to resist the powerful allure of "yes." But resist. Having the discipline to honor your reservation price is one of the best ways to insure that the deals you accept meet or exceed your status quo.

Your alternatives and your reservation price are important parameters for any negotiation, but if you focus only on them, you will systematically underperform in your negotiations. Rather than setting your sights on at least meeting your alternatives (your safety net) or using your bottom line as a standard for what is good enough, consider setting your expectations at a higher level. Because expectations drive behavior (see Chapter 1), you need to define them clearly at the outset of each and every negotiation.

Your aspiration is an optimistic assessment of what you could achieve in a given negotiation. And because aspirations are optimistic, they inevitably enhance your expectations for—and, as a result, enhance the outcome of—the negotiation.

Setting and focusing on your aspirations represents an often overlooked advantage in negotiation. Aspirations provide psychological leverage that makes you focus on the potential upside of a negotiation, rather than on your downside protection (your alternative) or your bottom line (your reservation price). This increases the likelihood that you will achieve better results. Indeed, research shows that the more challenging your aspirations, the better you will perform.[6] Even if you do not meet your aspirations, they will motivate you to perform better than if you had set more modest goals.

Your aspirations should be set independently of your alternatives. Alternatives offer a safety net and shouldn't get mixed up with your goals for a negotiation, but many negotiators treat them as a standard of performance.[7] Negotiators with poor alternatives often set their expectations lower, causing them to accept less. This result goes hand in hand with the general notion that better alternatives produce better outcomes, and worse alternatives produce worse outcomes.

In fact, your aspiration is the antidote to your natural focus on your alternative. Just because you may have poor alternatives does not mean that you should be pessimistic in setting your aspiration. Be mindful that the quality of your alternative plays a powerful role in enhancing or diminishing your performance, independent of your actual negotiation skill.[8]

Focusing on aspirations can make you a better negotiator, but it won't necessarily make you happier with the outcome of your negotiation. Consider a study in which researchers encouraged some participants to focus on their aspirations in the negotiation, while encouraging others to focus on their alternatives.[9] Once the participants completed the negotiation, the researchers assessed both their performance and their satisfaction with those outcomes. As you may have predicted by now, those who focused on their aspirations achieved better outcomes than those who focused on their alternatives. However, the aspiration group was less satisfied with their objectively superior outcomes. (See Figure 2.1.) Counterintuitively, you tend to get

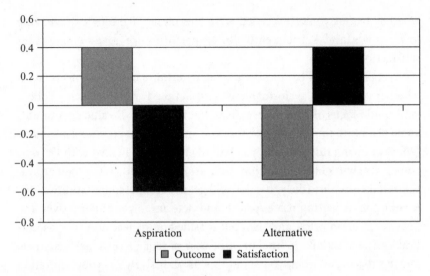

FIGURE 2.1 ASPIRATIONS VERSUS ALTERNATIVES

more but are less satisfied if you focus on your aspirations, but you feel more satisfied with a worse outcome if you focused on your alternatives. The alternative-focused negotiators got less, but they exceeded their alternatives, which satisfied them. By focusing on their alternatives, that alternative became the goal, the mark to beat. By contrast, the aspiration-focused negotiators got more, but less than they aspired to, which frustrated them.

This is the dark side of aspirations. Specifically, while optimistic aspirations lead to better negotiation outcomes, you will be less satisfied with your objectively better outcome. Consider the following example:

For decades, the World Value Survey identified the Danes as the happiest people in the world. Over the last thirty years, more than 67 percent of Danes have reported feeling very satisfied with their lives. What is the secret of this happiness, a secret they evidently have not shared with their Scandinavian neighbors? It appears to be low expectations.

Negotiators often act like Danes, who seem to set their expectations low about everything, including their happiness—and, as a result, feel content with their lives. Negotiators tend to focus on their alternatives, and when they exceed them, it makes them much happier than they would have been if they'd focused on their aspirations and failed to achieve them.

So focusing on alternatives means sacrificing performance for good feelings. This suggests that your subjective measure of getting a good deal is whether or not you've exceeded your alternative. Paradoxically, having lower goals and subsequently lower performance gives you greater satisfaction.

To cope with this paradox, you must determine before any negotiation whether your goal is performance or satisfaction. If you prefer satisfaction, you should focus on your alternatives, but if the overall value of your outcome is a more important measure, you should focus on your aspirations (while knowing full well that you will likely be less satisfied with the outcome). You will not likely achieve your aspiration, but having high aspirations makes it more likely that you will get a better outcome. Additionally, if your goal is getting more, you should determine your alternatives and your reservation price, and then put it aside and instead use your aspiration as the standard to anchor your assessment of your performance. During the negotiation, you should focus exclusively on your aspiration price. Only after you have negotiated the best deal possible, and just before agreeing to it, you should compare the value of your alternative and your reservation price, and accept the deal only if it meets or exceeds both of these parameters.

Once you have established your reservation and aspiration prices, the next step is to figure out how to achieve a deal that will approach your aspirations. Where are the opportunities for you to claim value? For that, you need to think about the structure of the issues over which you could be negotiating.

TYPES OF ISSUES IN NEGOTIATIONS

Issues can be classified into three types: congruent, distributive, and integrative. Congruent issues are those over which the parties have no dispute. For example, in an employment negotiation, both the candidate and recruiter may favor the candidate joining the same division. Similarly, the buyer and the seller may prefer an early delivery.

Some issues—price, for example—are not likely to be congruent. Although there may be issues about which the negotiating parties are in agreement, the parties may be unaware that they each prefer the same outcome. Identifying the congruent issues should therefore be one of the goals of the information exchange.

Identifying congruent issues can provide you with a strategic advantage if you know which issues are congruent but your counterpart does not. For example, the knowledgeable negotiator can benefit by offering to "concede" on the congruent issue in exchange for preferable terms on another non-congruent issue.

Distributive issues are those where the two parties have opposing preferences, often valued with equal intensity. That is, parties value each unit of the issue (for example, price paid, or days of delivery time) equally. Price is the most typical example of a distributive issue; the buyer prefers to pay less, while the seller prefers to receive more, and each incremental dollar benefits one party by the same amount as it hurts the other.

Most people think of negotiations almost entirely in terms of distributive issues, which is why negotiations are often characterized as battles to determine who gets what out of a fixed pool of resources.

Integrative issues are those where the parties have opposing but asymmetric values. All integrative issues have these two essential characteristics: first, the parties have opposing preferences; and second, the benefits and costs are not equal. For example, the benefits for the party that prefers more of the issue do not equal the costs to the party that prefers less of the issue. For instance, the number of vacation days offered in an employment negotiation could represent an integrative issue. The candidate likely prefers more vacation days, and the employer would prefer to offer fewer (hence opposing preferences), but the candidate may value each incremental vacation day more than the company wishes to avoid them. Such an issue offers an opportunity to create value by trading concessions on vacations days for an issue that the employer values more.

Trading integrative issues can make both parties better off. The exchange of information in a negotiation should therefore help identify integrative issues and assess their differential valuations so as to create value. Therefore, it is not only important to identify which issues are integrative but also to discover how the preferences differ in intensity; this will provide you with a strategic advantage (see Chapter 6).

Let's consider a real-world example in which each of these types of issues plays a role in setting up a negotiation.

SNOOP INC.

The sole proprietor of a business asked Thomas to serve as her advisor in valuing the company and devising the strategic approach to negotiating its sale. The value of its primary service of providing hiring organizations

with background checks of potential employees had grown with the increased security concerns in the wake of September 11. With the vast majority of her personal net worth tied up in the company, the owner hoped
to divest her stake to diversify her assets and to provide her with sufficient
liquidity to pursue other opportunities.

After discussing the company with the owner in detail, Thomas identified three issues to serve as the basis for the negotiation: price, risk, and the
owner's future involvement. It became clear that each issue featured a high
level of complexity. For example, the issue of selling price had two components: cash upon closing (dollars today) and an ongoing equity stake in the
business (dollars in the future). Thus, these two issues not only differed in
the timing of the amount to be paid/received but also in the risk (the first
being certain, the latter uncertain). Second, her future involvement in the
company was not a binary decision, but could fall anywhere along a con-
tinuum from the CEO's walking away the day after the sale to a much
longer, more involved transition plan. In between those two options lay
countless variations, where the selling CEO might stay on for a predeter-
mined time as a consultant.

This example reveals an interesting overlap between distributive and
integrative issues. While the selling price would likely be a distributive
issue—the seller values getting more money for the company and the buyer
values paying less—the exact nature of the payment could be integrative.
That is, while the owner wanted to receive more of the total selling price in
cash up front to reduce her risk and allow her to diversify her holdings, she
also valued future cash payments, albeit less than dollars up front. The
buyer, on the other hand, valued future payment more than current payments because it tied the owner to the business, allowing the buyer to benefit from her expertise. In addition, shifting payments to the future and
making them contingent on the subsequent performance of the business
(a so-called earn-out) shifted some of the valuation risk to the owner who
knew better what the business was actually worth. Because buyer and seller
did not value the earn-out equally, it was an integrative issue.

The owner's desire for an ongoing involvement in the business was
clearly a congruent issue; both parties wanted her to remain involved.
However, they differed in their preferred length and extent of her involvement. From the owner's perspective, if she remained too involved, she
would not make much progress toward her long-term life-style goals. She

was willing to remain highly involved immediately after the sale, but she wanted to disengage gradually from day-to-day operations within two years. The buyer preferred a longer, more consistent involvement—a logical preference, given all the expertise the owner had gained building the company from the ground up.

Once he had identified these issues, Thomas tried to understand each one from both the owner's and the buyer's perspective. The owner's alternative in this negotiation was straightforward: Because there was no alternative buyer on the horizon, the owner's alternative was the status quo, in which she could continue to own and operate the company. Using the existing business plan, Thomas valued Snoop Inc. at approximately $230 million from the perspective of a well-diversified investor. However, the owner had virtually her entire wealth tied up in the business (her only other major asset was her private residence). Thus, changes of the value of Snoop would have a very large impact on her well-being. To take this very high specific risk into account, Thomas increased the discount rate accordingly, which resulted in a lower value of Snoop Inc. to the owner. This adjustment resulted in a reduction in the value of the firm to $150 million. That is, while Thomas estimated that Snoop Inc. was worth $230 million to a well-diversified investor, in his assessment, taking the fact that virtually all of the owner's wealth was concentrated in Snoop Inc., the owner should be indifferent between keeping Snoop Inc. (high risk) or $150 million (low risk), which was Thomas's assessment of the owner's reservation price.

Next, Thomas established the owner's aspirations. Based on discussions with the owner, he estimated that combining Snoop Inc. with the buyer's existing business could generate synergies of approximately 40 percent or $92 million, resulting in a corporate value of $322 million ($230 million + $92 million). The owner hoped to capture 60 percent of those synergies or $55.2 million. Thus, the owner's aspiration price was $285.2 million ($230 million + $55.2 million).

The CEO was pleased with the work that Thomas had done—but despite their careful planning, other factors disrupted what might well have been a productive negotiation for both parties. The initial meetings were scheduled to begin in November 2008, just weeks after the Lehman Brothers bankruptcy filing, when capital markets froze, mergers-and-acquisitions activity plummeted, and almost unprecedented economic uncertainty cast a chill over the whole economy. The subsequent tightening of the credit markets prevented the buyer from successfully arranging the financing necessary to complete the transaction. The last time we checked, the CEO was still running the company, waiting for another suitor to appear.

SUMMARY

As negotiators, you must consider the unique aspects of your negotiations while recognizing that most negotiations have considerable commonalities. First and foremost, you must clarify your goals. Do you want to extract as much value as possible, or consummate a deal quickly to minimize risk and transaction costs? Would you prefer to enhance the relationship between you and your counterpart, or do you want to feel victorious?

With your goals defined, you must then identify the characteristics of a good deal:

- You need to know when to say yes, and when to say no; that is, you must know your alternatives. Consider the other options, partners, and opportunities you have.
- Once you understand those alternatives—and ideally, those of your counterpart—you must establish your reservation price or bottom line, the point at which you feel indifferent between taking the deal and walking away to take your alternative.
- You must also determine an optimistic assessment of your outcome: your aspirations. This should be significantly better than your reservation prices, sufficiently extreme as to challenge you to achieve more.
- Once you have identified your alternatives, reservation prices, and aspirations, you must understand the issues in the negotiation and their underlying structures; are they distributive, integrative, or congruent?

Later, in Chapter 5, we will walk you through a process that helps classify these types of issues in your negotiations. In the next chapter, however, we consider the value created by a negotiated exchange in which the issues are distributive: a situation that many people think of when they hear the word "negotiation."

CHAPTER THREE

CREATING AND CLAIMING VALUE

The Value of the Exchange

I n negotiations, what matters is how much value you claim. What form that value takes—more money, more influence in decisions at work, more control over your schedule, a better relationship with your partners— depends on your goals for the negotiation.

Any negotiation has two important reference points: your reservation price and your counterpart's reservation price. Whatever overlap exists between these reservation prices is called the bargaining zone. For example, between a buyer and a seller the bargaining zone is the difference between the most the buyer is willing to pay and the least the seller is willing to accept. The size of the bargaining zone determines how much value is available for you and your counterpart to claim; the larger the bargaining zone, the more value there is to claim.

As discussed in Chapter 2, value is created by an exchange even when no negotiation occurs. For example, for the buyer it is simply the difference between the price that the seller offers and what the buyer is willing to pay. To claim more, buyers must negotiate.

Attempting to claim more value than an exchange would otherwise grant is a fundamental part of any negotiation. In the bakery example from Chapter 2, for instance, the value created in the exchange is equal to the difference between the least the baker will accept for her bread and the most the buyer would pay (reservation price), which may or may not be equal to the baker's asking price. The value-claiming component of this exchange— and the aspect that makes it a negotiation, rather than a simpler transaction— is the buyer's willingness to give up some of the lesser-valued currency (dollars) in exchange for what the buyer values more—the bread. Likewise, the seller must be willing to give up what she values less (the bread) for what she values more (dollars). But notice that no additional value has been created beyond what existed in the original exchange. In the next section, we will expand on the tension that exists between value claiming and value creating as you attempt to create value.

MIXED MOTIVES IN NEGOTIATION

Intuitively, it seems that by creating more value, you would be able to claim more. The more value that exists, after all, the greater the amount available for you to claim. This intuition, however, can be misleading. Perversely, strategies that enhance value creation may actually hinder value claiming.

To create more value than what already exists in an exchange, counterparts have to share information. Information sharing, particularly when your counterpart does not reciprocate, gives a strategic advantage to her and may hinder your ability to claim value. Because this value-creating strategy is risky, choosing which information to share and which to withhold is crucial. Sharing too little information leaves value unrealized and unavailable for claiming, while sharing too much, jeopardizes your ability to claim value.

Successful negotiators must delicately balance the sharing and withholding of information. Sharing information may enable your counterpart to estimate your reservation price or bottom line. This information can help him calculate how much to demand—perhaps using your reservation price as his aspiration. However, if you can figure out your counterpart's reservation price, the roles are reversed; you can exploit that information and extract more, if not all, of the surplus of the created value by the exchange, leaving your counterpart with little more than his reservation price. (For example, if a buyer has exact knowledge of the dealer's costs on all attributes of a car—the cost of the car, cost of the service, loaner, warranty, etc.—the buyer can claim most if not all of the value in the deal. The converse is also true: if the dealer knows the car buyer's preferences, he can tailor the contract to claim most, if not all, the value created.)

This is one of the most significant challenges in negotiation: negotiators must weigh the benefits and the costs associated with value-claiming strategies, which are inherently competitive, against those associated with value-creating strategies, which are inherently cooperative. The juxtaposition of cooperative and competitive strategies and the need to balance when to cooperate and when to compete result in what researchers term the mixed-motive dilemma of negotiating.[1]

To distinguish between value claiming and value creating, imagine that when the parties simply bring each of their resources together, there is a pooling effect—the surplus created is the sum of what each party brings to the table. Consider a simple transaction with only one issue. This negotiation is purely distributive: The pie is fixed, and any benefit to one party comes necessarily at the expense of the other.

When the parties negotiate over multiple issues, however, the value of the exchange may exceed the sum of what each party brings to the table. In fact, multiple issues are a necessary condition for value-creating potential in the negotiation.

Value creation means that there is more value available to both parties when they negotiate than simply a sum of what they brought to the table. With value creation, the size of the pie depends on the particular trades that you and your counterpart make and the value that is created in those trades. You both may get more of what you want without either of you necessarily getting less of what you each bring to the table.

The value of an exchange can increase from the synergies the negotiators create by combining multiple issues into packages that reflect the relative importance of different issues. The difference between the value created by the exchange itself and the value created within the exchange when negotiators trade between and among issues is known as the "integrative potential." Identifying this integrative potential is an essential step in the preparation for any negotiation.

THE VALUE IN AN EXCHANGE

As we noted earlier, the value of a typical exchange is bounded by the reservation price of the seller (the least he is willing to accept) and the reservation price of the buyer (the most he is willing to pay). The bargaining zone is positive when the maximum price that the buyer is willing to pay exceeds the lowest price that the seller is willing to accept. By contrast, if the most the buyer is willing to pay is less than the lowest price the seller is willing to accept, there is no overlap in reservation prices, and the bargaining zone is negative. In this latter scenario, the parties should not reach an agreement because doing so would make at least one party (and possibly both) worse off than they would be without an agreement.

Only by sharing information can negotiators discover whether the bargaining zone is positive or negative. Because both parties are unlikely to divulge their respective reservation prices, all each can know with certainty is whether the deal violates his or her reservation price.[2] However, once an agreement is reached, the value created (or destroyed) in a purely distributive negotiation is always equal to the value inside the bargaining zone, independent of whether the bargaining zone is positive or negative.

When two parties are negotiating over a single issue and each has complete information—in this case, they each know their own and the other's reservation price—the value in the deal is whatever is contained in the bargaining zone. For example, if the seller will not accept less than $100 (i.e., $100 is her reservation price) and the buyer is willing to pay no more than $150 ($150 is his reservation price), then the value available in this negotiation is $50: the overlap of the parties' reservation prices.

However, even in simple cases like this one, approximately 20 percent of our students (whether they are MBA students or executives) and clients, violate their reservation price to get a deal. Therefore, knowing your reservation price is not enough. You need the discipline to adhere to it.

To increase the amount you can claim, you will need to estimate your counterpart's reservation price: how little that seller will accept or (if you are the seller) how much the buyer will pay. The same, of course applies to your counterpart. Thus, in this basic scenario, both buyer and seller approach the negotiation with knowledge of their own reservation price and an estimate of their counterpart's.

Your appraisal of your counterpart's reservation price will not always be accurate—or necessarily more accurate than their appraisal of *your* reservation price. You may not have access to all the information that you would like about the issues over which you are negotiating. Your counterpart may have an informational advantage, such as sellers of used cars know how well a car was maintained, how hard it was driven, and whether the odometer reading is accurate. Similarly, when buying art, some buyers may have superior information regarding the object's value, how the market may evolve, the recent sale prices for similar pieces, and so on. Such information helps determine the reservation price of the party that possesses it—and disadvantages the party that doesn't.

Because it is difficult to determine reservation prices with certainty, a number of factors unrelated to the true value of the reservation price may influence your assessment, but for ease of explanation, the examples that follow use reservation prices and aspiration values that are precise and certain. Reducing the errors associated with your assessment of your reservation price will be the focus of a later section in this chapter.

Consider a negotiation with a single distributive issue and a positive bargaining zone. Thomas wants to upgrade the tires on his truck. His current tires are in acceptable shape, but he covets a set of high-performance tires. He has identified dealers that carry such tires, but he can only justify the upgrade to his wife if it's a great deal. After investigating different brands and quality grades of tires, he decides that the most he is willing to pay is $160 per tire—this is the buyer's reservation price (RP_b). Thomas would be ecstatic if he could buy the tires for just $75 per tire—his aspiration price (AP_b).

Thomas finds that while most stores offer the tires for about $225 per tire, one dealer is offering a sale price of $210 each. Thomas expects that this is the seller's aspiration price (AP_s)—but just as the dealer does not know Thomas's reservation price, Thomas does not know the reservation price of the dealer.

Unbeknownst to Thomas, the dealer is willing to sell the tires for $125. This is the seller's reservation price (RP_s). Thus, because the reservation price of the buyer ($160) exceeds the reservation price of the seller ($125), a positive bargaining zone of $35 exists, making mutually beneficial deals possible. Because Thomas does not know this, he proceeds with caution— and the dealer does the same.

If both Thomas and the dealer had complete information about each other, the aspiration of one would be very close to the other's reservation price. If both parties are relatively uninformed about their counterparts or the value of the issues over which they are negotiating, each side's aspiration price might be considerably different from the other side's reservation price.

A pictorial representation of both sides of the negotiation would look like this:

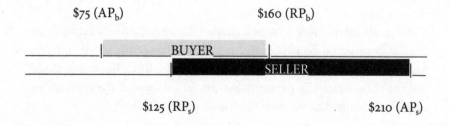

$75 (AP_b) $160 (RP_b)

BUYER

SELLER

$125 (RP_s) $210 (AP_s)

Because the gray and the black lines overlap, between $125 and $160 per tire, the bargaining zone is positive to the tune of $35. A reasonable deal could therefore be struck for any price between the two reservation prices and the value of this exchange is $35, regardless of the ultimately agreed-on price. If Thomas and seller agree on a price of $130 per tire, the value of this deal to him is $30 (his RP_b of $160 minus the price paid of $130) while the value to the dealer is $5 (the price received $130 minus her RP_s of $125). Together, these two amounts add up to the bargaining zone, or $35. This means that relative to an impasse (i.e., no deal), a deal between these two parties will create $35 of value that can be allocated between Thomas and the dealer. No matter how it's split, $35 is exactly the value that would be lost if no deal were struck.

You may wonder whether the amount of value in the deal shifts if one negotiator violates his or her reservation price. It does not. For example, if the dealer sells below her reservation price, say for $120, her benefits derived from the negotiation are negative (–$5 in this case), but those negative benefits accrue directly—and on a dollar-for-dollar basis—to Thomas, who would extract the entire $35 value plus a net transfer of $5 from the dealer. The wealth transfer from the dealer to Thomas is equal to the amount by which the dealer violated her reservation price (or $5 in our example). So in this case, the transaction benefits the dealer by –$5 and Thomas by $40.

Similarly, if Thomas pays more than his reservation price, the dealer claims the entire value represented in the bargaining zone plus a net transfer from Thomas. For instance, imagine that Thomas agrees to pay $180 per tire, violating his reservation price of $160. Here, his benefit is –$20 (again, his RP_b of $160 minus the price paid of $180 = –$20). However, the dealer realizes a full $55 of value ($180 – $125 = $55). But again, the value of the deal remains unchanged at $35.

In sum, the value of the exchange is *always* the difference between the two reservation prices, even if the parties strike a deal outside the bargaining zone. The situation is the same even when there is no overlap of reservation prices.

When the bargaining zone in a single-issue negotiation is negative, instead of positive, no deal exists that would simultaneously allow both parties to honor their reservation prices.[3] As a result, disciplined negotiators will not strike a deal. To demonstrate this, let's stick with the previous example but change Thomas's assessment of the tires' value.

Thomas feels a bit guilty purchasing these tires when he really doesn't *need* them, so he decides to make the purchase only if he gets an amazing deal of $110 (his reservation price), while hoping to pay only $75 (his aspiration price). Assume that the dealer's position does not change from the previous example. In this case the bargaining zone looks very different:

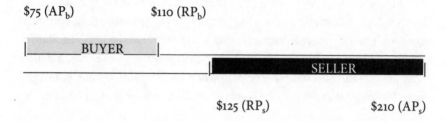

$75 (AP$_b$) $110 (RP$_b$)

BUYER

SELLER

$125 (RP$_s$) $210 (AP$_s$)

As the figure demonstrates, there is no overlap between Thomas's reservation price of $110 and the seller's reservation price of $125. The most that Thomas is willing to pay is less than the least the dealer is willing to accept.

If both Thomas and the dealer honor their respective reservation prices, no deal is possible. Given his preferences, Thomas would be better off walking away (guilt- and tire-free) than he would be after paying more than $110 per tire, and the dealer would be better off walking away than she would be if she accepted less than $125 per tire.

To strike at a deal under these circumstances, either Thomas or the dealer (or both, in the case of a price between $110 and $125) would have to violate their respective reservation prices. Consider the consequences of this outcome. Imagine that Thomas agrees to a price of $130 because he has gotten so caught up in the negotiation that he can no longer imagine walking away. Thomas ignores his reservation price of $110, which means that he receives −$20 of value (his RP$_b$ of $110 minus the price he pays of $130), while the seller improves her position by $5 ($130 minus her RP$_s$ of $125). Combining these two figures results in a value of −$15 (−$20 + $5), again the difference between the two reservation prices (i.e., RP$_b$ minus RP$_s$ or $110 − $125). While this deal is desirable from the dealer's perspective, it makes no sense for Thomas; it leaves him $20 worse off.

You may think that violating one's reservation price to reach such a deal is crazy, and that no one in his right mind would take a deal that made him worse off. Yet empirical evidence shows that because of a psychological bias in favor of agreement, it is not unusual for negotiators to agree to deals that make them worse off.[4] Time after time, we hear stories about people who do this, and we observe our students agreeing to proposals even though they know that the deal leaves them worse off than they would have been had they simply walked away. We can all come up with examples in our own lives.

When it comes to negotiation, it's important to know when to walk away. When negotiating, try to remember that no matter how badly you want to reach a deal, you improve your situation only if you get more than your reservation price. Opportunities to create value are missed when negotiators fail to reach an agreement when a positive bargaining zone exists, but also when negotiators do reach agreement when the bargaining zone is a negative. Although it can be difficult, avoiding such outcomes is a good rule to follow.

Our examples have focused on single-issue negotiations. Of course, negotiators often face scenarios that involve multiple distributive issues. Such scenarios are more complex, but also more potentially beneficial to all parties involved. For while you can create value with one issue—the value of the exchange—you can create even more value with two or more distributive issues—but that value is simply the pooled value of each of the exchanges.

CREATING VALUE WITH TWO DISTRIBUTIVE ISSUES

In the example of Thomas's search for new tires, suppose that the tire dealer prefers a high selling price and a later delivery date, while Thomas prefers a low selling price and an earlier delivery date. Suppose, too, that the benefits to Thomas of moving the delivery by one day exactly equal the costs that such a move would impose on the dealer. These issues are both distributive because moving the deal in any direction results in exactly offsetting gains and losses to the parties. That is, the value of every dollar that Thomas receives is equivalent to the value of every dollar that the dealer gives up. To reach a deal, Thomas and the dealer must now come to agreement on both issues; while this second issue seemingly makes the negotiation more complex, it also provides additional benefit. Thomas hopes to pay $75 per tire (his aspiration price), but is willing to go as high as $160 (his reservation price). In addition, he would like the tires delivered and mounted in seven days, but could accept, if necessary, delivery in as much as forty-five days. The dealer is asking $210 per tire, but will accept a price as low as $125 per tire. She prefers to deliver these tires in ninety days (when the next shipment of these high-performance tires can be bundled in with her regularly scheduled delivery from the wholesaler), but would be willing to deliver them in as little as thirty days.

Clearly, a positive bargaining zone exists in this negotiation—or rather, *two* positive bargaining zones exist, one for each issue. Pictorially, these two issues with their reservation and aspiration prices would look like this:

Price

$75 (AP$_b$) $160 (RP$_b$)

|_____BUYER_____|
|_____SELLER_____|

$125 (RP$_s$) $210 (AP$_s$)

Delivery Date

Within the next week (AP$_b$)   In 45 days (RP$_b$)

|_____BUYER_____|
|_____SELLER_____|

In 30 days (RP$_s$)   In 90 days (AP$_s$)

Any deal that satisfies both bargaining zones clearly makes both the dealer and Thomas better off, but there is more to the story. How much value does such a deal generate? Put differently, what is the value of a deal that satisfies both reservation prices?

When the issues are based on different metrics—in this case, days-to-delivery and price, it is difficult to evaluate the deal as a whole. To do that, you must be able to compare days to dollars. The answer is to create a common metric to allow the parties to trade one issue (price) for another (delivery date).

Successful negotiators recognize the importance of creating a common metric by which to evaluate the issues in a negotiation over multiple issues.

This is because negotiators can use such a metric to guide both the development and assessment of the proposals of their counterpart, thereby giving them a considerable competitive advantage. Finding a common metric provides you with a way to assess when you should say yes and when you should say no.

In the latest variation of the tire-buying example, in which price and delivery date are the two issues being negotiated, it is easy to calculate the value for the price as $35; as before, it's the reservation price of the buyer ($160) minus the reservation price of the seller ($125). The question is how to value the contribution of 15 days that results from the overlap between $RP_b - RP_s$.

Thomas faces an apples-and-oranges scenario, for he cannot add dollars and days and come up with a meaningful number; the two metrics need to be set to a common scale to allow a comparison. A simple way to do this is to determine how many dollars one day is worth. Admittedly, putting issues on a common metric like dollars can be tough. How many dollars is one day of waiting for delivery worth? What is your waiting time worth? Is a day of waiting the same as a day of working? Is every day worth the same?

From the perspective of both negotiators, let's assume that each additional day until delivery is worth $2. In other words, since the issue is distributive, this would mean that the dealer values an additional day at +$2 while Thomas values it at -$2. In that case the value in the exchange (VE) is:

$$VE = \$35 + (\$2/\text{day} * 15 \text{ days}) = \$65$$

Valuing the two issues on the same scale enables the negotiators to evaluate the proposal across both issues. It also allows them to identify and evaluate a single bargaining zone, rather than attempting to address two of them. Notice that in the example the common metric is dollars, but it could just as easily have been points or toothpicks!

With this common metric, Thomas and the dealer have a positive bargaining zone, one whose value is $65. No longer do the negotiators have to contend with two bargaining zones, one of $35 (price) and another of 15 days (delivery).

Having a common metric also allows Thomas and the dealer to exchange concessions on price for concessions on delivery date, thereby maximizing the value they receive from the deal. Indeed, as negotiations become increasingly complex, the value of packaging proposals rather than negotiating each issue individually proves increasingly beneficial for value claiming. Instead of an impasse, there are now $65 of value to be split between Thomas and the dealer.

Moreover, the bargaining zone in the negotiation grows significantly with the introduction of a common metric on which to assess the issues. Absent this common metric, the only feasible deals are those that simultaneously satisfy both bargaining zones; that is, deals with a price between $160 and $125 and a delivery date between 30 and 45 days. Once a common metric is established, one or both of the negotiators can set their reservation price at the deal level. This creates the opportunity to design deals that (had they focused on an issue-level reservation price) would violate their reservation price on one issue so long as they are compensated by a sufficient payoff on the other. For example, Thomas might pay just $120 per tire ($5 less than the seller's reservation price) but agree to get the tires in 60 days (greater than his own reservation price on delivery). In this example, the deal struck will create $65 of value to be divided among the parties. With this aggregate measure, *both* parties can do better than their individual status quo positions. The common metric represents the first step in crafting deals that create value.

The situation becomes more complex when multiple distributive issues in a negotiation create one bargaining zone that is negative, and another that is positive. In a case where both bargaining zones are positive, a mutually beneficial deal can be achieved by negotiating one issue at a time. However, creating a common metric facilitates an agreement in which parties sacrifice on one issue to be compensated by their counterparts' concessions on another.

In addition, a sequential negotiation of two distributive issues requires two positive bargaining zones; a sequential process is not likely to work if one bargaining zone is negative. In the example above, if Thomas had a reservation price of $110, Thomas and the tire dealer would not be able to come to an agreement because the least the dealer would accept is $125 per tire—even if they were to be able to agree to a delivery date between 30 days and 45 days if they insist on negotiating one issue at a time. However, if they yoke the two issues, they can negotiate complementary exchanges, creating mutually beneficial settlements that may exist outside one or both of the individual bargaining zones.

But it gets even better. Consider a settlement where Thomas and the dealer agree to a price of $175 and delivery in seven days. If negotiated sequentially, this deal would satisfy neither Thomas nor the tire dealer, because the price violates Thomas's reservation price of $110 while the delivery violated the dealer's reservation price of 30 days.

Price

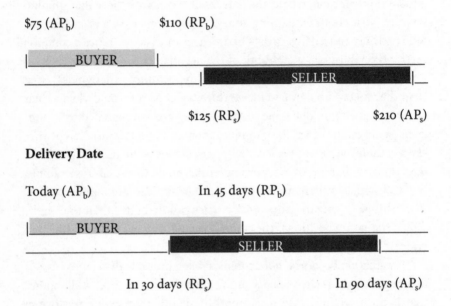

$75 (AP$_b$) $110 (RP$_b$)

| BUYER |

| SELLER |

$125 (RP$_s$) $210 (AP$_s$)

Delivery Date

Today (AP$_b$)   In 45 days (RP$_b$)

| BUYER |

| SELLER |

In 30 days (RP$_s$)   In 90 days (AP$_s$)

From Thomas's perspective, this deal is worth −$65 from price (because a price of $175 exceeds his reservation price of $110 by $65) plus 2 × (reservation delivery date of 45 days minus actual delivery date of 7 days) dollars for the early delivery. Thomas values this deal −$65 + (2 × 38 days) = $11. Thus there is value to be had negotiating by packaging these two issues that would not be available if each issue were negotiated separately—a strategy that is facilitated by valuing the issues on a common metric.

The dealer values the price at $50 (settlement of $175 minus dealer reservation price of $125) plus the negative value of the early delivery (equal to 2 × settlement of 7 days minus reservation price of 30 days) or −$46. Hence the tire dealer values this settlement at $50 + (−$46) = $4. The dealer would not have agreed to delivery in seven days, but she would be happy to take the price of $175 per tire. Because the dealer can extract a price that is so much higher than her reservation price to offset the negative value that results from a much earlier delivery date, negotiating the items as a package creates a deal worth $15 and leaves both the tire dealer and Thomas better off than they would be had they walked away.

This example shows that, even when multiple issues are distributive and the bargaining zones on a per issue basis are not all positive, reasonable deals may still be possible. Because of this potential, it is important to think about the negotiation as a package rather than focusing on one issue at a time.

Of course, it is only possible to think about the negotiation as a package if you develop a metric to compare issues that are denominated in different units, such as days and dollars. To accomplish this, you need to determine the minimum value that you are willing to accept for each issue, and a conversion rate that allows you to compare the relative values of each issue on an apples-to-apples basis. Only then can you evaluate a proposal against an aggregate reservation price that incorporates the individual reservation prices of all the issues.

It may not surprise you that deal-level reservation prices are more difficult to determine with the same precision that we have provided in this chapter's examples. In this example there were precise reservation prices for each of the two issues, but in the real world such precision is rare. Thomas would struggle to say with absolute certainty what his reservation price was on the price of the tires or the days to delivery. In reality, Thomas can only *estimate* his reservation price, and that estimate is subject to error.

But help is on its way. The magnitude of the errors in Thomas's estimation reflects how uncertain he feels about the accuracy of his estimate of his reservation price. If the errors were independent—that is, immune to influences from outside forces such as his emotions or urges and instead represent an accurate reflection of his willingness to pay, now given his various expectations regarding replacing his tires—then Thomas would be more confident about the accuracy of the reservation value of a multi-issue package than he could possibility be about the accuracy of each individual reservation price estimate. When aggregated to the package level, the individual errors could potentially offset one another, increasing the accuracy of his estimation. The more issues under consideration, the more confidence Thomas will have about the accuracy of his aggregate reservation price.

SUMMARY

Getting more of what you want in a negotiation is intimately connected to the potential value in the exchange. The total value available to the parties in the exchange is reflected in the bargaining zone. This is the value that exists even when negotiators place equal value on the issues but value them such that one party's gain is the other's loss: that is, when the issues are zero-sum or distributive in nature.

In considering your negotiations that focus on distributive issues, remember:

- In a situation with only distributive issues, the overlap of the parties' reservation prices delineates the value of the deal that is available to be claimed.
- Valuing multiple issues with a common metric can dramatically increase the range of potential agreements.
- Once you are able to value different issues on a common scale, you should set reservation prices at the level of the deal rather than on a per issue basis.
    ◦ Creating a deal-level reservation price allows negotiators to leverage the benefits that they can achieve on one issue to offset the potential cost they might incur on a second issue.
    ◦ Creating a deal-level reservation price also is likely to reduce the uncertainty of your estimate, because the errors you make in determining the reservation price of each issue are likely to offset each other.

In the examples in this chapter, both negotiators valued the issues, dollars and days, in the same way. While people commonly expect this to hold true—what is important to you is equally important to your counterpart, and what is of little value to you is of little value to your counterpart—expectations may not reflect the true value that your counterpart holds for the issues. These differences in the importance of issues or values across individuals create additional opportunities for negotiators to get more of what they want.

In the next chapter, we will focus on creating value within the exchange through trading issues that the parties value differently. This differential valuation is crucial for deals that effectively create value beyond what would exist if parties valued each issue the same, but opposite.

CHAPTER FOUR

VALUE CREATING

The Integrative Potential in Negotiations

Uncomfortable with the seemingly adversarial nature of value claiming, people often focus on negotiations as opportunities to create value—to find deals that can enhance the outcomes of all the parties. In this chapter we discuss how this occurs. However, while the primary focus of this chapter is on value creation, keep in mind that the ultimate goal of negotiations is to claim value—to get (more of) what you want!

Value creation in a negotiation has several seemingly self-evident benefits. First, it increases the amount of value that can be allocated between the parties. Think of this as enlarging the bargaining zone—the area between your reservation price and that of your counterpart. In isolation, enlarging the bargaining zone is a good thing: value creation has the benefit of potentially making at least one party better off without hurting the other party.[1] Widening the bargaining zone also makes it easier to find a deal that exceeds both parties' reservation prices thus reducing the likelihood of an impasse.

Value creation has a psychological benefit as well. By improving the deal for your counterpart, you increase his goodwill toward you. Even when you end up with objectively the same amount, he may give you credit for your cooperative engagement.[2]

For value creation to be possible, a negotiation must have at least one integrative issue—that is, an issue in which the parties value outcomes differently. This type of issue differs importantly from the zero-sum or distributive issues discussed in Chapter 3. With distributive issues, the cost of a concession made by one side exactly equals the benefit of that concession to the other side. Thus, value is created through an exchange but negotiating distributive issues within that exchange only offers parties the opportunity to redistribute that value.

Issues that are easily divisible or are valued for their extrinsic worth are more likely to be distributive while issues where the value is more intrinsic or subjective to an individual are more likely to be integrative. What makes an issue integrative is that it is valued differently by the negotiating parties such that the cost of a concession by one party is less than the concession benefits the other party.

Having a single integrative issue by itself is not sufficient for value creation, however, because a concession still leaves the conceding party worse off (even though by less than the counterpart benefits). Thus, while a necessary condition for value creation is the presence of at least one integrative issue, the receiving party must be a willing to concede on at least one other issue to compensate the conceding party. That additional issue can either be distributive or integrative. In that case, trading an issue that you value less than your counterpart in exchange for concessions on an issue you value equally (distributive) or even more (integrative) than your counterpart creates value. This strategy is called log-rolling (or horse trading), and it involves extracting concessions on issues that are of more value to you and giving concessions on issues that are of less value to you (or preference trades). The point is to realize the integrative potential through value-enhancing trades that get you more of what you want at a "cost" that you are willing to pay.

THE INTEGRATIVE POTENTIAL

Although the principle of value creation is straightforward, creating value in an actual negotiation requires negotiators to assess the relative value of issues for themselves and their counterparts. This is difficult for two reasons. First, many negotiators strongly believe that negotiations are zero sum, leading them to miss the value-creating potential of many negotiations. Second, overcoming this zero-sum presumption requires information to identify integrative issues.

Take our tire example from Chapter 3; let's see what changes when Thomas and the dealer value the issues of price and delivery time differently. The basic structure of the scenario is the same as before, a bargain-ing zone on price between $125 and $160 per tire and a delivery date between 30 and 45 days.

Price

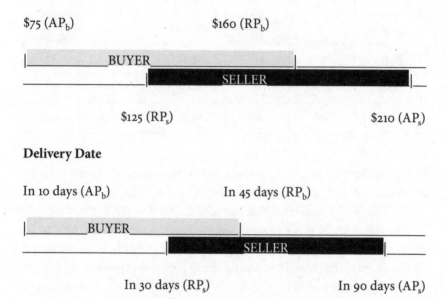

$75 (AP$_b$) $160 (RP$_b$)

BUYER

SELLER

$125 (RP$_s$) $210 (AP$_s$)

Delivery Date

In 10 days (AP$_b$)   In 45 days (RP$_b$)

BUYER

SELLER

In 30 days (RP$_s$)   In 90 days (AP$_s$)

The dealer is content to continue using the metric of $2 per day to value the delivery so that these two issues can be evaluated on the same scale. However, Thomas now assigns a different value to the delivery date: an early delivery is now essential. In fact, he is willing to raise his price by $10 per day to obtain as early a delivery as possible.[3]

This asymmetry in the valuation of the delivery date changes the total value of different combinations of price and delivery dates. Using the dealer's perspective of price and delivery dates as a starting point, the value of an earlier delivery swamps the value available in the price range under discussion from Thomas's perspective. Table 4.1 shows how the issue-value matrix looks. Note that Thomas's reservation price on each issue is highlighted in grey; while the reservation price of the seller is highlighted in black.

In the split-the-difference example ($145 and 37 days), the deal is worth $95 to Thomas ($15 + $80) and $34 to the dealer ($20 + $14), for a total of $129.

TABLE 4.1 ISSUE-VALUE MATRIX

Price			Delivery date		
Price/Tire	Buyer	Seller	Delivery	Buyer	Seller
$75	85	−50	10 days	350	−40
$125	35	0	30 days	150	0
$145	15	20	37 days	80	14
$160	0	35	45 days	0	30
$210	−50	85	90 days	−600	120

However, had the parties taken advantage of the asymmetry in the value of the delivery date, the outcome would be quite a bit different—considerably more value would be created that could be claimed by the parties.

Recall that Thomas is willing to pay $10 more per day for the tires to be delivered sooner. In contrast, the dealer requires only $2 per day to speed up the delivery. Because Thomas and the dealer value the delivery date so differently, the best deal here would be a combination of a high price per tire associated with a delivery date within thirty days. Both parties are better off when Thomas is willing to give concessions on price while receiving concessions resulting in an earlier delivery time.

Consider how the integrative value of the deal is affected by this trade-off. If Thomas were willing to go to his reservation price on price while the dealer went to her reservation price on delivery, the deal would be worth $150 ($0 + $150) to Thomas and $35 ($35 + $0) to the dealer, resulting in $185 in total. They have significantly enlarged the pie (from $129 to $185), and each has claimed some of that additionally created value.

Yet the dealer, in this case, is not extracting as much value as Thomas. Obviously, this would change if the dealer realized how valuable early delivery was to Thomas. If she paid attention, she might realize that delivery date is an integrative issue. However, Thomas should avoid divulging how much he actually values an early delivery as this would induce the dealer to demand more. Going back to the idea of packaging issues to achieve a reservation price, the dealer could propose to get the tires delivered within the next ten days (the buyer's aspiration price) if Thomas were willing to pay the dealer's asking price of $210. If the parties were able to agree to a $210 price and delivery within ten days, the dealer would realize $45 ($85 − $40) of value while Thomas would realize $300 (−$50 + $350) of value. Hence, the integrative value in this situation would increase to $345.

So a better deal can be reached—even though it might violate the reservation price of individual issues—so long as the benefits received in exchange for this violation on price are sufficiently valuable. Since Thomas is in a big hurry to get the tires (reflected in his valuation of the delivery issue), he might be willing, even eager, to take this deal; in the aggregate, after all, it creates $300 in value for him even though it violates his reservation price on price per tire. The same is true for the dealer. Given the dealer's concern with price, she should be willing, even eager, to deliver the tires in ten days even though the delivery time violates her reservation price on that issue, because the deal gives her $45 in combined value.

As this scenario demonstrates, value creation hinges on the parties' ability to discover that they value issues differently and to use that information to propose packages that make them better off. Often this isn't easy—but if it's accomplished, the value available to be claimed by one or both parties can be much greater than in a purely distributive negotiation.

Thus, the challenge of realizing the integrative potential of a deal requires that you understand the issues and your preferences as well as the issues and preferences as valued by your counterpart. This is important for three reasons. First, it provides information that allows you to agree only to deals that do not violate your package-level reservation price. Second, it allows you to make trades that create value. Finally, it allows you to claim more of the value that has been created.

But herein lies the danger. Realizing how highly Thomas values an early delivery allows the dealer to extract more value from Thomas. By revealing that each delivery date is worth $10 per tire to him, Thomas and the dealer may find a deal that maximizes value—but that value may be claimed entirely by the dealer.

In negotiations not only can you gather information during the preparation phase, but also the negotiation itself can provide numerous opportunities not only to verify the information you gathered in the planning phase but also to expand your knowledge. In the next section, we demonstrate strategies and tactics that allow you to exchange information while minimizing the impact of this information exchange on your ability to claim value.

THE INFORMATION-GATHERING CHALLENGE

I t seems reasonable to expect that increasing the size of the pie will allow you to claim more of it. But is that necessarily true?

To create value in a negotiation the parties must share information that will allow them to identify the issues; determine which are distributive, integrative, and congruent; and for integrative issues, allow trades that reflect their respective differences in value. Yet sharing too much information (or the wrong kind) can put you at a competitive disadvantage. Specifically, value creation does not change either party's reservation price. As a result, your counterpart could claim all the value created (and then some) if she could infer your reservation price from the information shared.

From an economics perspective, sharing information in the value creation process creates two challenges: First, separating the negotiation into a value-creating phase and a value-claiming phase runs the risk of limiting the value you can claim. Once both sides know the size of the pie, the negotiation becomes distributive (zero sum), and value claiming becomes contentious: whatever you get comes out of your counterpart's pocket. Second, the negotiator who first realizes the value differential between the parties has an increased capacity to claim the value created. To illustrate this first challenge, consider the implications of a full-disclosure strategy.

Sharing information indiscriminately is potentially disastrous: If such sharing behavior is not reciprocated, you run the risk that if a deal is consummated, all you would claim is your reservation price. But when all information is shared by both parties, you may be able to create the largest pie possible, but you almost certainly won't be able to claim more than half of it because your counterpart will be attempting to claim as much as possible as well. Perhaps you don't see that as a problem. However, if, for example, you bring more critical resources to the deal than those brought by your counterpart, you may find yourself less than satisfied. Moreover, attempting to extract more than an equal split will result in an extremely contentious process, so much so that one party may choose an impasse over losing her claim to equal distribution. In short, when all the information is shared, then the only task left is to fight over who gets what. The negotiation becomes adversarial—it is only about value claiming.

To illustrate this challenge, suppose the dealer discovers that delivery time is five times more important to Thomas than it is to her. For every day earlier, Thomas is willing to pay $10, whereas originally the dealer would have been willing to charge only an additional $2. With this knowledge, the dealer can offer Thomas earlier delivery for $9 per day. From Thomas's perspective, this offer nets him an additional $1 per day. The outcome exceeds his reservation price—but not by much, and most of the value created ends up in the dealer's pocket.

It's important to understand, too, that not all information is equally strategic. Revealing information that allows the parties to figure out which issues are integrative may be necessary for value creation; revealing the exact integrative potential for these issues is highly strategic, because understanding how each party values the integrative issues provides a strategic advantage in value claiming. (This principle will be emphasized in Chapter 6.)

The bilateral full-disclosure strategy is great if you are certain that you are both happy with splitting the resources equally and will share all the information openly. This is much more likely to be the case when you are negotiating with counterparts with whom you have a long-term relationship. In fact, research demonstrates that if the relationship is an important issue, then an equal split of the value that is created is exactly what most people want.[4]

But what if the full-disclosure strategy were unilateral? For example, while you reveal all your information, your counterpart misrepresents her interests. Knowing all your information, she can find the deal that maximizes value creation in the negotiation. But what part of that value will you get? The deal will likely be struck just at, or slightly in excess of, your reservation price. After all, your counterpart, knowing all your information including your reservation price, could fashion a deal that provides you with the absolute minimum that you are willing to take.

In conclusion, since there is no way for you to verify whether your counterpart is speaking or obfuscating the truth, the full-disclosure strategy is dangerous because you may well end up with not much more than your reservation price. This is particularly true if this were a one-time negotiation because your counterpart need not take the long-term consequences of her behavior into account.

So, if you want to claim more value, what other options will protect your value-claiming potential? Next, we show you how you can reduce the general risk associated with sharing information.

MITIGATING THE RISK OF INFORMATION EXCHANGE

In some situations information exchange can be relatively safe: for example, when you negotiate among friends. Ongoing relationships such as friendships inhibit one party's short-term exploitation of the other for strategic advantage.

Yet there are reasons why you might withhold information even from your friends. Perhaps you are concerned about generating conflict if you push too hard—paradoxically this may include additional information that might make you both better off. So rather than engaging in that hard work, you opt for a quick, easy solution that avoids conflict even if it significantly reduces the potential value created. In such a scenario, the relationship has actually made information sharing more difficult. The mutual desire to maintain the comfort level of the interaction often results in sacrificing the quality of the deal.

From our perspective, there is nothing wrong with accepting a bad deal for the good of a relationship, as long as it is done intentionally. Yet easy-solution strategies are often adopted because of parties' aversion to conflict rather than a thoughtful assessment of what they would lose or gain.

Just as negotiating with friends and partners can be difficult, negotiating with strangers (or in a one-time deal) has its challenges, as well. You are likely to know less about which issues matter and how much they matter to a stranger, making the prenegotiation preparation more challenging. In addition, you may be less adept at interpreting the information conveyed by strangers during the negotiation. And the process of sharing information may be riskier, as well. First, because there is less chance of a future interaction, the cost of misrepresentation is much lower. As a result, each party should be more suspicious when interpreting information and triangulate it with other evidence to assess its reliability. Second, value claiming will likely be more contentious, because there is no benefit to creating good will or long-term reciprocity when (in the context of the negotiation, at least) there is no tomorrow.

Finally, value creation is hampered: you and your counterpart are more likely to expect the issues to be distributive, thus justifying more aggressive strategies such as exaggerating, misrepresenting, and withholding information.

But regardless of whether you negotiate with friends or strangers, high aspirations—or high expectations—are beneficial. Moreover, there is another necessary condition: you need to be ready to problem-solve—that is, to craft proposals that take advantage of the asymmetries in preferences between you and your counterpart to *create* value without unnecessarily sharing information that could damage your ability to *claim* value. This requires focused information gathering and thoughtful sharing.

In the next section, we consider ways to gather and share information in a negotiation. Some of these strategies are better at protecting your value-claiming potential while others are more conducive to value creation. Choosing ways to share information is a strategic choice—and the right strategy depends on the particular situation, your counterparts, and your goals.

CREATING AND CLAIMING VALUE: AN EXAMPLE

This example continues our vehicular theme, but gives Thomas and the tire dealer a break; rather, it concerns Margaret's real-life purchase of a new car. This negotiation appears—at first glance—to be very similar to our first example of Thomas and his tires: it concerns a single, distributive issue (price). Yet by focusing on issues other than the dollar value of the car, Margaret was able to create considerably more value and get a better deal.

Margaret could have conceived of the transaction as simply an exchange in which she was willing to trade cash for a new car. Naturally, Margaret wanted to pay as little as possible for the car while the dealer wanted to extract as high a price as possible. The dealer set a price (i.e., the first offer); if Margaret willingly accepted it, then value has been created by the exchange because Margaret must value the car more than she values that cash (and vice versa for the dealer). If, on the other hand, Margaret were successful in negotiating the dealer's offering price, then she would have managed to claim additional value—and the dealer would have lost value, all by negotiating over a single, purely distributive issue.

Yet within this exchange there was opportunity to create more value, so long as Margaret and the dealer were willing to include additional issues in the negotiation—especially issues they valued differently (i.e., integrative). Indeed, before she started to negotiate, there were a couple of issues that Margaret wanted to discuss that had the potential to increase the value of the deal to her.

The first issue was trading in her ten-year old SUV. She could have sold it to a private party, but she placed a premium on selling it quickly and was willing to sacrifice some money for the convenience of having the dealer take the car as a trade-in. In addition, by trading in her old car, she would also save on the sales tax on her new car, because its final purchase price (on which sales tax is assessed) would be reduced by the value of the trade-in. Having done her homework, Margaret believed that if she were lucky she could get $7,500 through a sale to a private party; however, the dealer was only willing to pay $5,000. From Margaret's perspective, the convenience of leaving her old SUV at the dealership was worth more than the potential $2,500 she would forgo by not selling it herself. Knowing this, we can calculate that Margaret values every dollar that the dealer offers her for the car at least at $1.50. The extra fifty cents per dollar represents the cost of the hassle of selling her car privately as well as the additional taxes she would have to pay.

A second issue with value-creating potential was the asymmetric value associated with the cost of the routine maintenance. The value of that maintenance was more to Margaret than the costs to the dealer. Therefore Margaret was willing to pay a higher price to extend the length of time that the dealer would cover routine maintenance.

Fortunately, there was another issue that the dealer cared more about than Margaret: a high rating of the dealership on the customer-satisfaction survey conducted by the automobile manufacturer. Thus the dealer extended the length of time that the warranty covered routine maintenance while Margaret agreed to convey her satisfaction about the interaction in the strongest possible terms. Thus, value was first created by the sale itself: the trade-in, increasing the coverage of routine maintenance, and ensuring Margaret's satisfaction with the process were all ways in which additional value was created.

We have been focusing so far on two related mechanisms for value creation—trading among issues that you and your counterpart value differently (or log-rolling)—and adding issues—making it easier to find value-enhancing trades. In the final section of this chapter, we will focus another useful method to create value—contingency contracting.

CONTINGENCY CONTRACTING: PLAYING ON YOUR DIFFERENCES TO CREATE VALUE

In some negotiations, the true value of an outcome can only be known at some time in the future. Think about executive salaries as a compensation for managing the firm well or compensating a television producer for obtaining high the ratings of his television shows. In each situation, the actual value of the issue cannot be determined at the time of the negotiation. The ultimate value may be a function of how the contract creates incentives for future effort by the parties as well as the differential beliefs that each party has about the future.

Because such issues are difficult to value, they are good candidates for inclusion in contingency contracts. Think about contingency contracts as bets.[5] The executive believes that she can do a great job at running the firm. By accepting the compensation in stock options, she is betting that the future stock price will be higher than the exercise price of her options, while the producer's compensation will increase as his television show is watched by more people (higher ratings mean more viewers and more advertising revenue).

Contingency contracts are challenging to design and typically appear at a relatively late stage in the negotiation—often as a last effort to avoid an impasse. To see their challenges and benefits, let's explore how a contingency contract saved Thomas a lot of money on his new home.

Thomas had interviewed a number of architects with excellent reputations in Chicago's North Shore. After much deliberation, he and his wife Franziska chose one and then spent about eight months designing the home they had always wanted. Of course, the design had to be completed before the price could be negotiated. When both Thomas and Franziska were both relatively comfortable with the design, the builder (Out-of-this-World Architectural Design—OAD[6]) priced the construction of the house they had designed.

While Thomas and Franziska negotiated with the architect, another change occurred. From the time when the first price was proposed to the point of the negotiation, the economy had contracted, and prices on most building materials had dropped precipitously. As you might imagine, Thomas wanted the benefit of that price reduction. The OAD contracts person, Rod, held the position that any benefit from cost reductions from the subcontractors belonged to OAD (interesting to note that OAD was not expecting to absorb the subcontractors' cost increases—those would be absorbed by the subcontractors themselves). Thomas thought that the amount of potential cost savings could be very large; after all, the initial price points had been solicited in early 2008—in a much different economic environment from late 2009. After some heated discussion, the parties reached a stalemate with both parties seriously considering calling off the entire project.

One evening, after a long day of discussions for both parties, Rod left with this parting comment: "I cannot believe that you are going to walk away from this deal for a dispute worth less than $3,000." Thomas was stunned—for two reasons. One, he had calculated the potential benefit as being much higher than Rod's comment indicated. Second, if he were going to walk away from this deal for a mere $3,000, so was Rod and OAD. After all, negotiation is an interdependent process. As such, Thomas was sure that the actual benefit had to be higher than $3,000 or Rod's behavior would make no sense. The next morning, Thomas contacted Rod with the following proposal: OAD could have the first $3,000 in cost savings and then they would split the remainder of the savings: 25 percent would go to OAD and 75 percent to Thomas and Franziska. Thomas knew that if Rod were accurately representing his true beliefs about the size of the cost savings, then this deal should be very attractive because it gave him 100 percent of what he calculated would be the potential savings: OAD would be kept whole. However, if the cost savings were much larger than $3,000 (as Thomas suspected), then this deal would look much less attractive to Rod. After a few more rounds of discussion—which included the principal of the firm—a deal was finally struck. The contingency contract was modified to a 50-50 split between Thomas and OAD of any cost savings beyond the first $3,000. Thus, it seems that this $3000 figure was, in Rod's mind, a real and significant barrier to an agreement.

Thomas had been the one to propose increasing OAD's proportion of the benefit from 25 percent to 50 percent—but he was not simply being generous. Rather, he wanted OAD to seek out cost reductions whenever possible. As such, he was concerned that a 25–75 split would not give them sufficient incentives to press their subcontractors, so he proposed a 50-50 split to which OAD happily agreed—and the construction on Thomas's new home began.

As this example illustrates, contingency contracts make sense when the parties differ in their expectations about the size of the future benefit (as Thomas and Rod did) or when they differ in their risk profiles or time horizons. Such differences result in the parties valuing these factors differently, thereby creating integrative potential. However, remember that contingent contracts reflect the parties betting on different future outcomes, and they both cannot be right. For at least one—and maybe both— the deal they expect might end up being quite a bit different from the deal they actually get.

In deciding whether to propose a contingency contract, there are at least three criteria to consider. First, contingency contacts require that the parties have a continuing relationship—that both parties are around when it comes time to settle up.

Second, contingency contracts should be transparent. Consider the differing levels of transparency if your compensation is based on company profits or company sales. Sales are a much more transparent metric than profits because it is easier to determine when a sale occurs than when profit is realized. In addition, organizations have considerable leeway in defining what expenses should be deducted from revenues to compute profit. There are numerous stories about successful films in Hollywood that have never achieved profitability, often told by movie stars and backers who agreed to contingency contracts that kicked in once "profitability" was reached.

Third, contingency contracts must be enforceable. Part and parcel of the first two criteria is the requirement that both parties have the ability to insure that the bet gets paid. Think about the level of interest that credit card companies charge high-risk customers. This is a contingency contract. The credit card company will loan you money to purchase a variety of goods and services. In exchange, they expect this loan to be repaid at a specified future date and with interest. The specific interest rate depends on how the bank assesses the risk of the enforceability of the contract. Do you have the means to repay the loan? Will you still be around to pay the debt or to go to court if you fail to pay? If this or the other two criteria cannot be met, then it's best for you to stick to more standard, fail-safe ways of creating value in a negotiation.

SUMMARY

Value creation is an important aspect of negotiation and is intimately connected to value claiming. Simply put, creating value allows you to claim it—to get more of what you want. Value creation comes in two forms: the value that is created by the exchange itself, and the value represented by the integrative potential of the multiple issues that may be valued differently by the parties.

In considering value creating opportunities, remember:

1. Value creation is in the service of value claiming. What really counts is how much value you can get out of your negotiated interactions.
2. While it may be easier to claim more value when more value is created through the interaction, the information exchanged to create value may handicap your ability to claim value.
3. To search for issues that you and your counterpart value differently because having multiple issues that are valued differently can increase the value of the negotiation.
4. Setting your reservation price at the level of the deal or package rather than at the issue level facilitates your ability to create value by increasing the potential trades to which you can agree.
5. Figuring out which issues are valued differently—and how differently they are valued—provides an important window into the value-creating opportunities.
6. When different expectations of future events, risks, or time threaten the agreement, consider exploring a contingency contract where parties can bet on their beliefs.
7. If considering a contingency contract, only do so if the following three conditions exist: (1) there is a continuing relationship between the parties, (2) the contract is based on transparent aspects of the deal, and (3) the contract is enforceable.

In these first four chapters you have explored the basic structures of a negotiation. In the next chapter, we walk you through the planning and preparation process, with a focus on identifying what you want and, equally important, assessing what your counterpart wants. The information that you gather during the planning process is critical to success because in negotiation, what you don't know can really hurt you.

CHAPTER FIVE

MAPPING OUT THE NEGOTIATION

What You Don't Know Can REALLY Hurt You

By now, we hope we've convinced you that getting a good deal should be the goal of any negotiation. However, although understanding what constitutes a good deal is central to success, negotiators often are confused about what they should be trying to achieve—especially about which trades among the issues at hand make them better off and which don't. Only through careful planning can they obtain clarity about these crucial aspects of the negotiation, and maximize their chances of getting more out of it.

The first step when planning and preparing for a negotiation is to identify your goal for the negotiation—exactly what is it that you want more of? But this is only the first step. In this chapter, we outline the steps necessary to systematically plan for a negotiation and enhance your chances of getting a good deal.

The planning process is divided into three phases: (1) figuring out what you want; (2) figuring out what your counterpart wants; and (3) developing your negotiation strategy based on what you know about yourself and what you discover about your counterpart. The first phase focuses on identifying your goals, your issues, your preferences, and your reservation and aspiration prices. The ultimate objective of this phase is to derive an issues-value matrix or a comprehensive list of settlement options and the relative value of each of those settlement options to you.

In phase two the focus switches to the goals, preferences, and reservation price and aspiration of your counterpart to create an issue-value matrix from her perspective. Obviously, this is a much more difficult task, and undoubtedly there will be some aspects that you cannot accurately assess. Therefore, in addition to the preparation before the negotiation, you should supplement and verify your information as the negotiation unfolds.

Finally, combining the two perspectives of the issue-value matrix allows you to develop your negotiation strategy. With this roadmap, you will be better able to assess alternatives, make creative proposals, and decide whether to accept your counterpart's proposal or to walk away.

Now, before you decide to skip the first step as being obvious or even trivial—after all, why would you ever engage in a negotiation without knowing what you want—our experience shows that many negotiators do in fact start negotiating without really understanding what they are trying to achieve. As it turns out, knowing what you want is harder than it appears, and even experienced negotiators forget or change their goals in the heat of a negotiation.

Because of the competitive nature of negotiations, negotiators often shift their objective from getting more of what they want to simply beating the other side. This is best demonstrated by an exercise we often conduct entitled Competitive Advertising. We separate our students into teams and instruct them (both orally and in the written instructions) that the goal of the game is to make as much money for their team as possible. In each of the ten rounds, teams must simultaneously decide whether to cooperate (not advertise) or defect (advertise). The payoffs are highest for teams who advertise while their counterparts do not advertise. The payoffs are intermediate when both teams do not advertise, highly negative when they both advertise, and even more negative for teams who do not advertise when their counterparts advertise. After round three we allow the teams to "negotiate" and resume the game, then "negotiate" again after round seven. The teams resume the game again for the three last rounds, at which point the game is over and the total profits and losses are tallied.

This game confronts students with a classic example of the prisoner's dilemma—a scenario in which both parties have incentives to undermine their opponents even when they would both be better off if they cooperated. As one would expect, most teams lose money in this game. When confronted with this fact, some teams very quickly point out that they lost less than their counterparts, even though they admit that they lost money.

In fact, if you eavesdropped on their conversations, you would observe that most teams quickly transform their objective from making as much money as possible to beating the other team. What's more, most of the teams that beat their counterparts do so by losing less, not by making more. As a result, because the goal is shifting from one of doing well for one's team to beating the other team, negotiators and their counterparts are both worse off.

One of the main lessons of this example—and of this chapter—is that losing sight of your goal can be very damaging to both you and even to your counterpart. The good news is that careful planning can help you maintain the clarity and focus on your goal. It is challenging enough to figure out and commit to your reservation prices, alternatives, and aspirations without the interference of an ongoing negotiation. Without clearly defining these parameters, you are likely to be at the mercy of your counterpart in ways that will increase not only the likelihood that you will get less than you could, but also the risk that you will accept a deal that makes you worse off than you would have been had you not negotiated at all.

PHASE ONE: FIGURING OUT WHAT YOU WANT AND CREATING THE ISSUES-VALUE MATRIX

This first phase of the planning process—the one in which you assess your own goals for the negotiation—has six steps: (1) determine what you want to achieve; (2) break down your overall goal into individual issues; (3) rank the issues by importance in achieving the overall goal; (4) identify possible settlement options for each issue; (5) assign relative values to each issue; and (6) determine your overall reservation price and your overall aspiration value.

1) What Do You Want to Achieve in the Negotiation?

Why are you negotiating? What do you want to achieve in this interaction? At this stage, focus on the high-level goal rather than on a particular issue or issues. For example, you may be negotiating to get a new job, buying a car, improving the control you have over your work schedule, or having more influence in your work team.

To illustrate the preparation process, imagine that you are in the market for a new car. Your goal is to purchase the coolest car at the best price. Thus, the motivation for your negotiation is to claim value in the form of the cool new car but to pay as little as possible for that coolness and not to violate your budget constraint!

While setting that overall goal, you are implicitly also determining what is *not* your goal. For instance, when buying a car, you goal should not be to make the dealer happy, or (presumably) to establish a long-term relationship with the dealer. It is very important not to lose sight of what is important to you in the negotiation and what is not!

2) What Are the Issues over Which You May Be Negotiating?

Once you have determined the overall objective, list the attributes that characterize the outcome. These are the issues over which you will be negotiating. As we saw in Chapter 4, the more issues there are in play, the more opportunity there will be for value creation.

So what are the issues, and what are your positions on those issues that, in the aggregate, can satisfy your overall goal? You need to be creative and inclusive about what issues to include in the discussion. Since your overall goal is to buy a really cool car, what are the attributes that are critical for maximum coolness? Once you have identified the make and model, likely issues that relate to an affordably cool car are the price, delivery, warranty, extended warranties, color, dealer-installed options, and financing. For the purpose of this illustration, consider issues related to costs: price and financing terms; and issues that affect coolness: color and audio components.

3) How Important Is Each Issue to the Achievement of Your Goal?

Once you have identified your goal and its attendant issues, rank those issues in terms of their relative contribution to your goal. The ultimate objective is to establish your trade-off values among the issues. This will help you maximize the chances of achieving your overall goal. Understanding these relative trade-offs highlights potential substitutions among the issues, thus increasing the number of possible deals.

Because this is a difficult task, we recommend that you begin by ordering the issues by relative importance. You can do this best by first thinking about each issue and then comparing how achieving it moves you closer to meeting your overall goal. Those that are most central will be the most important. So for example, when buying a car, the size of the engine may be more important than whether the car has a metalized paint.

Assume that you view costs and coolness as approximately equally important. Within the cost component, you view price much more important than financing, while within the coolness component, you view audio twice as important as color.

To quantify these relative ranks, you need to compare one issue to another. The best way to do this is to create a metric on which you array the issues. For example, you decide to use a metric of 100 points. Of this total and based on what you value, you allocate 46 points to costs and 54 points to coolness. In turn, of the 46 costs points, you allocate 40 to price and 6 to financing, while of the 54 coolness points, you allocate 36 to audio and 18 to color. This approach allows you to construct a value matrix that will help you make trades among the various issues.

4) For Each Issue, What Are Potential Settlement Options?

While different settlement options may be available for the issues under consideration, you might prefer some of these over others. For example, in an employment contract, when you were negotiating fringe benefits, there may be five health care plans that you would consider while there might be three different bonus plans that include differing amounts of cash salary and stock options. Be creative, because these settlement options will constitute the proposals that you present to your counterparts.

Returning to our cool car example, you notice that the manufacturer's suggested retail price of the car is $45,799.00, whereas you would be thrilled if you could buy it for $37,500. On the financing side, you will consider an interest rate of 8 percent, 6 percent, 4 percent, and 2 percent. For audio, you consider single-CD, six-CD player, premium, and top of the line; while your color preferences are white (least desirable), red, and silver (most desirable).

5) What Is the Relative Value for Each of These Settlement Options?

Once you have identified settlement options for each issue, assign each one a set of points out of the total metric you settled upon in Step 3 (100 points, in this example). The value you assign to each one reflects how important that option is to achieving your overall objective. While you could simply rely on the more-is-better-than-less rule of thumb, a more careful consideration of what you prefer may reveal this rule to be inadequate. Understanding how your preferences change as you move through the settlement options can give you insights into how much more of that issue you want.

In our cool car example, you decide on the following allocations:

Price: $47,499 (MSRP) 0 points, every $1000 drop in price is worth 4 points, until 40 points for $37,500.
Financing: 8% 0 points, 6% 2 points, 4% 4 points, and 2% 6 points.
Audio: Single-CD 0 points, 6 CD player 12 points, premium 24 points, and top of the line 36 points.
Color: White 0 points, red 9 points, silver 18 points.

6) What Are the Parameters for This Negotiation?

Now to the specifics: First, with your issues-value matrix, you can determine your reservation price across the issues under consideration. As discussed in Chapter 3, setting the reservation price at the package level rather than at the level of each individual issue provides greater flexibility to construct creative combinations of issues that meet your underlying interests.[1] Because you have valued multiple options for each issue, you can now explore a precise aspiration and reservation price at the package level. In addition, you can use this fine-grained understanding of the issues to evaluate your alternatives. Now, you can begin to compare directly the proposals that your counterpart may offer with the value of your alternative.

Returning to our cool car example, first determine your reservation price (your bottom line) by considering your alternatives: You could simply keep your current car. You have determined that this alternative is worth 30 points. But that is not all. You reasonably expect that you could achieve 50 points by playing one dealer against another (taking the value of your time into consideration). In this case, your reservation price for this negotiation is 50 points.

Next, you need to set your aspirations. One possibility is to aim for the 100 possible points. But this would mean that you would have to get the maximum value on every single issue. But for you to get 100 points means that your counterparty might have to concede on every issue, essentially settling for their reservation price on the deal. Although possible, this may be extremely optimistic, even by the standard of an expert negotiator like Thomas (and downright impossible by most normal people's standards).

PHASE TWO: YOUR COUNTERPART'S PERSPECTIVE

Now, that you have analyzed your objectives and parameters, repeat the analysis from your counterparts' perspective. Revisit the five steps you took to figure out what you wanted; start at Step 1, but this time, run through the steps from the perspective of your counterpart. Naturally, you have less information on each of the steps than you have from your own perspective. Make a note of these gaps, and use the negotiation process to learn more about your counterpart.

1) What Are Your Counterparts' Goals in This Negotiation?

Consider the negotiation from the perspective of your counterparts, and fill in as many of the blanks as you can. Why are they negotiating with you? What aspects of your respective goals do your counterparts hold in common with you? The more you understand your counterparts' preferences, the more you can craft proposals that take advantage of value-creating opportunities. You will often have little direct insight into what your counterparts really value because of incomplete or limited information, but do the best you can and (as above) make note of gaps in your knowledge.

It also might be useful to see if you know someone who might have some insights into how an individual counterpart thinks: for instance, someone who has negotiated with your counterparts or with someone who is similar to them. Those insights could be particularly useful as you try to put yourself into the mindset of your counterparts.

2) What Are Your Counterparts' Issues?

Think creatively about the issues that your counterpart might wish to negotiate. These may be the same issues on your list, but may also include ones that do not overlap with yours. As you consider the goals and aspirations of your counterparts, what additional concerns or opportunities arise from the issues that they might raise? Pay particular attention to issues that do not appear on your list. Knowledge of those issues will give you a strategic advantage because you could concede on them without sacrificing your objective. Consider how to break down complex issues into their components. This may help you figure out ways to yoke different issues together.

Although it is highly likely that you will not have as much information about how your counterparts value these issues as you have about how you value them, identifying and assigning values to possible settlement options from your counterparts' perspective will be very beneficial in deriving your negotiation strategy. In our cool car example, the dealer has two issue categories: profitability (price and financing) and customer satisfaction. In this case, customer satisfaction may be based on many different attributes of the car and the experience. But for the sake of simplicity, assume that the two most important attributes are the audio system and the color of the car.

3) What Is the Relative Importance of These Issues from Your Counterparts' Perspective?

What issues are likely to be more important to your counterparts, and which ones less important? It is helpful to realize that the more different your counterparts are from you, the more likely they are to value the issues differently. These differences can reflect culture, experience, expertise, or background—but the greater the differences, the more potential value there is to be created through negotiation.

As you think about the differences between you and your counterpart, be mindful of your unconscious biases. When you expect differences, you are more willing to see differences—and it is these differences that signal the asymmetry necessary for value creating. As you perceive your negotiating counterparts to be more similar, you expect the situation to be predictable: Their interests will be the mirror image of yours. What you want more of, they want more of.

These are the basic assumptions that result in the fixed-pie mindset of adversarial negotiations. In what is known as the false consensus effect, people assume that their preferences and opinions are widely shared by others.[2] In negotiations, this can easily lead you to believe that achieving your preferred outcomes on issues is incompatible with your counterparts' achieving their desired outcomes on these same issues (e.g., if salary is your most important issue, it must also be the most important issue for your potential employer—and there is a limit to how many salary dollars the employer can provide).

When you and your negotiating counterparts are obviously dissimilar—perhaps because you differ in culture of origin, profession, experience, or demography—the mere presence of these differences makes the negotiation less predictable and can motivate you to engage in a more elaborate and systematic search for information. At the same time, the greater the differences, the more potential there is for value creation. Thus, while the negotiations are likely to be more complex, they are likely to be also more beneficial. However, because these differences change how reliably you can assess your counterpart's preferences, you need to find out as much as possible when negotiating with counterparts who are different from you and with whom you have less experience negotiating.

Researchers found that people who expected to face dissimilar counterparts had plans that were more elaborate and with more information than were the plans of those who believed they would face similar counterparts.[3] The more different your counterparts are, the more motivated you are to plan and prepare for the negotiation. You will be more likely to seek out information about the issues, and this additional information search can enhance your ability to persuade your counterpart in line with your preferences. Thus, the perception of differences changes how you plan by increasing your information search and the subsequent elaboration of your arguments.

The more uncertain you are about how the negotiation will unfold, the more useful it is to engage in the difficult work of creating an issue-value matrix. Figuring out which issues have integrative potential—and which are congruent or distributive—requires that you compare your preferences on issues with those of your counterpart. Expecting to find differences in how your counterpart values the issues in the negotiation can improve your assessment of the category (integrative, distributive, or congruent) of each issue. In addition, writing down your beliefs about what your counterpart wants in this matrix form also provides a useful template for revision when you verify your assessments in the information-exchange component of the negotiation. Reflecting this in our cool car example, you believe that the dealer values profitability much more that customer satisfaction. Moreover, within the profitability category, price is more important to the dealer than financing, while within the customer satisfaction category, the dealer is more open to concession on color options because, from the dealer's perspective, it is cheaper to provide than a high-end audio system.

4) What Are Your Estimates of Your Counterpart's Parameters?

Using the information you have gathered in the preceding steps, you should now rank the issues by your counterpart's sense of relative importance.

Then try to deduce your counterpart's reservation prices, aspirations, and relative values of the issues. In many instances—particularly if this is the first time you are negotiating with these counterparts—it will be difficult to determine their parameters beyond rank ordering the issues. We will return to this issue in the next phase, when we discuss information gathering during the negotiation.

Still, by careful sleuthing (e.g., using your social and business network connections), you may find useful information about your counterpart. You can also match what you know about your counterpart with what others with those same characteristics are likely to do. For example, individuals who have written books on negotiation are more likely to negotiate—and are more likely to have higher expectations! Or, as research shows, women have lower expectations than men so aspirations are likely to differ by gender.[4]

Now let's apply this to the cool car negotiation. Based on your knowledge of the car dealership and what you know about sales people more generally, out of 100 points, you are expecting the dealer would have assigned 70 points to profitability, with 40 points to price and 30 points to financing; and assigning 20 to customer satisfaction, with 18 points to color and 12 to audio.

Within each of those subcategories, you assess the dealer's settlement options as:

Profitability:
  Price: $37,500 (employee discount) 0 points, $47,499 (Manufacturer's Suggested Retail Price) 40 points.
  Financing: 8% 30 points, 6% 20 points, 4% 10 points, and 2% 0 points.
Customer satisfaction:
  Audio: Single-CD 12 points, six-CD Player 8 points, premium 4 points, and top of the line 0 points.
  Color: white 0 points, red 9 points, and silver 18 points.

5) Are the Potential Settlement Points That You Have Identified Sufficient?

Are there other outcomes that your counterpart would consider? As you gain more insight into your counterpart, you may be able to rework the settlement points that you identified when you were focusing solely on your own interests.

PHASE THREE: DEVELOP YOUR NEGOTIATION STRATEGY

After all of this analysis of your goals and those of your counterparts, you are ready to prepare your negotiation strategy. To begin, consider the following four questions.

1) What Information Are You Missing?

Decide on an information-gathering strategy—that is, a way to obtain more information about your counterpart during the negotiation itself. This will be important to fill the holes in your knowledge. Based on what you were able to establish in phase two, you may need to focus on confirming whether the issues you identified for your counterpart are indeed relevant. If your prediction of what is and is not important to your counterparts maps onto what they say and do in the negotiation based on their words and actions, you can update your assessment of their reservation price and quality of their alternatives.

In general, your counterpart's willingness to share information will be related to how strategically valuable they perceive the information to be. Given that criterion, it is likely that they will be least reluctant to share information about the issues, more reluctant to share information about the rank ordering, and most reluctant to share information about reservation prices and aspirations.

One strategy that we have found to be effective is to open the negotiation with a discussion of what you and your counterparts are trying to achieve, what is important to each of you, what the potential issues are, and even what possible outcomes or settlement options could be. But understand that, while this discussion will allow you to fill in some of the blanks (and confirm what you already know) in what you believe is your counterparts' value matrix, it will also provide information about you to your counterpart. So start with more general issues and look for reciprocity—are your counterparts forthcoming and truthful? Compare their answers to facts you already know to see if they're being straight with you.

You won't get all the information you want. Obviously, what you would like to know are your counterparts' issues, settlement options, and their relative values. Of course, it would also be very useful if you had some information about your counterpart's reservation price—that is, the point at which they would be willing to abandon the negotiation and take their next-best alternative.

While your counterparts should be reluctant to share their reservation prices, they may be more forthcoming about their alternatives. With knowledge of a counterpart's alternative, you can begin to triangulate a reservation price. For example in the car-buying example, the dealer might ask you how much you like your current car, what other dealers have you visited, how soon you want to complete the purchase and take possession of the car, what other cars you are considering, and so on. All of these questions allow the dealer to infer your alternatives and from those to triangulate your reservation price.

In turn, you can obtain information about the dealer's cost of the model you are considering, how many days' supply are on dealers' lots, and what the average selling prices for this model are. All of these can give you information that will help in triangulating the dealer's reservation and aspiration prices.

Finally, reservation prices can also be inferred from negotiators' behavior. Research shows that those with superior alternatives will be more aggressive in their demands than will those with inferior alternatives. These aggressive demands can help you to assess the value of the alternatives and focus in on your counterparts' reservation prices.[5]

2) Which Issues Are Likely to Be Distributive, Integrative, and Congruent?

Using the information from the first two phases of your planning—concerning the issues, potential settlement options, and your and your counterparts' ranking and valuation each of those options—you should now determine whether the issues are likely to be congruent (no disagreements), distributive (you and your counterpart value them equally but in opposite directions), or integrative (you and your counterpart value them in opposite directions but not equally). At first, this seems to be a relatively straightforward assessment. The only way you can do that is to compare how you value each issue with your best assessment of the value that your counterpart places on these same issues. And this is the challenge because you are relying on your incomplete knowledge of counterparts' preferences.

Compare how you ordered the issues for yourself and how you ordered the issues for your counterparts. Where are the issues about which you and your counterparts do not feel equally strongly? The greater such a discrepancy, the more potential value that could be realized by yoking these mismatched issues; that is, if they make a concession on an issue that they care less about, you would make a concession on another issue that you care less about. For example, if an issue, such as compensation, is your most important issue, but your counterpart sees considerable upside to the stock options and bonus, then designing a proposal that gives each side more of what they care about can create additional value over and above a simple split-the-difference strategy.

On the other hand, if you both view an issue as very important, particularly when that issue is denominated in dollars, the issue is likely to be distributive. Congruent issues are likely to be those that reflect the common interests of the parties, while integrative issues reflect the different importance parties place on particular issues.

For example, the combined issue-value matrix (Table 5.1) in our car buying example looks as follows:

TABLE 5.1 COMBINED ISSUE-VALUE MATRIX

	Buyer	Dealer
Price (Distributive)		
$37,500	40	0
$40,500	30	10
$42,500	20	20
$44,500	10	30
$47,499	0	40
Financing (Integrative)*		
8%	0	30
6%	2	20
4%	4	10
2%	6	0

(continues)

TABLE 5.1 (*continued*)

	Buyer	Dealer
Audio (Integrative)		
Single CD	0	12
6 CD Player	12	8
Premium	24	4
Top of the line	36	0
Color (Congruent)		
White	0	0
Red	9	9
Silver	18	18

*While integrative, the financing is more important to the dealer. In contrast, the outcome on the audio-component issue is more important to the buyer.

Comparing the relative values assigned by the buyer and the dealer allows you to identify the type of each issue. First consider price: As you can see, at each price point, an increase in price reduces the value claimed by the buyer by a constant 10 points while increasing the value claimed by the dealer by the same 10 points. Thus, price is a distributive issue as both buyer and dealer value price equally but in opposite directions.

Next consider financing. The buyer's claimed value increases by a constant 2 points for each reduction of a percentage point in financing. Thus, conceding on the financing rate reduces the value claimed by the buyer by much less than it benefits the dealer. Taking in isolation, financing by itself could be viewed as "distributive," but combine financing with price, taking a midpoint as a starting point. Compare a settlement at $42,500 and a financing rate of say 4%. Such a deal is worth 24 points to the buyer (20 + 4) and 30 points to the dealer (20 + 10). If the dealer were to trade a price reduction by an additional $2000 for an increase in the financing rate by 4 percentage points to 8%, the trade would benefit the buyer by a net 6 points while benefiting the dealer by a net 10 points (−10 + 20), hence creating a net increase in the value claimed by both the dealer and the buyer of 16 points. Thus, integrative issues can be used to enhance the value claimed by both parties when combined with another distributive and (as we will show shortly) integrative issue.

Next consider the audio option—also an integrative issue. Although the buyer prefers to get top-of-the line audio and the dealer prefers to sell a car with the single-CD player, the magnitude of those "opposite" preferences is not equal: Each concession costs the dealer 4 points but benefits the buyer by 12 points. So now, consider combining the two integrative issues (as opposed to the integrative and the distributive issues discussed in the previous paragraph),[6] beginning at a financing rate of 4% and a six-CD player. That deal is worth 16 points to the buyer (4 + 12) and 18 points to the dealer (10 + 8). Now, have the dealer concede on the audio and the buyer concede on the financing: If they move to top-of-the-line audio and financing terms of 8%, that deal is worth 36 points (a net gain of 20) to the buyer and 30 points (a net gain of 12) to the dealer. Thus, both parties are better off by a sum total of 32 points.

The final issue is color. As you can see from the combined value matrix, both the buyer and the dealer prefer silver. Thus, color is a congruent issue: There is simply no dispute, because while the buyer really likes the silver color, it turns out that the dealer has too many silver cars on the lot and is motivated to move that particular color.

Consider two strategic approaches with congruent issues. First, assume that the dealer recognizes first that the issue is congruent. The dealer could simply reveal that fact to the buyer, and the parties would settle on silver, with both the buyer and the seller realizing 18 points. Second (and more likely), assume that the dealer decides to play it strategically, offering white first. Then, suggesting to the buyer that he just found a silver car, but that car was more expensive than the white one (for example, going from $42,500 to $44,500). The buyer would agree to that trade, gaining 18 points on the color but sacrificing 10 on price, for a net gain of 8. In contrast, by not revealing the information to the buyer and playing it strategically, the dealer could gain 28 points, 18 for silver and another 10 for the new price of $44,500.

3) Where Are the Gaps in Your Plan?

What information do you hope to learn during the negotiation? Because no planning process can be totally accurate or complete, you need to identify the information about which you are least certain—the questions that still need answers. Be specific. Once you enter into the negotiation, you can use these answers to these questions to augment your strategy.

In addition to the parameters of your counterparties' preferences that you don't know, there may also be some parameters that you thought you knew but really did not. One strategy to uncover such errors is to predict your counterpart's responses to your questions and proposals, and pay attention when their responses differ significantly from what you expected. For example, you offered a trade on an issue that you believed very important to them in exchange for a concession on what you thought was a relatively unimportant issue to your counterpart—yet they did not accept. Although very strategic counterparts may not clearly indicate that the trade you propose is advantageous to them, unexpected behavior deserves more of your attention and exploration. What did you miss? Is it that your counterpart is misrepresenting his interests, or that you misunderstand his preferences? You need to distinguish between these two interpretations by asking additional questions (e.g., why is this trade not good for you?) or asking them to propose alternative trades that reveal their preferences on the issues in question or reveal that they are simply misrepresenting their interests to confuse you.

4) What Strategies and Tactics Will You Employ to Achieve Your Goals, Taking into Account the Preferences, Goals, and Strategies That Your Counterpart Is Likely to Use?

Reflect back on the goals you have set for yourself and the goals you expect your counterpart has established. Use these as the filters to select strategies that are consistent with achieving your goals. Clearly, the strategies and tactics that Thomas uses when he is buying a new car differ from the strategies he would use when negotiating with his nephew about the responsibilities inherent in driving that new car. Matching your strategies to your goals in a specific negotiation requires you to choose your strategies and frame your negotiations in ways that will be most persuasive to the person across the table. Use what you know about your counterpart to guide your choices.

Consider what you know about your counterpart from her reputation, your common negotiating history, and the type of relationship you have. All of these factors help you predict and interpret your counterpart's behavior and select approaches that will be much more effective in achieving your goals for this interaction. Armed with all this information about you, your counterpart, and your negotiation strategy, there are still two very important aspects of planning that you should keep in mind.

THINGS TO CONSIDER WHEN YOU PLAN

1) Planning Can Change Your Expectations; Expectations Can Change Your Experience

The planning you do in advance of a negotiation alters your expectations of what will happen and therefore can change what you experience in the negotiation. Consider the following research: In one study, all participants saw three truly funny cartoons, followed by three not-so-funny ones.[7] Half of the participants were told nothing about the contents of the cartoons, while the remaining participants (the misinformed group) were told that all the cartoons would be funny. The misinformed group rated the less-funny cartoons to be as funny as the truly funny ones. Those who were told nothing (the control group) found the truly funny cartoons significantly funnier than the less-funny cartoons. A videotape of the facial expressions of participants in the misinformed group backed up this self-reporting by indicating that positive expectations improved their cartoon-viewing experience; their facial expressions suggested that they found all the cartoons equally funny.

In another related study, participants were asked to taste and rate their preferences for beer.[8] In one beer, an odd flavor (balsamic vinegar) was added. It turns out that participants disliked the adulterated beer more when they knew about the additive *prior* to their tasting the beer. Disclosing the additive after tasting did not significantly reduce participants' preference for the beer as compared to a control condition in which they received no information about the additive.

These studies reveal the power of information to change perception. Having the information prior to the experience creates anticipatory expectations that can change not only your preferences but also the experience and interpretation of the others' behavior. Thus, if a negotiator has, prior to a negotiation, an expectation that the negotiation will be adversarial—more like a battle—the behavior of the counterpart will be interpreted and evaluated though the adversarial filter. Alternatively, if the negotiator expects a more collaborative interaction, the behavior of the counterpart and the negotiation itself may be evaluated through an entirely different filter of collaborative problem solving.

2) Uncertainty Is Good—in Moderation

Engaging in the planning process prior to negotiating can reduce the un-certainty or unpredictability of the negotiation. That certainly seems like an advantage. Yet, as you plan for the negotiation, what you don't know becomes clear, which may raise the specter of unpredictability. If you are too confident about how the negotiation will unfold, your perception of predictability can have the unintended, negative consequence of making you less effective at creating value.

Consider the following example of the connection between uncertainty and value creation. Participants in a research study were either certain or uncertain that their counterpart had behaved extremely selfishly in a prior interaction.[9] Negotiators who felt certain of their opponent's bad behavior included fewer value-creating and more fixed-pie strategies in their preparation, while those who felt uncertain about whether their counter-part had behaved selfishly included more value-creating and fewer fixed-pie strategies in their preparation. Not only was there a clear difference in the strategies that negotiators developed, but their outcomes also reflected those differences. Those who were more uncertain realized better outcomes with more joint value because their strategies including more opportunity for value creation.

Too much uncertainty is as bad for value creation as too little uncer-tainty. When people are overwhelmed by uncertainty, they rely on their most well-learned or familiar routines or practices. Even if uncertainty were an aversive experience and you were willing to exert considerable effort to resolve the uncertainty, too much uncertainty can create a condi-tion known as threat rigidity. When faced with revolutionary and unex-pected changes in their environments, people often revert to their most overlearned, dominant behaviors.[10] When levels of uncertainty go from being useful (by motivating negotiators to think more deeply about value-claiming and value-creating strategies) to overwhelming, negotiators often revert to their most well-learned behaviors—behaviors that typically include expectations of adversarial interactions, split-the-difference compromises, and fixed-pie frames.

How you manage uncertainty often depends on your available mental resources. To some extent, your mental resources are of course intrinsic, but research has identified three factors that can affect your reserve of mental energy and, thus, your responses to uncertainty: need for closure, time pressure, and accuracy motivation.

Individuals vary in how much information or knowledge they need to make a choice or a decision. This difference is their "need for cognitive closure."[11] Individuals high in need for closure hold their thoughts and opinions more strongly, are quick to make decisions, and rely on incomplete but easily available information. When encountering uncertainty, high need-for-closure individuals will be more motivated to reduce the uncertainty by making a decision quickly—in negotiation, high need for closure is reflected in a desire for quick agreements that eliminate the uncertainty associated with negotiating. Individuals low in need for closure are more willing to entertain multiple interpretations or conflicting opinions, prefer to gather information more systematically before forming an opinion or making a decision, and are more willing to suspend judgment. Those low in need for closure are willing to tolerate uncertainty by postponing judgment until they have systematically assessed the situation.[12] In a negotiation, those with a low need for closure are motivated to gather information to resolve or mitigate the uncertainty rather than reaching a quick deal.

Either because of a formal, immediate deadline or the feeling that the time is running out, time pressure can affect how negotiators process information. Time pressure in a negotiation affects information-processing strategies. Negotiators who perceived a high level of time pressure took less time to propose counteroffers and to reach final agreements, reported less motivation to process information, made less persuasive arguments, and used more heuristics than negotiators who perceived less time pressure. As a result, negotiators who perceived high time pressure used more heuristic processing strategies and achieved agreements of significantly lower joint value than did those who perceived low time pressure and processed information more systematically. This was true even when all negotiators had the same amount of actual time to complete their negotiations.[13]

Finally, negotiators may differ in their concern for accuracy—their "accuracy motivation."[14] Higher levels of accuracy motivation typically occur when negotiators are held accountable, either to a constituency or to a third party,[15] for the quality of their agreements and are associated with greater engagement in systematic and thoughtful information processing.[16] In negotiation contexts, those who expected to have their negotiation behavior evaluated by a third party were less likely to fall prey to the fixed-pie bias, and they achieved outcomes of higher joint value than negotiators who did not expect to be evaluated.[17]

To be sure, the planning process outlined above is challenging. Even being motivated by your desire to get more of what you want, not all negotiations require this level of planning. In fact, the last time Margaret engaged in this full-blown planning process was when she was facing her negotiation with Stanford. Since then, the planning that she has done for the more routine negotiations with her husband, coauthors, friends, and colleagues is an abbreviated version of this three-phase process.

The amount of time spent preparing for a negotiation should be consistent with its relative importance. The issue is more or less planning—not planning or no planning. Even in relatively mundane negotiations, your baseline is knowing your alternatives, reservation price, and aspirations as well as the issues to be discussed both from your perspective and the perspective of your counterpart. And contrary to the natural predilections of most negotiators, it is better to err in the direction of too much planning rather than too little!

Even if you were to produce a three-phase plan in considerable detail that reflects the points of this chapter, it would still be incomplete. There would be aspects of the negotiation, particularly of your counterpart's interests, preferences, or options that would be unknown to you. With your plan in place, however, you would have a better idea of what those unknowns were and could tag those points for attention during the actual negotiation.

The topic of the next chapter is strategic thinking—that is, taking what you have developed in your plan and choosing strategies and tactics that can help you get more of what you want. If this chapter has been all about obtaining basic information about yourself and your counterpart, Chapter 6 goes deeper: In that chapter, the focus is on understanding your counterparts and predicting their likely reactions to various strategies and tactics that you employ.

SUMMARY

Effective planning and preparation are critical to achieving success in negotiation. While the importance of a particular negotiation will influence how detailed your preparation is, the preparation before a negotiation should include three important phases:

1. Figuring out what you want and creating an issue-value matrix to quantify it.

    a. What do you want to achieve in the negotiation?
    b. What are the issues over which you will be negotiating?
    c. How important is each issue in achieving your goal?
    d. What are the potential agreement options for each issue?
    e. What is the relative contribution/value of each settlement option to your goal?
    f. What are your parameters in this negotiation?

2. Figuring out what your counterparts want and creating their issue-value matrix.

    a. What are your counterparts' goals in this negotiation?
    b. What are your counterparts' issues?
    c. How important is each issue to achieving their goals?
    d. What are your counterparts' parameters?
    e. Are the potential settlement points you have identified sufficient?

3. Developing your negotiation strategy.

    a. How do you gather the additional information you need?
    b. Which of the issues are likely to be distributive, integrative, or congruent?
    c. What are the holes in your plan?
    d. What strategies and tactics will you employ to achieve your goals, taking into account the preferences, goals, and strategies that your counterpart is likely to employ?

As you plan, be mindful of the assumptions and expectations that are embedded in your plan. What you do in advance of the negotiation can influence your expectations of what will happen. In addition, while planning can reduce your uncertainty, you don't want to be too sure of yourself and of how your counterparts will react. Uncertainty in moderation is associated with more value-creating outcomes in negotiations. So, a moderate amount of uncertainty is good. Too little can make you too confident; too much, and you quickly revert to your most well-learned and dominant behaviors—which, in the case of negotiation, are likely to be manifested as an inflexible commitment to a zero-sum, split-the-difference perspective on negotiation. How much uncertainty is too much depends on at least three factors: (1) need for closure (how comfortable you are with ambiguity and how willing you are to tolerate indecision); (2) time pressure (how powerfully you are influenced by deadlines); and (3) accuracy motivation (whether you have to justify what you did to an outside observer or authority).

Chapter Six

IT TAKES AT LEAST TWO TO TANGO

Thinking Strategically in Negotiation

I n negotiations, there is tension between behaviors that create value (by enlarging the pool of available benefits/resources) and those that claim value (by allocating benefits/resources among the parties). Information sharing helps to create value, but revealing information to your counterpart can handicap your ability to claim value.

Recall the one-sided full-disclosure strategy we discussed in Chapter 4: Revealing all your information to your counterpart allows her to determine the largest feasible pie of resources. By revealing all your information, she might offer you the smallest increment over your reservation price that she believes you are likely to accept, leaving you with essentially your reservation price, and claiming all the remaining value for herself.

Developing strategies to determine the right kind and amount of information to share is a major challenge. The total pie might be smaller when you share less information (it certainly can't be larger), but you may manage to claim more than you might be able to get from a larger pie.

The challenge really has three aspects. First and foremost, if getting more of what you want is your goal, then value creation is a means to that end, not the end in itself.

Second, by its very nature, value creation is cooperative. By contrast, value claiming is *inherently* adversarial. Thus, while value creation may facilitate the value available to be claimed, some value creation strategies may handicap your ability to claim value.

Finally, the distinction between actions that create value and actions that claim value is fluid. Because opportunities for value creation exist when negotiating parties value some issues differently from one another, the selective claiming of positions on issues with asymmetrical value can increase the size of the pie that you can ultimately claim. Indiscriminate information exchange can leave less for you, even if it were to increase the size of the pie.

Knowing what information to share, and how to share it, is an important strategic consideration in most negotiations. For most people, strategic thinking does not come naturally—but luckily, there is help. An entire area of study—game theory—focuses on strategic thinking in social interaction. In this chapter, we rely on tenets of game theory to help negotiators get more of what they want.

THE RATIONAL PERSPECTIVE

Game theory assumes that parties pursue their interests in a rational manner, fully understanding that their counterparts will do the same. Thus you must consider that as your counterparts pursue their objectives and you pursue yours, your ultimate objectives may be unaligned. For example, the buyer should understand that the seller's actions are based on the seller's information, motives, aspirations, and goals (which, of course, include what the seller knows about the buyer). Symmetrically, the seller must accept that the buyer's actions are based on the buyer's information, motives, aspirations, and goals (including what the buyer knows about the seller).

Game theory is not useful in situations in which parties can pursue their objectives while ignoring the action of their counterparts. While negotiators sometimes may act (or at least appear to act) *as if* achieving their objectives were not dependent on their counterparts, the only real-world circumstance in which you can choose to ignore the behavior of your counterpart is when you have complete command-and-control power over the situation.[1] However, if your counterparts cannot walk away, then it is not really a negotiation, is it?

Game theory also assumes that negotiators pursue their objectives in a rational manner. While game theory necessarily makes an assumption about the cognitive ability of the actors and their interactions, this allows it to identify what might be attainable between two rational actors. This rationality assumption does not mean that the actors will not make mistakes—only that mistakes are random and unpredictable. Of course, considerable research has demonstrated that humans are fallible and often deviate or violate these assumptions of rationality in predictable ways. But when mistakes are predictable, knowledge of these systematic errors or biases can allow you to predict and exploit the behavior of your counterpart as well as avoid mistakes you are likely to make yourself.[2]

The hallmark of a strategic interaction is taking your counterpart's likely actions into account. So just as in a game of chess where Player 1 has to take Player 2's likely reaction to a specific move or set of moves into account, a skillful negotiator will look ahead and reason back, taking the likely actions of her counterpart into account.

A good example of the look-ahead-reason-back rule can be found in the way negotiators must analyze their strategic options in a Truel. This is a three-party version of a duel in which three players—in our example, White, Grey and Black—engage in a three-way, sequential gun battle. Let's say that White is a bad shot, and hits about one third of his targets. Grey is somewhat better: he hits 50 percent of his targets. Finally, Black is 100 percent accurate; he is truly dangerous! Because the contest is patently unfair, White is allowed to fire first, followed by Grey (if he were still alive), then Black (if he were still alive) then White again (if he were still alive) and so forth until there is only one person standing.

Imagine that you are asked to advise White. What should he do to maximize his chance of survival? Using the look-ahead-and-reason-back rule, you can see that shooting at Grey would be a disastrous decision because, if White were successful (and, frankly, there is only a one-third chance that he would be), he would die next at the hands of the sharpshooting Black. So reasoning back makes it obvious that shooting at Grey would be a grave mistake.

Shooting at Black would clearly be better than shooting at Grey—but not for the reason you think. At first glance, this might seem to be the case because if White were to kill Black, Grey will shoot at White—and that would be better for White than facing a shot from Black. So if White kills Black, he ends up in a duel with Grey, with Grey firing first. But what if White were to miss Black? Then Grey would have to decide where to fire, and clearly he will fire at Black. If he misses, Black will fire back at Grey, since Grey is a more dangerous adversary than White. If Grey misses, moreover, Black's perfect accuracy means that he will inevitably kill Grey, and then it will be White's turn again.

So if White shoots at Black first, White has a one-third probability of hitting him, and living—but then he would have a 50-50 chance of being killed by Grey. If White misses Black, however, and Grey then manages to kill Black, then White and Grey will face each other again—but this time White will fire first. For this to occur, however, White has to miss Black in the first round.

So White's best chance of winning the Truel is to shoot at Black and miss. While he is likely to do so by pure chance, he shouldn't rely on his bad shooting! Your advice to White should be to miss Black intentionally, increasing his odds of missing Black from 67 to 100 percent.

Looking ahead and reasoning back allows you to identify White's optimal strategy and choose a course of action that increases his chance of surviving the Truel. To do this, of course, you have to consider the likely behavior of his counterparts Grey and Black—and in this situation you were able to do this with complete accuracy, since all the information was known by all the parties.

In a negotiation, by contrast, parties have incomplete information and must seek out additional facts—but that is only the first step. Once that additional information is revealed, it is important to understand what to do with it.

Strategic considerations are a hallmark of all our social interactions. Taking advantage of information revealed in social situations is surprisingly difficult. Consider the following experience we had in a recent consulting assignment.

Our client, a large Real Estate Investment Trust (REIT), made an offer for the assets of a smaller Canadian REIT at $15.00 per share, as part of an auction in which the bidders agreed to submit a best-and-final-offer at a particular date and to abstain from further bidding after that date. The Canadian REIT's board accepted our client's offer, although it still needed the approval of its shareholders.

Following the offer, (but prior to the shareholder vote) the target's stock price settled in a narrow band in the $14.90s per-share range. A few weeks before the shareholder vote, however, the competing company violated its prior agreement and submitted a new offer of $18.00 per share. As the shareholder vote was approaching, the target stock price traded above $17.00 per share.

Obviously, because the value of their stock had increased, the target shareholders were not going to approve the sale at $15.00 and, as such, our client had to assume that the bid would fail. The simplest way to see this is to consider the three options faced by target shareholders: (1) vote in favor of our client's offer and receive $15.00 per share; (2) vote no and hold out for a higher offer, possibly higher than $15.00 per share (which may or may not occur, as our client sued the interloper for "tortious interference with contract"—meaning that the interloper illegally interfered with a valid contract that our client had); or (3) sell the stock in the marketplace.

While the payoffs to the holdout option are uncertain, it is clear that as long as the stock price was above $15.00 per share, alternative (3) is more attractive to the target shareholders than alternative (1). Thus, while it is not clear whether selling or holding out is a better strategy, as long as the stock price is trading above $15.00 our client's original $15.00 offer will be rejected. Predicting this, our client threatened to lock up the deal in lengthy litigation, causing the stock price to drop to the mid-$16 range. Then, our client raised the offer to $16.50 and acquired the target for that price. (As it turned out, our client also recovered the additional $1.50 per share from the competitor from the tortious interference with contract lawsuit that followed the acquisition.)

In both of these cases—the Truel and the three-way interaction between our client, the competitor and the target shareholders—the actions taken were sequential. Whether you are negotiating through words or through actions, it is not enough to know what you want; that is, to know your aspirations, alternatives, and reservation price. Because of the strategic nature of negotiation, the importance of analyzing the likely behavior of your counterpart(s) is also critical for your success. Not knowing what you want or ignoring the systematic—and, thus, predictable—behavior of your counterpart dramatically reduces your ability to achieve a better deal.

Taking into consideration the likely behavior of your counterpart requires you to engage in the look-ahead-and-reason-back strategy. In this way, you are more likely to consider your explicit goals as well as understanding the motivations and aspirations of your counterparts. If you appreciate the critical role that such information gathering plays in your success, you are much more likely to undertake a serious (and systematic) planning process.

Of course, predicting human behavior is more complex than simply relying on the tenets of rationality. Many psychological factors shape the choices that individuals make—and one of these factors is the perception of what is fair.

FAIR VERSUS RATIONAL

Consider the following situation: Two anonymous parties are offered a chance to split $100. One party—the allocator—is tasked with dividing up the $100. The other party—the decider—will then decide whether to accept the allocation as presented.

The allocator can divide the $100 anywhere in the range of $99 for the allocator and $1 to the decider to $1 for the allocator and $99 to the decider. The allocation is then sent electronically to the decider, who must choose between one of two options: If the decider agrees to the allocation, the money will be allocated as indicated between the allocator and the decider; and the game is over and will never be played again. If the decider says no, no money is distributed and the game is over, never to be played again. In both outcomes, neither the decider nor the allocator will ever know the identity of the other.[3]

Suppose you were assigned to the allocator role. How much would you allocate to yourself, and how much to your counterpart? If you were trained in Thomas's world of classical economics, the answer is clear: you'd allocate $1 to the decider and the rest to yourself. Following the "look ahead and reason back" rule, you must conclude that the decider faces a simple choice: get $1, or get nothing. Any reasonable decider would obviously choose the $1, right?

Wrong. Imagine yourself in the role of the decider. Across your computer screen comes the allocation: $99 for the allocator, $1 to you. Do you hit the YES button or the NO button?

When faced with this decision, most people seem to choose to forgo the $1 simply for the satisfaction of knowing that the greedy allocator who wanted the other $99 will get nothing. (In fact, most deciders don't start agreeing to the allocation until a 70/30 split is offered; a substantial minority agree to a 60/40 split and most deciders will agree to a 50/50 split.)

What if the game were for a much larger pool of money? Would the size of the allocation to the decider change your mind? Most people, in thinking about this, agree that it would. But researchers have found evidence that most people do not actually change their behavior when the amount in the game is increased.[4] In allocating the equivalent of 10 months of wages, deciders were highly unlikely to agree to a 90/10 split; they began to agree to a 70/30 split. A substantial minority agreed to a 60/40 split and almost all agreed to a 50/50 split.

Why does this happen? Researchers have yet to find a simple answer, but it seems likely that the deciders simply cannot bear to see themselves be used as the instrument of the allocator's gain, even for the equivalent of ten months of wages. They simply say no.

When deciders have more information about the allocators in this game, however, that knowledge can influence their decision. For example, if deciders know the allocators have earned their position, rather than having been randomly assigned to it, then the deciders are often willing to take less. More controversially, when male and female deciders knew that their allocators were women, they demanded more to say yes; conversely, when male and female allocators knew their decider was female, they allocated significantly less to her.[5]

Consider the implications of this for negotiations: factors such as fairness, legitimacy, justifications, and even the identity of the counterpart can influence how willing parties are to agree to a particular deal. Wise negotiators are those who understand this notion of voluntary agreement and frame the proposals as solutions to their counterparts' problems so as to make their offers more attractive. Of course, in some situations you may not know enough to craft your proposals in this manner—a challenge we confront in the next section.

STRATEGIC THINKING WITH ASYMMETRIC INFORMATION

One of the biggest challenges in negotiation is the presence of asymmetrical information: knowledge that your counterpart has but you do not. For example, in many purchase negotiations, sellers typically have an information advantage about the sale item, including what truly might have motivated their decision to sell. As a result, rationally, a buyer should ask "Why this item? Why now?" Consider what happened when Thomas wanted to purchase a used car.

In 1989, after he was awarded tenure at Kellogg, Thomas decided to reward himself by purchasing a red Corvette convertible. Chevrolet had just come out with a brand new six-speed manual transmission made by Zahnrad Fabrik Friedrichshafen AG in Germany (ZF for short), an obvious must-have for every newly tenured faculty member! Unfortunately, professor salaries—even for those who just received tenure—limited Thomas's choices. He could only afford a used Corvette. Yet he knew he

AKERLOFF'S MARKET FOR LEMONS

In the 1970 paper "The Market for Lemons: Quality Uncertainty and the Market Mechanism," George Akerlof describes a market with extreme information asymmetry: the market for used cars where sellers have more precise information about the quality of the cars than buyers. Therefore, if the seller is willing to accept the sale price, then the buyer should infer that the quality of the car is lower than implied by that price. As a result, buyers should follow the age-old principle of caveat emptor and rationally discount the prices of used cars, as people are more likely to keep their good cars and sell their bad cars! This in turn is more likely to drive out good cars than bad cars from the market, which in turn results in even lower prices, driving more good cars out until only lemons are left. Hence the title of the paper.

While this may seem like a relatively unimportant subject for an economic paper, it not only provides the economic foundation of Groucho Marx' famous line: "Please accept my resignation. I don't want to belong to any club that will accept people like me as a member," but Akerlof's work on information asymmetry took him further: In 2001 he, Michael Spence, and Joseph E. Stiglitz were awarded the Nobel Prize in Economics for "their analysis of markets with asymmetric information" which stimulated the development of an important new area—information economics.

should only buy one that was a few month old, as the previous model had a clunky 4+3 transmission, which clearly was not acceptable.

As luck would have it, Thomas was able to locate a beautiful specimen, red with black leather interior and a black roof—his favorite color combination. He was in love. With his mechanic friend in tow, Thomas embarked on a careful inspection— under the hood, under the car, and any other place that the two could think of. They could not find anything wrong. The car looked absolutely perfect—almost brand new and over 30 percent off the new car price.

As a last check, Thomas asked the owner why he was selling such a beautiful car, after only six months. The owner, looking very sad, pointed to a young woman who was sitting on the porch: "my daughter" he explained, "is turning sixteen next week and will start driving. This is way too much car for her, and I doubt I can keep her from driving the 'Vette' rather than the family station wagon (an Oldsmobile Custom Cruiser)!" Hearing this explanation, and to the surprise of his mechanic friend, Thomas decided to pass on the opportunity. Can you think why?

The answer is quite straightforward: Thomas simply did not find the seller's explanation persuasive. When the seller purchased the car six months ago, he surely knew that his daughter would soon be turning sixteen. While it is possible that he was rich enough to buy the car in full anticipation of selling it six months later, a 30 percent discount seems like a steep price to pay for such a short-run pleasure. Besides, if the seller were really that wealthy, then it is not clear why he would sell the car in the first place rather than buy another interesting, but safer car for his daughter's birthday—like a Mustang with an anemic six cylinder engine. The danger that the sale was motivated by a serious problem with the "Vette," one that Thomas and his mechanic friend were not able to identify, was simply too high. To put it differently, Thomas felt that he simply was not wealthy enough to take that risk.

Asymmetrical information is not limited to negotiating a used car purchase. In fact, it exists to a greater or lesser degree in all negotiations because negotiations in which there is complete information on both sides are very rare indeed. Yet just because negotiators constantly experience asymmetrical information does not mean they've developed good coping skills for this challenge. Consider what you would do if you were confronted with the following situation:

You represent Company A that wants to acquire 100 percent of Company T from its owner for cash. The value of T depends directly on the outcome of an oil exploration project it is currently undertaking. If the project fails, T will be worth nothing—$0/share. If the project succeeds, the value of T under current management could be as high as $100/share. All share values between $0 and $100 are equally likely.

T will be worth 50 percent more in the hands of A than under its current management. For example, if T were to be worth $50/share value under its current management, the company would be worth $75/share under A's management. (Technically, the combination of A and T creates a synergy of 50 percent to T's stand-alone value.)

Your task is to acquire Company T profitably. T's owner will delay their decision on your bid until the results of the project are known to him (but not to you)—and accept or reject your bid before the drilling results become public. From A's perspective, you are deliberating over offers in the range of $0/share (i.e., no offer) to $150/share.

What price per share would you offer?[6]

If you answered $60/share, then you are like a large number of our students who seem to base their offer on the following reasoning: The unconditional expected value of the firm to its owner is $50/share, and hence the expected value to A is $75/share. Thus, A can make a reasonable profit by offering less than $75 and reasonably expect their offer to be accepted by offering something greater than $50/share. On average, our students suggest an offer of $60/share.

At first, this may seem a reasonable offer as it in the middle of the average of T's value to its owner and of A's synergistic value (i.e., between $50 and $75 per share).[7] However, this offer will, on average, lose money for A. To understand why, consider what A will learn about T's private information if it were to accept A's offer. Because T's owners have an accurate assessment of the value of their shares (they know how much oil is present), they rationally will only accept a deal that is profitable to them. So T accepting your $60 offer means that the range of possible values is not $0–$100 but rather it is $0–$60; because they will not accept an offer that is worth less than the oil that they have. Since all values are equally likely, the average value of any offer accepted by T then is $30. Because T is worth 50 percent more to A, A's expected value of T when A's offer is accepted is $45. Thus, if A's offer were accepted, A's $60/share offer results in a loss of $15 ($60 – $45)! In fact, by offering $60/share, acquirers will lose money 67 *percent* of the time (since A breaks even only if T has more than $40 worth of oil there is a two-thirds probability that T's oil is valued between $0 and $40 and a one-third probability that T's oil is valued between $40 and $60).

The previous example highlights two important facts about information in negotiation. The first is quite obvious: not all participants have equal (or all the) information. In the previous example, A knows the distribution of the amount of oil held by T, while T knows the exact amount of oil it has.[8] Such information asymmetry has an important impact on the negotiation success of the parties.

But there is a second, more subtle truth embedded in the previous example: The actions of the parties reflect the information they have. So, for example, when T's owners accept A's offer of $60 per share, A realizes that the amount of oil owned by T must be equal to or less than $60. Thus, applying our principle of looking ahead and reasoning back, before making an offer of $60, A has to ask: "If I were to make an offer of $60, what do I learn if it is accepted?" The answer is that T has no more than and probably less than $60 worth of oil. But if the offer were accepted, T on average has

$30 worth of oil and "I will lose money; hence I should not make that offer in the first place."[9]

By now it should be abundantly clear that your success depends on taking advantage of information that you gathered during the planning phase and supplemented during the negotiation. But some types of information have more impact on your ability to claim value than others, and thus are more strategically important. So let's consider different types of information and the effect that having (or not having) that information has on your ability to get more of what you want.

RESERVATION PRICES. Arguably, a party's reservation price is the most strategic piece of information it possesses, because it helps negotiators distinguish between good and bad deals—and it allows their counterparts to claim more value than might otherwise have been theirs. For example, if your counterparts were to learn your reservation price, they might simply package their offers to give you the smallest increment over your reservation price they assess you would accept, make that offer, and hold out until you agree and then they claim the rest.[10]

So we strongly advise you not to reveal your reservation price. But what if you face an impasse? Are there any situations in which you should reveal your reservation price?

Consider the following scene: Your counterpart, after negotiating for a while, says, "Look, this is my best and final offer. I simply cannot afford to pay a dime more." She supports this statement by disclosing what she claims to be her reservation price. Do you believe her? If you are like most, you would not. Here is why: If she told you her true reservation price and you reach a deal, then she gets no more than her reservation price. But then, she is no better off than taking the impasse and simply walking away. Knowing that, she is likely to misstate her reservation price. Thus, if she tells you that this is her best and final offer, you can rationally assume that she may have a few more concessions available. Thus, rather than giving you her reservation price, you believe your counterpart has given you her *faux* reservation price. And this, in turn, implies that there is still more potential value that you may be able to extract from the negotiation.

When you are tempted to share your true bottom line with your counterpart, you should reconsider—because as the previous example demonstrates, you can't be certain that your partner will believe you, or will respond in kind. Of course, it would save time if you could simply tell your counterpart your reservation price, have her reciprocate, and then split the surplus equally. But there are a few problems with this strategy. First, while sharing equally may have some romantic appeal, it may not necessarily reflect an equitable allocation from an economic perspective given the different contributions and alternatives of the parties. More importantly, revealing your reservation price carries considerable risks over and above simply identifying your tipping point between a yes and a no. This is because neither you nor your counterpart can reliably distinguish when each of you is telling the truth and when you are misrepresenting your reservation price.

There is another dangerous effect of oversharing, as well. For instance, suppose the ticket scalper that we first met in Chapter 2 makes an opening offer of $60 for a theater ticket, and you respond that you will pay no more than $30.[11] The scalper suspects that you are actually willing to pay more than $30, but she does not know how much, so she concedes and lowers the ticket price to $50. You hold the line at $30, and she tries one more time, offering to accept as little as $45 for the ticket. You repeat that $30 is the most that you can pay.

How will this negotiation end? Our research suggests that the outcome is counterintuitive: Sharing your true reservation price actually increases the likelihood that the negotiation will reach an impasse, and it is the party that receives rather than the party that reveals its reservation price that is more likely to walk away, claiming that the party revealing its reservation price is not bargaining in good faith.[12] Thus, truthfully revealing your reservation price—something your counterpart did not expect and cannot reasonably verify—results in more impasses, because the recipient of this truthful revelation—the scalper in this case—will likely suspect you are giving a *faux* reservation price, and will walk away when you stick to it. Hence, what seems like a more direct strategy for efficient value claiming is more likely to result in an impasse.

In summary, revealing your reservation price, or revealing information that would allow your counterpart to triangulate it accurately, is a grave mistake in a negotiation. Of course, the same applies for your counterparts—revealing their reservation price to you will either allow you to claim most if not all of the surplus created in the negotiation or hasten your walking away because you cannot verify that this is their true reservation price.

CONGRUENT ISSUES. Next, consider whether you should reveal issues in which there is no disagreement—where both parties want the same thing. For example, assume that the tire dealer in our earlier tire-purchase examples has multiple locations and that both the dealer and Thomas would prefer to have the tires delivered in location A, which is closest to Thomas's office. But, prior to the negotiation, neither party knows the preference of the other party; that is, the dealer does not know where Thomas's office is located and Thomas does not know that the dealer has a surplus of tires at that location. Because both the dealer and Thomas favor the same location (say A), the location is a congruent issue.

Assume now that the dealer discovers that Thomas prefers to pick up the tires at location A, but Thomas is unaware that the dealer also favors location A. Thus, knowing that location is a congruent issue gives the dealer a strategic advantage. She can appear generous and offer location A to Thomas while demanding nothing in return. This is called a "direct strategy," and it's most useful to the dealer if she wants to establish a rapport with Thomas or establish better long-term relations. Alternatively, she can offer location A in return for a concession, such as a higher price. This is called a "trading strategy," and it is most useful when the dealer's goal is to exact as much value as she can from the exchange.

Thus, while revealing congruent issues does not put you in as much strategic disadvantage as revealing your reservation price, doing so is potentially costly and therefore requires some thoughtful analysis. For example you can simply give that information away to create goodwill or you can capitalize your informational advantage by trading it for another concession from your counterpart. Your choice between direct and trading strategies will depend on what you value in the negotiation. But either way you are obtaining something in return for your knowledge.

INTEGRATIVE ISSUES. The last item on the list of strategic information that should be shared with caution is information relating to the integrative issues in the negotiation. To see why this is the case, consider the earlier tire example, in which Thomas was willing to increase his purchase price by $10 for each day that delivery could be accelerated, while the dealer was willing to accelerate delivery for $2 per day. Accelerating delivery thus created $8 in net benefits for each day ($10 per day of incremental benefits for Thomas minus $2 of incremental costs for the dealer). This created value can be claimed by the parties in the negotiation.

But who will be able to claim that additional value? Research shows that if both the parties are aware of the value creation potential, then they are more likely to split it equally. In our example, Thomas and the dealer then would each get $4 for each day that they agree to accelerate delivery.[13]

But assume that Thomas realizes that the dealer is willing to accelerate delivery, but is uncertain of the costs to the dealer. Not knowing those costs, Thomas might offer to increase the purchase price by $3 for each day delivery is accelerated.

For simplicity assume that the dealer accepts Thomas's $3 offer. Now Thomas captures $7 of addition value while the dealer captures $1 for each day that delivery is accelerated. Thus, if Thomas knows that the delivery date is an integrative issue, and even better if he knew the value of each additional day for both parties (i.e., $10 for Thomas and $2 for the dealer), he could be much more effective at creating value and claiming most of that value.

But here lies the dilemma: To create value, you need to identify the integrative issues and triangulate the value that is created by the differing preferences of you and your counterpart—but you have to do so without sharing too much information. The first step, of course, is in the planning and preparation phase, when you should try to obtain as much information as possible prior to the negotiation.

In your preparation, you have identified the relative importance of the issues under consideration for both you and your counterpart. You should consider issues where there is a considerable difference between the way in which you value the issue and the way in which, in your assessment, your counterpart values it, because these issues are likely to be integrative. For example, in the tire purchase case, Thomas has identified that he is willing to pay up to $10 for each additional day that the delivery is accelerated from his reservation delivery date. Next, analyze the situation from your counterpart's perspective—what are the dealer's costs of accelerating delivery? For example, can the dealer get the tires from her supplier on short notice? What are the additional expedited transportation costs? Is there a queue for mounting the tires? Thomas may be able to answer some (but probably not all) of these question prior to the negotiation.

Once Thomas concludes that the dealer cares more about price than about delivery date, the next step is to figure out what her costs of accelerating delivery are. Let's say that Thomas estimates that her costs to expedite delivery are somewhere around $3 per day. Thus, Thomas could propose a price increase of $3 per day of expedited delivery. Notice that once Thomas has made that offer, the dealer can infer that expediting the delivery is worth *at least* $3 per day to Thomas. So if the dealer were thoughtful and strategic, she probably would not accept Thomas's offer of $3 per day but instead counter with an offer of $5 per day. Countering is actually optimal as it provides an opportunity to increase her profit but reveals only minimal information to Thomas: While it confirms that delivery date may still be integrative, it does not allow Thomas to triangulate her true cost as the counteroffer only places an upper limit of $5 on her costs to expedite delivery.

At this point, the parties might go back and forth for a while, but suppose they eventually agree to say $4 per day. This agreement still creates $8 per day of additional value (remember, while Thomas thought that the dealer's reservation price was $3 per day, in reality, her reservation price was $2 per day), allocating $6 ($10 − $4) per day of that value to Thomas and $2 ($4 − $2) per day to the dealer.

Notice again how important planning and preparation is. Because Thomas suspected that delivery date might be more valuable to him than the costs the dealer would incur, he offered what he thought was her reservation price of $3 per day. Without that preparation, he might have thought that delivery was distributive and offered closer to his value of $10. If he were to offer $10 per expedited day, the dealer might have accepted and captured all the value. If he had offered $9 and the dealer were to accept that offer, he would have learned that delivery is integrative—but this would have been an expensive way of learning, as the dealer would have gotten most of the value created in the process.

In this example, the initial identification of the integrative issue was based on planning and preparation. In fact, however, much of the information that is necessary for identifying integrative issues requires this information to be exchanged between the parties during the negotiation. Information can be exchanged in a number of ways, whether through reciprocity or explicit proposal exchange. Relying on reciprocity encourages your counterpart to match your exchange of information while mitigating the adverse effect to you of one-sided information exchange.

Encourage Reciprocal Information Sharing

Sometimes you may hesitate to share information because you are concerned that your counterpart will take advantage of you. Although this concern is justified, it is less acute when you already have an established relation with your counterpart and you both expect future interactions.

But the fact remains that to create value negotiators need to get the information exchange process started. Taking the first step and sharing some information can initiate the process of reciprocal information exchange. The challenge is what and how to share.

The information that you choose to initiate the sharing process should open up the conversation without risking significant harm to your strategic position should your counterpart not reciprocate. For example, you might open the negotiation by discussing the characteristics of a good deal—what is important to you to achieve in this interaction (and of course, learning what is important to your counterpart). In the tire purchase example, for instance, Thomas might reveal that early delivery is important to him. In response, the dealer might indicate that she could accommodate Thomas's desire, but that she would need a higher price to defray the additional costs. Although Thomas does not know the exact magnitude of those costs, he can obtain a reasonable estimate by asking her what price increase would be acceptable. Comparing her proposal to his reservation price of $10 per day may confirm to him that the delivery date is likely to be an integrative issue.

The information that you gather can help you choose between a direct strategy (your counterpart asks, you agree) or a trading strategy (your counterpart asks, you propose to give your counterpart what he wants in exchange for a concession on another issue). Suppose you chose the trading strategy. You should propose this by asking your counterpart her preference about the congruent issue and then you agree to accommodate her preference in exchange for a concession on another issue. In this way, your counterpart is unable to infer whether that issue is congruent, distributive, or integrative.

Package Your Proposals

One strategy to claim value is to package your proposals, rather than negotiating issue by issue. For example, Thomas might make the dealer an offer that specifies price, location, and delivery date. There are several advantages to such an approach. First, by offering a packaged offer, you open up the opportunity for trading among multiple issues. Second, packages are very effective means to solicit counteroffers—and thus move toward value-creating trade—without revealing too much information.

In contrast, consider a diametrically opposed strategy often used in collective bargaining negotiations: "solve the easy issues first!" One reason that some may find this strategy attractive is because it creates momentum towards agreement: Once you have agreed to the first issue, finding a way to agree on the second issue seems like less of a hurdle. In addition, as you and your counterpart reach agreements on successive issues, walking away from what you have achieved becomes increasingly difficult: with every agreement, the negotiators may perceive that they have more to lose, and thus each becomes more committed to reaching an agreement.

However, there are some significant disadvantages to the solve-the-easy-issues-first strategy. First, because it necessarily requires an issue-by-issue approach, it hinders your ability to take advantage of the integrative potential within the negotiation, which requires multiple issues that are packaged. Remember that creating value within a negotiation requires at least two issues that are valued differently by the parties.

Second, if you were to solve the easy issues first, what ultimately remains is the most difficult issue—and you now have nothing to trade. Your remaining option to resolve this last, difficult issue is through the contentious strategy of domination—who will win as neither you or your counterpart have any other issues that you could trade in exchange for concessions on this last issue. Even if you get a deal, you and your counterpart have now ended the negotiation in the most contentious way possible—as a winner or as a loser! Obviously this doesn't bode well for future negotiations, if you have a continuing relationship with your counterpart.

The third, and less obvious, drawback of the solve-the-easy-issues-first strategy is that it assumes that *your* easy issues are also *your counterpart's* easy issues. What if an issue that was relatively unimportant to you was your counterpart's most important issue? Resolving this issue early would put you at a decided disadvantage in the negotiation going forward. You would lose an opportunity to trade a relatively minor concession for a concession on an issue that was important to you.

The value of solving the easy issues first is based on the common assumption that issues are equally important to both you and your counterpart. If this is the case, then the strategy may be useful to garner commitment and momentum in fashioning an agreement. If this is not the case, then you run the risk of reducing the quality of the value created and, in like measure, the value that you claim.

Packaging issues is more likely to lead to negotiation success. But should you combine all the issues into one package and negotiate it? Or would it be better to offer your counterpart multiple packages, each differing in settlement options but similar in the value of the package to you? As we'll show in the following section, the latter approach can provide some important tactical advantages.

Propose Multiple Packages

You may find yourself in a situation in which it becomes clear that your counterpart has done little in the way of preparation for the negotiation or acts as if every issue and potential concession is a life-and-death struggle. One strategy that may help both of you figure out what is more and less important among the issues to your counterpart is for you to design and propose multiple offers and present these offers simultaneously to your counterpart. Unlike a fast food menu, this option does not allow your counterpart to cherry pick a single aspect from each of the different packages (for instance, combining option A in Issue 1 in Package 1 with option C in Issue 2 in Package 3). Rather, you offer your counterpart a choice among the packages you offered. Even if your counterpart were not prepared to choose a package, it is useful to have her rank-order the packages or, at the very least, to tell you which is most preferred and which is least preferred among the packages.

This strategy has a couple of real benefits. First, asking your counterpart to rank packages provides you both with information about each issue's relative importance to both of you, without revealing too much information. Second, providing your counterpart with a choice among multiple packages may increase her sense of control over the outcome of the negotiation. This increased sense of control can increase her commitment to what she chooses, so that implementing the actual deal is more palatable. In addition, since this strategy has much less of the take-it-or-leave-it flavor, it appears less adversarial and more of a problem-solving approach.

However, these benefits can come at a cost. When you propose multiple packages that are similar in value from your perspective, you also provide information that allows your counterparts to triangulate the values that you place on individual issues. Thus, while this strategy can enhance the value-creating aspect of your negotiation, it may well limit the amount of value that you can ultimately claim in the interaction.

Of course, these costs are offset by the benefits of the information about your counterpart's preferences that you can infer from her. While this is an important point to keep in mind, however, you must understand that no strategy has only an upside potential—that is, no strategy can help you create value without creating collateral problems in value claiming. The converse is also true; there are few strategies for value claiming that do not affect opportunities for value creating. The task of the strategic negotiator is to create a productive balance between those strategies, creating value as long as that value creation is likely to increase the ultimate value that can be claimed.

SUMMARY

This chapter has explored the ways in which negotiators' interests intersect with the interdependencies of the negotiation process. Thinking strategically in negotiation requires that you not only focus on your preferences, interests, motives, and goals but also focus on your counterpart's preferences, interests, motives and goals.

- Acquiring and using information requires that you identify the outcome you wish to achieve and then figure out how to get there from here; that is, you look ahead and reason back (remember the Truel).
- Look out for other systematic aspects of human behavior such as fairness which is likely to influence the behaviors of you and your counterparts. But even if getting more of what you want does not depend on fairness, you still must consider this factor, as it is likely to affect your counterpart's behaviors.
- Information asymmetry is a constant challenge for negotiators. Sellers typically know much more about what they are selling than the buyer does, and that information often becomes evident only after you have completed the deal. Thus, an important question that should be answered prior to making an offer is "what do I learn if my offer is accepted?"
- Remember that if all information is known by all parties, then the negotiation becomes purely distributive and adversarial. In this situation, value claiming will likely be more of a function of who is more

powerful—particularly in terms of who has the better alternative and the discipline to demand more while being willing to walk away.

At this point, you are finally ready to negotiate. You have determined your reservation price; you have established your aspirations and have investigated your alternatives. You have scoped out the issues that will be discussed in the negotiation, and you've figured out what your preferences are—and you have a good idea of the preferences and interests of your counterparts. You know which of these issues are distributive, which are integrative, and which are congruent.

What's next? In the next chapter we address the first strategic question facing negotiators: Should you make the first offer?

PART TWO

THE NEGOTIATION

CHAPTER SEVEN

WHO SHOULD MAKE THE FIRST OFFER?

Is S(he) Who Speaks First Truly Lost?

One of the most common questions that negotiators raise is "Who should make the first offer?" This is an important question, since a negotiation can only start in earnest once one of the parties makes a first offer and the other party responds.

In some of your negotiations, you may have made the initial offer, and, in others, you may have received it. So, in your experience, was there a difference when you made the first offer compared to when you received the first offer? Even if you kept track of the outcomes of both kinds of exchanges, negotiations are often very different, and it may be hard to compare directly the result of one negotiation to that of another. Still, the odds are that you strongly prefer one way to the other.

When asked, executives as well as graduate and undergraduate students (and their parents!) overwhelming believe that receiving the first offer gives them a competitive advantage. Indeed, about 80 percent of participants in our negotiation workshops and classes prefer to receive rather than make the first offer. When asked why, the typical response is that whoever makes the first offer gives away information, giving the receiving party an informational advantage.

Receiving the first offer certainly gives you information about the issues and the positions on those issues that are attractive to your counterpart. You now have a starting point. Having this information advantage can give you insight into how you might want to respond. Think about negotiating the salary of a new position. What if you waited for your potential employer to make an offer and it turned out to be significantly higher than your aspiration. What a great outcome! You are being offered much more than you expected, and this was only the start of the negotiation! The point is that it is possible for someone to value your potential contributions more highly than you yourself value them. The employer might have said, "What would it take to get you here?" If you had made the first offer, you might have named a relatively low figure—and probably would have gotten it and would settled for significantly less than you might have received otherwise!

Second, by making the first offer, you allow your counterparts to identify any congruent issues—thereby giving them an advantage in the negotiation. For example, Thomas's request that the tires to be mounted at the location next to his office would alert the dealer, who also happens to favor that location, that location is a congruent issue. She might simply agree, or she might use that information strategically by demanding a concession on another issue in return for agreeing to Thomas's preferred location.

Some of our students have suggested that Thomas might be better off by not asking for his favored location in his first offer, thus denying the dealer the opportunity to identify location as a congruent issue. However, such a suggestion implicitly assumes that Thomas knows that location is a congruent issue. If he did not, the location he misleadingly proposed might actually be the dealer's favored one—one she would surely accept.

There can be substantial risks associated with making the first offer so perhaps the 80 percent who prefer to receive the first offer are on to something. Consider Margaret's experience when she was in the market to purchase a new home. Her real estate agent (with whom she spent a considerable amount of time touring potential properties) spontaneously offered the advice that "he who speaks first has lost." Margaret was a bit surprised by the emphatic nature of her statement and asked the agent how she came to that conclusion. She looked at Margaret, surprised at her question, and said, "Everyone knows that making the first offer is a bad thing to do."

On the long drive to the next property, Margaret thought about the agent's statement. She was a successful real estate agent in an industry where sellers list their homes for sale and set a listing price. In effect, they have made the first offer. If making a first offer were such a bad idea, why wouldn't sellers, rather than listing a price, simply advertise that their homes were for sale and that they were willing to entertain offers?[1] In fact, according to realtors, the selling price is typically between 95 and 97 percent of the listing price.[2]

In contrast, the scientific literature indicates that making a first offer is often advantageous. So there is obviously a disconnect between most peoples' intuition ("receiving the first offer is better than making the first offer") and what academics recommend. As we will discuss next, the decision is more nuanced than to *always* or to *never* make the first offer.

The most powerful effect of a first offer is to create an anchor. Much as a physical anchor creates a drag, the first offer in a negotiation anchors the starting point of the negotiation, setting the agenda and starting points for valuing the issues and allocating the benefits. Experienced negotiators expect the first offers to be extreme: The offering party is asking for more than he reasonably expects to get. As a result, when your counterpart receives your first offer, he will rationally discount that offer. If you list your home for $1.5 million, potential buyers expect that you would be willing to take something less than $1.5 million. But of course, potential buyers do not know how large the discount is that you will accept.

In a world of rational actors, the discount (or adjustment as it is often called) by the potential buyer would, on average, exactly offset the seller's exaggeration, offsetting the effect of the anchor. However, psychologically, it is a much different story because you are unsure about the "true" value of the object.

In response to this uncertainty negotiators search for clues to assess the worth of the issues under consideration—an obvious reference point is the (first) offer they just received. As a result of using it as a reference point, they are influenced by that offer. From this reference point, they adjust their assessments based on a variety of factors, such as their knowledge that the counterparty's offer must be in its best interest and the reliability and perceived diagnostic value of the clues, to arrive at their estimate of value.

The power of an anchor has less to do with the quality of the information than it does with how vivid or salient the receiving party perceives that information. In fact, even an arbitrarily chosen reference point or anchor will influence value estimates,[3] and the adjustments you make away from these points will be insufficient.

Perhaps one of the earliest and most impressive demonstrations of the strength of the anchoring effect was conducted by two psychologists, Amos Tversky and Daniel Kahneman.[4] You may recognize Kahneman's name as a winner of the Nobel Prize in Economics in 2004 and as the author of the recent book *Thinking Fast and Slow*.

In an early experiment, Tversky and Kahneman had participants estimate the percentage of African countries in the United Nations. Each person was given a starting point that was determined by the spin of a random
number wheel. They then had to decide whether the number generated by
the wheel was higher or lower than what they thought the correct percentage of African countries in the United Nations was and then give their best
estimate of the correct percentage.

Even though the participants were aware that their starting point was
the result of a random process (the wheel was literally spun in front of
them), their final estimates were influenced by the number generated by the
wheel. Although the wheel appeared to be generating random numbers
from 1 to 100, in reality it was rigged, stopping at either 10 or at 65. And
here is the surprising result: the median estimate of African countries in
the United Nations of those who saw the wheel stop at the number 10 was
25, while the median estimate of those who saw the wheel stopping at the
number of 65 was 45.

So how could this random number affect the participants' estimate of
the percentage of African nations in the United Nations? Obviously, there
was no logical reason to expect that the number generated by spinning
the wheel had any relation to the actual number of African nations in the
United Nations—and hence it could not have been informative, or in any
way diagnostic, of the true number. So it is unlikely that the participants
believed that the random number generated by the wheel had any relation
to the percentage of African Nations in the United Nations—yet the participants in the experiment were clearly influenced by this anchor when
answering the experimenter's question. Further, even when the researchers offered to pay the participants based on their accuracy, the anchor still
had a significant impact on their estimates.

So if such an obviously nondiagnostic anchor were influential, think
how much more powerful the effect of an anchor would be if it appeared to
be diagnostic of the actual value. Margaret investigated this question in a
study coauthored with her colleague Gregory Northcraft, when both were
colleagues at the University of Arizona.[5] The two of them talked a real estate agent in Tucson, Arizona, into helping them identify a house that was
about to go on the market. Then, they got permission from the owner of
the house to use the property in an experiment and assembled a group of
real estate brokers to serve as a focus group. They asked what type of information brokers would need to value a residential real estate property. In

addition, they asked the focus group how skillful they were in estimating the true or appraised value of residential real estate. Although they used different words to describe their expertise, the brokers reported that they could assess the value of a residence within 5 percent of its true value.

Then Margaret and Gregory took the results of this focus group and created a ten-page packet of information about the house. The first page of the packet was a facsimile of the standard Multiple Listing Service (MLS) sheet for the property that was about to come on the market. The remaining nine pages included a copy of the MLS summary of residential real estate sales for both the entire city and the immediate neighborhood of the house for the last six months, information including listing price, square footage, characteristics of the property for houses in the same neighborhood that were currently for sale, that had recently sold, that had sold but the sale was not complete, that had previously been listed but did not sell and had been removed from the market, and the MLS listing sheets for homes in the immediate neighborhood currently for sale.

They then created four different packages. While each package had the same last nine pages, the first page—the facsimile of the MLS listing sheet had one major difference in each of the four packets: listing price. As their real estate focus group had indicated that they could assess the value of a residence within 5 percent of its true value, taking the average assessment of the property by three independent appraisers, they created an MLS sheet that had a listing price that was 12 percent higher than the appraised value, 4 percent higher, 4 percent lower, or 12 percent lower than the appraised value.

If the focus group were correct, they would not be able to distinguish between the "house" that was listed at 4 percent higher or lower than the appraised value; but they should clearly be able to tell that the "house" with the listing price 12 percent higher than the average appraised value was overpriced; and that the one with a listing price 12 percent lower was underpriced.

The actual house was then included in the realtors' weekly real estate tour. Agents viewed it as they normally would with any property just coming on the market. When they arrived at the house, they received one of four packets and were asked to assess its appraised value; the listing price they would set for this house were they the seller; the most they would pay if they were the buyer; and finally, the least they would accept if they were the seller. They were also asked to describe how they arrived at these four

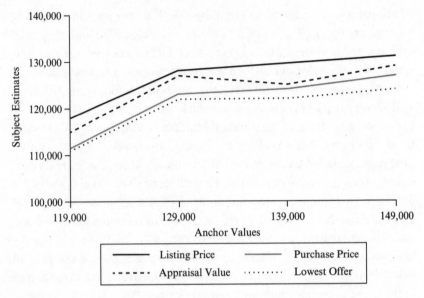

FIGURE 7.1
Based on data from G. B. Northcraft and M. A. Neale, "Experts, Amateurs, and Real Estate: An Anchoring and Adjustment Perspective on Property Price Decisions," *Organizational Behavior and Human Decision Processes* 39 (1986): 228–241.

figures and to identify important considerations in making their assessments.

So how did the agents assess the value of the house? Figure 7.1 illustrates the findings of this study. As you can see from the figure, the listing price had a major impact on the agents' assessment of the value of the property. The higher the listing price, the higher the agents' estimation of the value of the property.

Figure 7.1 illustrates the stark discrepancy between what the agents said they did and what they actually did. While the results showed that listing price was highly influential in the valuation of the property, only 19 percent of the agents mentioned listing price as a factor they considered. In fact, slightly fewer than 75 percent of the real estate agents described their valuation decision as a computational process in which they took the average price per square foot of houses that had recently sold and multiplied that number by the number of square feet in our property. They then adjusted that figure for the unique aspects and conditions of the house. What you should notice is that if they, indeed, had used such a strategy, the arbitrary variations in the listing prices would have had no effect on their assessment. But since listing price was the only thing that varied across the four packets, the differences observed by Margaret and Gregory must have come from the influence of the listing price!

But even when explicitly asked about listing price, the majority of the focus group indicated that they paid no attention to it. After all, how are listing prices determined? If deciding on a particular real estate agent, the potential seller might identify a small number of agents who have been successful and then ask each of them to assess the property. While the agents would also discuss many issues with the potential seller (the specific marketing strategy of the agent, the state of the real estate market in that location, the type of improvements that should be done before the house would be ready to be shown, etc.), the one thing that is most likely to grab the attention of the seller is the price at which the competing agents believe the house should be listed. If there were multiple agents, the potential seller may favor the agent who names the highest price. So clearly agents have an incentive to overstate the listing price. In turn, it seems completely reasonable that realtors should ignore listing prices. Yet, as the results show, they are woefully unsuccessful at doing so. And the more subjectivity or uncertainty associated with the object, the more influential the anchor.[6] And these are trained professionals!

While this may surprise you, it turns out there was no difference between amateurs and experts in how influenced they were by the anchors of listing price. The only difference was that the experts claimed that they had a very explicit computational strategy while the amateurs admitted that they looked at the listing price and decreased their assessment of value depending on the condition of the property. Thus, what the experts said they were doing was not what they were actually doing. They may not have explicitly considered the listing price in the way that the amateurs did, but the anchoring effect was as powerful on them as it was on the amateurs!

Why do first offers have such impact? An important reason is that they focus the receiving party's attention on his or her reservation price and that of the issuing party on the aspiration price.

To understand this effect, consider that your first offer should be an optimistic assessment of what you could achieve in this negotiation (i.e., your aspiration). Thus, when you make a first offer, you are focused on an aspirational level of outcomes. At the same time, such a first offer focuses your counterpart on his or her reservation price. In fact, if your offer were below his reservation price he might be thinking about strategies that could get him to the level of his reservation price so that an agreement would be possible. Thus, by making the first offer, you take advantage of your counterpart's urge to come to an agreement and focus him on his reservation price while maintaining your focus on your aspiration. You maintain your expectations about an optimistic outcome and, at the same time, subtly prime your counterpart to focus on getting to his reservation price.[7]

However, the anchoring effect on the party receiving the offer is less effective the more prepared he is, mainly because careful preparation creates alternative anchors such as aspirations. Indeed, this positive effect of preparation is reinforced if the receiving party keeps its focus on its aspiration.

But interestingly, preparation also works for the party making the first offer by helping that party maintain focus on its aspirations. Think back to Chapter 2. Your aspiration influences your expectation and can direct your focus and offset the power of your counterpart's first offer. Having optimistic aspirations or challenging goals can enhance your ability to achieve better negotiated outcomes.[8]

To maximize this effect, when preparing for a negotiation, excessive focus on your alternatives may make you an underachiever! Using your alternatives as a standard by which to judge an acceptable outcome makes your safety net your goal, and will cause you to systematically underperform in your negotiations. Keeping your aspiration firmly in mind, on the other hand, will provide additional psychological leverage that can help you extract more value in the negotiation.

Designing a First Offer

Let's assume for a moment that you have decided to make the first offer. What are the characteristics that make a first offer more effective? First, you probably want to make a first offer that will set the anchor as favorably for you as possible, subject to it not being dismissed out of hand by the receiving party. That means that you want to make as aggressive a first offer as you can, "just this side of crazy."[9] But while that is a colorful description, of course it is hardly an actionable prescription.

When situating your first offer just this side of crazy, your offer has to be considered by your counterpart and not just dismissed out of hand. So while you typically do not expect your counterparts to accept your first offer, you want them to give your offer serious consideration and not simply walk away.

The challenging aspect is that what your counterpart will perceive as crazy depends on a number of factors, such as cultural expectations (how extreme is extreme?), your counterpart's level of preparation, the justification for your offer, and—surprisingly—how "rounded" or "precise" is your offer.

What makes an offer extreme differs considerably across cultures. When traveling internationally, you get a first-hand opportunity to observe different definitions of extreme. For example, we have observed that the first offers and counteroffers that are given by carpet sellers in Istanbul are quite different from the equivalent offers and counteroffers by a carpet seller in Zurich (even when the sellers were of Turkish origin).

However, culture is not something that changes only when you cross national boundaries. Cultures and their impact can differ dramatically within a country, a region, or even across organizations within a region. The culture of one group or division can differ dramatically even within the same organization. Imagine how negotiations between engineers and marketers in a high-tech firm might differ in what they think of as this side of crazy.

Second, the effect of an anchor also depends on the uncertainty of the value of the issue or issues. The more uncertain or ambiguous the value is, the more influential the anchor will be. Issues may be more or less ambiguous because of their inherent uncertainty or lack of predictability. However, it is more likely that the uncertainty stems from a lack of preparation. The less prepared you are for a negotiation, the more power the first offer has to influence your judgment of what is reasonable.

Third, the presentation matters. First offers, counteroffers, or requests in general are more influential when they are accompanied by an explanation or justification. Classic studies in social psychology clearly demonstrate this. For example, people standing in line are more likely to allow others to "cut" if they give a justification for their request ("I am in a hurry"). Interestingly, the quality of the justification is not as important as the fact that a justification is given. But if you are going to provide a justification for your offer, the more objective justification is the more powerful anchor. For example, when you are negotiating a move forward in the airport security screening line, "I am in a hurry because I am about to miss my plane" is likely to work better than simply "I am in a hurry."[10]

Fourth, the more relevant the anchor appears to be, the more it will influence the receiving party.[11] For example, researchers asked people "Is the freezing point of vodka 32 degrees F?" followed by a request to identify the freezing point of vodka. Most of us would view the anchor of 32 degrees F as diagnostic because 32 degrees F is the freezing point of water. Thus, much as we would be influenced by the listing price of a residence, we would more influenced by this anchor than we might be by an anchoring question such as "Is 30 the average number of days in a month in the Gregorian calendar?" in trying to figure out the freezing point of vodka.

Probably the most surprising effect of the effectiveness of anchors is that the numerical form of a first offer—that is, how round or seemingly imprecise it is—significantly influences how informative recipients view that offer and how much influence it has on the ultimate outcome. Research has found that the more (seemingly) precise an offer, the more it binds the target; the more "round" the offer, the less influential—or the more the receiving party will adjust away from the anchor.[12] What this suggests is that the precise offers are more anchoring than are their less precise cousins (but equally accurate—remember that high school math class where the distinctions between precise and accurate were discussed?). It turns out that, for example, houses sell for more when their listing prices were precise ($1,423,500) rather than round ($1,500,000) even when the round number was larger than the "seemingly" precise number!

So, what makes an anchor powerful? Anchors influence assessment of value because negotiators are rarely in a situation where they have perfect knowledge of the deal and of their counterparts' alternatives and aspirations. In trying to assess a likely point of agreement for a deal, negotiators look for cues that provide information about the interests and preferences of their counterparts. Anchors can provide that perspective. More important, the power of an anchor lies in its subtle ability to influence negotiators' judgments of value. The more unprepared you are for the negotiation, the more influence anchors will have on what you think is reasonable. The more objective the anchor appears, the more it appears to be a reasonable starting point. And the more objective and precise the first offer, the more easily you accept its validity.

YOU MADE THE FIRST OFFER: WHAT'S NEXT?

You just made the first offer to your counterpart. Now what? There are at least three possibilities: Your counterpart could (1) end the negotiation by accepting your first offer; (2) she could simply walk away by saying you should come back when you have a reasonable offer; or (3) she could make a counteroffer.

From a purely rational perspective, you might think that (1) is the preferred outcome. After all, you made the first offer, and you got what you wanted. Yet as we discussed in Chapter 2, while this might hold true economically (although it tells you that your counterpart values the item more highly than you expected), it isn't the case psychologically: Having your counterpart accept your first offer almost guarantees that you'll feel less satisfied than you would have if you and they had negotiated a different outcome—even one that made you worse off. When you made the first offer, you did not expect it to be accepted precisely because of your assessment that it was an extreme and one-sided outcome. So, when that offer is accepted, it calls into question your basic assumption—that the first offer was extreme and one-sided.

Indeed, research shows that negotiators are much more dissatisfied when their first offer is accepted than they are with the *same* objective outcome if an agreement is reached after rounds of offers and counteroffers.[13]

If, on the other hand, your counterpart takes option (2) and walks away after saying she will not even respond with a counteroffer, it will be pretty clear that you have wandered into crazy land. This puts you in a difficult position: Without a counteroffer, the only way to continue the negotiation is for you to make a unilateral concession. You have to make another offer—and that offer is likely to entail a significant concession from your first offer. And in making this unilateral concession, you have let counterpart know how important an agreement is for you: that you are not willing to let her walk away.

At that point, you have lost significant power in this negotiation. When you make that unmatched concession, you have essentially rewarded your counterpart for not negotiating! You made a first offer, she started to walk away, and you conceded. Now your counterpart is even less likely to make a concession; it makes more sense for her to hold out, keep walking, and see how much more you will concede.

One alternative is to have a partner who can step into the negotiation and replace you, because by conceding you have made it too clear that you won't walk away from this negotiation. If there is any hope of getting a reasonable deal, it will require someone else to take over, preferably someone whom the counterpart does not associate with you, someone who can reestablish his own willingness to walk away. But you are done.

So stepping into crazy land is something to avoid—as is making too low an offer. You don't want to get your first offer accepted, nor do you want your counterpart to end the negotiation by walking out. Rather, what you want is a counteroffer. So the best first offer really is the most extreme offer that your counterparts will seriously consider. Once they make a counteroffer, you will have achieved the goals of the first offer: You will have anchored your counterparts with an offer, and they will have responded with a counteroffer, creating that range between the two points that defines the playing field for a particular negotiation.

Now consider the choice that most folks believe is the better option: receiving the first offer. When is receiving the first offer a good idea? What is it about receiving the first offer that makes it so attractive to negotiators?

WHEN TO WAIT FOR THE FIRST OFFER

Receiving the first offer gives you a strategic advantage when the potential value of the information conveyed by the offer outweighs the value of the anchoring effect of making the first offer. This will occur when your counterpart is poorly prepared—and you are well prepared.

If you are negotiating with a counterpart who does not do much in the way of systematic planning or preparation to understand her perspective or yours, she may make an error in her assessment of what she wants, and that error may be in your favor. Your unprepared counterpart may also reveal much more in her first offer about how she values the issues, giving you insights into what she believes to be an extreme opening position. Since you are well prepared, you can learn about how she values the issues while remaining relatively uninfluenced by the effect of the anchor contained in the first offer.

Consider a negotiation where you have unique and private information and you are confident that your counterpart does not know. If you were trying to buy a painting, the value of that painting may be quite different to you if you were a casual buyer of art from what it might be if you were an art collector. As an individual collector, the value of a particular painting may depend on your knowledge of the artist, the state of your personal collection, and other factors that might be unique to the specific interaction between you and this particular piece of art. So the value that is potentially available in this interaction is a function of you. Another art collector might value this same piece of art in a very different way. In contrast, if you were simply a buyer of art, the unique component of the perspective that you bring to the table might be much more equal to that brought by your counterpart (you bring the money, the counterpart brings the art).

Let's move from the world of art sales to the more mundane setting of a flea market. You are spending a Saturday afternoon, strolling through a flea market—looking for something interesting. Passing a small kiosk, you notice a large work table that was fashioned out of cement blocks that is for sale. Although singularly unattractive, it, nonetheless, caught your eye. The seller had glued some interesting tiles to the center of the work table to make it more attractive. It is these tiles that have attracted your attention. The tiles, it turns out, were made by Grueby—a famous arts-and-crafts artisan. Given the context (flea market, concrete table), you conclude that it is highly unlikely that the seller is aware of the famous provenance of his decorative tiles.

So, in this case should you make the first offer? Will the anchoring effect or the informational effect dominate? Since you recognize the value of the Grueby tiles, that knowledge is likely to anchor you to a much higher value than your counterpart is expecting if he were ignorant of their provenance. If you propose a price dramatically higher than the seller expects, however, you may raise his suspicions about either your state of mind ("I have a real sucker here") or, more importantly, the knowledge that would cause you to offer such a high price for his tiles. Either way, odds are he'll try to get you to pay considerably more than he had planned because of your first offer. What should you do? The answer: Let him make the first offer and then use that offer to assess what he knows. If he makes a first offer that demonstrates his lack of knowledge about the tiles, then you can negotiate at the level that he has set with his first offer. If you are successful at reaching an agreement, then the seller will be happy with the sale of the work table, and you will be happy with your purchase of those rare Grueby tiles. Now all you have to do is to figure out how to get that cement block table home so you can remove the tiles!

In the same vein, if you truly believe that your counterparts have a very different, higher metric for valuing the issues over which you are negotiating, then you should entice them to make the first offer. If you truly believe that your potential employer will make you an offer that is substantially greater than your current compensation, you don't want to anchor her with your current compensation figure, possibly signaling that you would be willing to take less than she was offering. So if you honestly believe that your counterpart values your capabilities much more highly than your current compensation would suggest, see what she has to say first.

Finally, you may choose to receive the first offer if you have great uncertainty about the value of the object to your counterpart. For example, assume that you know that your counterpart's reservation price is either 10 or 1,000—but you don't know which. If you were to make the first offer, you either run the risk of making it too high or having her walking away. Thus, by having her make the first offer, you can infer whether her valuation is high or low.

Of course, by receiving the first offer, you subject yourself to the anchoring effect of your counterpart's offer. However, the better informed you are, the less impact the first offer will have in anchoring you.[14] The more you know about the issues over which you are negotiating, the more certain you can be about what you want and what you value. The more certain you are, the less your assessment of value will be swayed by that first offer. The better prepared you are compared to your counterpart, the more resistance you have to the anchoring effect and the greater the potential to take advantage of the unexpected information contained in the counterpart's first offer. But don't get confused: No matter how well you have prepared, you will be influenced by your counterpart's first offer. It is not a question of if but rather a question of how much.

BOTTOM LINE: WHO SHOULD MAKE THE FIRST OFFER?

So, let's go back to the original question—should you make or receive the first offer? There may be times in which you want to receive the first offer, and situations in which you will do better by making the first offer. Recent research helps us distinguish which is preferable in various situations.

Researchers recently looked at the impact of making the first offer across different cultures, when negotiators had differing levels of power, when negotiations were over single issues (such as price), or when the negotiations involved multiple issues that were distributive, integrative and congruent in nature. In all of these situations, negotiators who made the first offer did better. Further analysis of the data suggested that it was on the allocation of the distributive issues (such as price) that the first offers had their effects. Making the first offer did not influence the relative outcomes on the integrative or congruent issues.

To help you make the decision, let's consider what happens when you make the first offer and there are congruent issues. Assume first that neither party is aware that a given issue is congruent. The receiver can exploit this information by choosing a trading strategy that accepts that extreme offer (which, of course, is not extreme since the issue is congruent) in return for a concession on another issue. Alternatively, she can choose a direct strategy and accept the counterpart's offer on the congruent issue, possibly gaining goodwill. Either way, the person receiving the offer has a choice.

Now assume the negotiating parties are not equally well informed and that the better-informed party knows (or suspects) that some of the issues being negotiated are congruent. Then the choice of whether to make the first offer depends on weighing the relative impact of forgoing the benefits from setting the anchor compared to the value of knowing which issues are congruent and having the option of choosing a trading or direct strategy.

As this example indicates, information and preparation are key in any negotiation. So in deciding which approach makes you better off—making or receiving an offer—you need to assess both your and your counterpart's relative preparation. To help you do that, we have organized your options into a table that has sixteen different possibilities. How prepared are you about your interests (high or low) and about your counterpart's interests (high or low)? How prepared are they likely to be about what they want (high or low) and how much insight do they have about your interests (high or low)? For example, you could be very knowledgeable about your interests and not knowledgeable about the interests of your counterpart or you could be knowledgeable on both or knowledgeable on neither. In each of these sixteen possibilities, we have made a recommendation.

Take a look at Matrix 7.1. To make it more accessible, we have blacked out the possibilities that reflect your not being prepared about what your interests and preferences are. After getting this far in the book, that simply is not an option! More importantly, consider the grey and white possibilities. In the grey zone, you should proceed with caution. You have not analyzed the negotiation from your counterpart's perspective. Some of these possibilities reflect mutual ignorance—you both don't have insight into the interests of the other. The white possibilities reflect the sweet spot in your preparation. You are knowledgeable about you and your counterpart. In some of these situations, your counterpart is also quite knowledgeable and, in others, less so. You know your interests and your counterparts know theirs. But each of you has little insight into the other.

MATRIX 7.1 SHOULD YOU MAKE OR RECEIVE THE FIRST OFFER?

Counterpart's information about own negotiating parameters	Counterpart's information about your negotiating parameters	Information about your negotiating parameters			
		Your information about counterpart's negotiating parameters (L)		Your information about counterpart's negotiating parameter (H)	
		L	H	L	H
L	L			*Can receive (but make also good)*	*Receive*
L	H			*Make*	*Make*
H	L			*Make*	*Make*
H	H			*Make*	*Make*

What may be very surprising to you is the dominance of "make" recommendations: 75 percent of the recommendations are "make the first offer." Compare this to our survey findings that 80 percent of negotiators prefer to *receive* the first offer. At the very least, you may need to be more proactive in making the first offer than you'd prefer. But more important, remember that this is not a simple, binary question. To get more of what you want, you need to analyze the situation, your behavior, and the behavior of your counterpart to determine the best course of action for yourself. Sometimes that will require you to make the best offer; at other times it will require you to wait for it.

SUMMARY

Who knew that figuring out when you should make the first offer would be this complicated? Here, we attempt to distill the lessons in this chapter to their most important elements. In sum, you should consider the following in deciding how to initiate the negotiation:

- Analyze the situation to determine if the effect of the anchor or the effect of the information asymmetry is more powerful. If it were unclear, ambiguous, or equivalent, consider making the first offer.
- Anchors do work, even when negotiators are knowledgeable about the value of the issue. They are just more effective the less precise the knowledge of the receiving party is.
- The offer should be as extreme as you can make it while still getting your counterpart to respond—unless you are trying to get an auction going. We discuss that exception in Chapter 13.
- The numbers contained in the first offer should appear precise rather than rounded (even if no such accuracy objectively exists).
- The basis or justification for the offer should accompany the offer. The more objective that basis or justification appears to be, the more influential the offer.

CHAPTER EIGHT

MANAGING THE NEGOTIATION

Supplementing and Verifying What You (Think You) Know

You have completed your prenegotiation planning, made the decision about making the first offer, and are now ready to start the negotiation. But unless your situation is very unusual, there are still gaps in what you know. For example, your knowledge about many aspects of the negotiation and the issues and their values, particularly from your counterpart's perspective, is likely to be incomplete. So you—like any sophisticated negotiator—should therefore regard the negotiation as an opportunity to extend and verify much of what you've learned in planning and preparing for the negotiation.

To take advantage of the information exchange during the negotiation, you should prepare a list of the things you still don't know and a list of items you would like to confirm. While the optimal time to gather information is at the planning and preparing stage, some information simply cannot be obtained before the negotiation; furthermore, some information may be obtainable beforehand, but will be imprecise. Despite the necessary incompleteness of their preparations, however, few people treat the negotiation itself as a chance to update, confirm, or revise their knowledge particularly of their counterpart—and to enhance their assessment of the potential solutions.

But negotiators face a challenge: As you prepare for the negotiation, invariably you base your preparation on a series of assumptions—assumptions about your and your counterpart's interests and issues and their value to each of you. In Chapter 1 you learned about the power of expectations to drive behavior. Your assumptions are the filter through which you evaluate information you uncover or receive. For example, negotiators who assume that their counterparts are cooperative are more likely to ask questions about their counterpart's intention to cooperate; while negotiators who assume their counterparts are competitive ask questions about their counterpart's intention to compete.[1]

But assumptions are just that—assumptions. You should test and, if necessary, update them, and the negotiation provides a real opportunity to do just that. However, this approach also creates a real danger fueled by your urge to reach agreement, which may encourage you to abuse or neglect the information you receive—for instance, by adjusting your reservation price simply to make it easier to conclude the deal.

The first step in taking advantage of the information available in the negotiation is to set the right tone—and the right expectations—for both you and your counterpart. The tone should focus on information exchange rather than on who gets what. We recommend that you use the first phase of the negotiation to identify what you and your counterpart are trying to achieve, including what the characteristics of a good deal from each party's perspective would be and how you and your counterpart will know when you both have found that deal. Although this first phase will undoubtedly identify issues on which your and your counterpart's interests differ (e.g., the buyer wants as low a price as possible and the seller wants as high a price as possible), it is important to highlight the common interests (e.g., a price that is acceptable to both the buyer and the seller, to establish an ongoing relationship, etc.). By identifying and emphasizing those common interests, you are framing the negotiation as a means to solve a problem that brought both you and your counterpart to the negotiation, you can create a more collaborative setting that counteracts the presumption of an adversarial relation and enhances information sharing in the negotiation.

This reframing to a more collaborative interaction minimizes the potential to interpret the negotiation as adversarial and to use a different filter by which you and your counterpart assess each other's behavior. Consider how a fixed-pie perspective might influence your assessment of a proposal from your counterpart. If you assume that a negotiation is purely adversarial, then any offer proposed by your counterpart must be a bad one for you (and vice-versa). As a result, you will value a particular proposal less, simply because it has been offered by your counterpart. This effect is called reactive devaluation.[2]

An experiment demonstrated reactive devaluation: Participants (who were all U.S. residents) were randomly assigned to three groups, each being asked whether they would support a drastic bilateral nuclear arms reduction program. Participants in the first group were told that the proposal came from President Ronald Reagan; 90 percent of them said it would be favorable or even-handed to the interests of the United States. Participants in the second group were told the identical proposal came from a group of unspecified policy analysts; 80 percent of them thought it was favorable or even-handed to interests of the United States. Participants in the third group were told it came from Mikhail Gorbachev; only 44 percent thought that this very same proposal was favorable or neutral to the interests of the United States. While all three groups saw the same proposals, the only difference was who the participants thought crafted the proposal: the United States, a neutral party, or a cold-war enemy; and that information had a dramatic impact on how the participants viewed the proposal.

The second step in the opening phase of the negotiation is to identify the issues that are important to you and those that are important to your counterpart. Of course, this process requires reciprocity; that is, you will have to share what is important to you as well as finding out what is important to your counterpart. But be judicious: All information is not of equal strategic importance, and reciprocity is a two-way street. So share information, but require your counterpart to do the same. Start with coarse information such as identifying issues, before exchanging more granular (and hence more strategic) information such as the rank ordering of issues by their importance. We recommend that you do not share the most strategic information, such as the specific values of issues, or if this becomes necessary, reserve it for late in the process (if at all) when you are in the process of finalizing the negotiation.

Even when you attempt to supplement and verify what you have discovered about your counterpart's preferences, your information search is likely to be biased by your expectations. As a result, your conclusions are likely to be consistent with your expectations, even if those expectations do not reflect the true nature of your counterparts' preferences. But reactive devaluation is not the only informational filter that affects negotiators.

Often negotiators fail to take advantage of the information that can readily be inferred from how the negotiation unfolds, thus overlooking ways to assess the preferences and beliefs of their counterparts unobtrusively. In the remainder of the chapter, we discuss how to extract information from the way your counterpart concedes, the impact of the relational horizon (long-term vs. short-term), reputation, and bargaining history. Paying attention to these aspects of the negotiation can increase your effectiveness by supplementing and verifying the information you have collected in advance. In the next section, we consider additional sources of information, as well as filters that influence how you are likely to interpret the behaviors of your counterparts and how they are likely to interpret yours.

THE PATTERN OF CONCESSIONS

An important marker that you can use to assess the progress of the negotiation is the concessionary behavior of your counterparts. How much do they concede from one proposal to another? Are they making concessions early or late in the negotiation? How do your counterparts justify their concessions? These are all sources of information that can be gained as the negotiation unfolds. These three tell-tale behaviors can influence your assessments of your counterparts' value of the issues or items under consideration as well as the counterparts' satisfaction with you and with the outcome.[3]

Margaret was attentive to presence of these three "tells" when she was trying to buy a new horse. She talked to horse people who had a reputation for dealing honestly to see if they had any horses that would suit her—both in terms of her riding ability and the horse's potential for working cattle. One of these people, a friend she had known for many years, told her he knew of a person with a really nice horse for sale. Margaret contacted that seller to assess the horse: She first observed the owner ride the horse, she then rode the horse herself, and finally she had the horse examined for soundness by a veterinarian. So now she was ready to discuss the sale. To illustrate the significance of the pattern and timing of concessions, let's assume that the negotiation itself was simply about price. The seller was asking $11,000, and, based on the information she gathered, she countered with $9,000.

If you were Margaret, would there be any difference in your assessment of the value of the horse if the seller immediately accepted your offer (that is, made a unilateral concession of $2,000)? Would you evaluate the value of the horse differently if the seller gradually conceded on price over four rounds, eventually settling on Margaret's asking price of $9,000? Or how would you evaluate the value of the horse if the seller took a hard line, making no concessions until Margaret was about to walk away—and then conceded to Margaret's offer of $9,000?

Note that in each of the three scenarios, the asking price was $11,000 and the final price was $9,000. Thus, if one were to simply focus on the final outcome, there would be no economic differences among the three scenarios. So, from a purely rational perspective (i.e., Thomas's perspective), Margaret should not care how she got to the price she wanted to pay. Yet, it is highly likely that Margaret (and even Thomas) would be much more satisfied with the purchase and her assessment of the value of the new horse in the second scenario of gradual concession more than the third with its hard line and, with the third scenario more than the first with its quick agreement.

In the first scenario, Margaret is likely to believe that the horse was worth less than she had originally believed, interpreting the seller's concession as indicative that he knew the horse was not that valuable. Maybe there was something wrong with it that she had not identified? In the second scenario, she was likely to be more comfortable with her assessment of the value of the horse and more satisfied with the interaction and the seller, assessing the concession as indicative that the seller wanted to sell the horse (rather than that the horse was worth less). In the third scenario, she was more likely to believe that the horse was worth more but would also be less satisfied with the behavior of the seller. She may not want to negotiate with him again or recommend him to her horse-owning friends. (We return to this issue when we discuss the impact of the expectation of future interactions on negotiators' behavior.)

The seller could further enhance Margaret's satisfaction by justifying his concession to sell the horse for $9,000. For example he could disclose that completing this deal by week's end was important to him because his son's college tuition payment was due. Note that from Margaret's perspective, that justification provides a credible justification that his concession had little to do with the horse and more to do with his financial situation. As a result, it is much more palatable than her attributing his rapid concession to the possibility that the horse was worth considerably less than she thought. This justification also reduces the likelihood of her experiencing buyer's remorse: a buyer's subjective and negative experience after completing a transaction that she may have paid too much and, having second thoughts about whether she should have made this purchase.

The value of a concession may also change depending on that the timing of the concession. Consider how willing you would be to give a $20,000 price concession in exchange for a more favorable closing date when selling your home. Research shows that sellers' willingness to concede is greater when they have already surpassed their cost basis in the house and even greater once they surpassed the $500,000 tax exemption that the U.S. government provides (assuming you are married and filing jointly).[4]

Notice that there is no economic justification for the first benchmark: every dollar you concede costs you a dollar, irrespective whether you have surpassed your cost basis or not. The purchase price is sunk, and thus irrelevant from a rational perspective. This first benchmark is purely psychological. However, once you have surpassed your cost basis by $500,000, then every additional dollar you concede costs you about $.75 (assuming capital gains and state taxes total 25 percent)—a clear economic impact.

If the more favorable closing date were worth at least $15,000 to you (perhaps because you don't have to move twice), then the $20,000 price concession might cost you much less and, depending on how much you value the earlier closing date, this package of concessions could increase the value you could claim in this negotiation. Of course, if your counterpart knows the cost basis in your house because he has already researched the price at which you bought it, he has insight into how expensive the trade-off is for you and can use this to make offers that are more favorable to him.

ASKING AND ANSWERING QUESTIONS

It is surprising how accommodating people are when asked direct questions. Most of us don't think twice before we answer. In fact, most often don't even think once. A great negotiator, on the other hand, is like a great diplomat: She can think twice before saying nothing.

If your counterparts are like most people, they are likely to answer a direct question, even if it may reveal information that is strategically detrimental to them. Moreover, you can enhance the likelihood that they will reveal useful information by asking a question and then simply waiting. Most people are surprisingly willing to fill up the silence.

Taking advantage of this human tendency is useful, but—to be successful—you need to consider how and when you ask your questions. Clearly they should focus on complementing and confirming what you already know, as well as finding out what you are missing. But even so, the type of questions you should ask, when you ask them, and the order in which you ask them all matter because of reciprocity and whether you can trust the answer you get.

As an example, let's revisit the reservation price. It would be really advantageous if you knew your counterpart's reservation price, but you're not sure how to go about asking for it. In Chapter 2, we suggested that sharing your true reservation price is a bad strategy if your goal is to get more of what you want. But where does this leave you? After all, if you were to ask your counterpart to reveal her reservation price, you not only should expect her to misrepresent, but also to ask you to reveal yours.

There is a solution to this dilemma, however: developing skills in directing the conversation. Rather than asking your counterpart to reveal her reservation price, you could engage her in a conversation starting with what she is trying to achieve in the negotiation, moving to her alternatives, possibly even asking her what she paid for the item—information that would allow you to triangulate her reservation price.

The solution of directing the conversation works in other situations, as well. For instance, in the course of a negotiation it's likely you'll be asked direct questions that you just don't want to answer. Explore potential answers that convey the level of information that you want to share but do not expose you to follow-up questions that you may not want to answer. For example, if your counterparts ask about your bottom line, consider asking them what is important for them to achieve in this negotiation— that is, what the characteristics of a good deal are for them. You are redirecting them from a "who-gets-what" question (the answer to which they are not likely to believe) to one aimed at information exchange, the heart of value creation—something we recommend you attempt at the beginning of the negotiation.

Of course, a major challenge in any negotiation is to assess the reliability of the information you obtain. As mentioned in Chapter 4, one strategy is to ask questions to which you know the answers, with a reasonable level of confidence, in addition to questions where you don't know the answers. Your counterparts' answers on the former can help you triangulate just how trustworthy your counterpart's answers are on the latter.

Asking specific, targeted questions can help achieve more of what you want—but be judicious. Ask questions you believe your counterpart would be willing to answer. Before asking a question, however, ask yourself if you would be willing to answer that question if your counterpart asked it of you. In general, a series of small questions is more effective than fewer but bigger questions. But remember to pay attention to the answers both to enhance what you know about the negotiation and your counterpart and to assess the veracity of your counterpart's responses.

But this is just the start. To fill in the knowledge gaps, one of the more effective strategies to enhance information exchange—and perhaps open doors you had not even considered—requires that you leverage the negotiation situation. Specifically, you can use specific aspects of your negotiation to interpret the information that you receive and even to predict the likely behavior of your counterparts. In the next section, we discuss when and how reputation, bargaining history, relationships, and your own ability to read and understand your counterpart's point of view will help you get more of what you want in your negotiations.

THE POWER OF THE FUTURE

I s there a tomorrow in the present exchange? Is the negotiation part of a continuing interaction, or is it a one-time event? The expectations of continued interaction change the dynamics, both from an economic and a psychological perspective, so it's important to assess whether there is a future when entering a negotiation.

When there is a future, reputation matters. Parties are more likely to take the long-term implications of their actions into account, influencing both their communications as well as their positions. The good news is that negotiators who expect future interaction are much more likely to communicate truthfully, act less competitively, feel more dependent on their counterparts, and be more motivated to develop a working relationship than negotiators who do not expect any future interactions.[5] In addition, negotiators with high aspirations reach more integrative agreements when they expect future interactions as compared to those with high aspirations who expect the negotiation to be a one-time event.[6]

At the same time, a future may also complicate the negotiation. For example, negotiators may also be less likely to concede when a concession has a precedence value that negatively affects their long-term interests. For example, a long-term supplier may be less likely to concede on price because doing so may increase your expectations that she will also have to concede in the future. However, she may be much more willing to customize payment plans to meet her counterpart's unique circumstances at a particular point.

The potential of future interaction also provides a different filter through which you and your counterparts interpret each other's intentions, behaviors, and the choices that each of you make. That filter can be composed of each negotiator's reputation and your unique histories. Even the type of relationship that you have or expect to have is an important input. For example, when either current or future negotiations are expected to be contentious, negotiators may be less willing to make concessions— particularly early ones—to establish a reputation of toughness.[7]

Reputation is perhaps the most obvious factor in a negotiation that contains the potential of future interaction. A person's reputation is an aggregation of available information. It is shorthand for conveying information, both objective and stereotypical, and is useful at predicting that person's actions. Experienced negotiators often consider a counterpart's reputation when deciding whether to enter into a negotiation in the first place. For example, when Margaret was looking to buy a horse, she initially contacted people based on their reputations.

Your counterparts' reputation, for example, can help you predict what actions they will take and, more importantly, influences your interpretation of their underlying intent.[8] Through the filter of reputation, you attach meaning to your counterparts' behaviors. If your counterparts identify an issue as important, they could either be exchanging this information to create value or strategically justifying a bigger concession on another issue in return for a concession on this issue. Thus, when your counterparts are known for their tough bargaining techniques, it is likely you would interpret their statement about the importance of an issue as a precursor to claiming more. Your response to this revelation would be very different if, in contrast, your counterparts were known for their value-creation orientation.

Reputation has been empirically shown to affect performance in negotiation. In one study, half the pairs, or dyads, were told that their counterparts were particularly adept at distributive bargaining.[9] Negotiators in the other half of the dyads were not given any such information. In negotiating the outcome of a multiple-issue negotiation with integrative potential, negotiators facing a counterpart with a distributive reputation were less willing to share information and were more sensitive to attempts to control the interaction. Interestingly, those negotiators with no reputational information about their counterparts actually did significantly better. They were more effective in value creation when they had no information about their counterparts' reputation than when they knew the reputation to be distributive.

In addition, negotiators with a distributive reputation achieved outcomes of significantly less value than negotiators with no reputational information. Their distributive reputations—and subsequent counterpart expectations—overwhelmed their capabilities as negotiators. This is particularly important because negotiators were randomly assigned to the distributive reputational condition: In reality, there were no differences between the experts' skill at distributive negotiating. On learning of the distributive reputation of their counterparts, negotiators were influenced in what they expected and how they interpreted their counterparts' behaviors, leading to a greater emphasis on distributive behaviors. Their counterparts reciprocated in kind, meeting these more aggressive, value-claiming actions with increased distributive responses, even though these negotiators were unaware of their own reputations. This type of reciprocity created a destructive conflict spiral that left both parties worse off.

There has to be the opportunity to interact in the future for reputations to matter, even if that opportunity were as short as the one-time negotiation above. This becomes clear when you think about negotiating with a counterpart who is local versus one who is transient. When negotiators interacted with transient counterparts (i.e., those with a high likelihood to be present only for a short time), they demonstrated shorter time horizons, and this focus on the "now" resulted in more adversarial interactions. In contrast, when negotiators interacted with local counterparts, they were more likely to accept short-term sacrifices to realize additional long-term advantages. This exchange required that negotiators be confident that their counterparts would reciprocate short-term sacrifices in a future negotiation—making the long-term gain possible and increasing the importance of the respective reputations of the negotiators. Thus, when appropriate, you can facilitate the negotiation by stressing the long-term aspect of your interactions.

Clearly, the reputations of your counterparts set your expectations even before you interact with them. Yet reputations are subject to change or modification. How does your experience in negotiating, especially your experience negotiating repeatedly with the same counterparts, influence your expectations about the interaction? That is, how influenced are reputations by bargaining history?

When there is a future, often there has been a past as well. What happened in your last interaction can significantly impact what happens in your next one. When negotiators reached an impasse in a prior negotiation, as compared to those who reached agreement, they were more likely to assess those outcomes as failures, were angrier about and frustrated with their performance, and intended to choose more competitive strategies in the future.[10] What were the ultimate effects of these intentions? Did it matter if you were negotiating with the same counterpart in either situation—or someone completely different? The short answer, again, is yes. Your prior negotiation experience (impasse or agreement, in this case) affects your future negotiations, and this is true even when negotiators change counterparts.

When you change negotiation counterparts, your expectation of a cooperative or competitive interaction in the subsequent negotiation predicts the outcome of the present one.[11] When negotiating with the same counterpart, your expectations have no effect although prior negotiating history does. If you reached an impasse in the prior negotiation, you are significantly more likely to reach impasse in the next one. Likewise, if you have reached agreement in a prior negotiation, you are more likely to reach agreement in the subsequent one. This finding suggests that the outcome of your last interaction may be an important consideration when deciding to keep or change negotiators.

It is within the context of relationships that negotiators have a future that is influenced both by bargaining history and reputation. Are relationships simply the sum of reputation and history—or is there more?

Bargaining histories require repeated negotiations, so it's inevitable that negotiators build relationships with one another—but relationships aren't based purely on the negotiator's behavior in the current negotiation. Rather, relationships incorporate both bargaining histories and future expectations. Just like reputation, relationships add a temporal dimension to the effectiveness of negotiation strategies and tactics, and hence the value that can be created and claimed. In addition, when relationships are stable, negotiators are not limited to the present set of issues or values. Preferences for outcomes today and in the future can be combined and leveraged. Thus, from an economics perspective, relationships offer the opportunity to extend the value horizon to include value today and value in the future. But remember, the effect of relationships is a two-way-street, providing you with both advantages and disadvantages.

To illustrate the impact of relationships on your negotiations, compare the issues that you would face when buying or selling a used car when your counterpart is either a relative with whom you socialize and regularly exchange holiday gifts or a stranger with whom you do not expect to interact in the future.

The costs and benefits are quite different depending on whether your counterpart is a relative with whom you share a relationship or a stranger with whom you do not. It's probably obvious that it's better to buy a used car from a relative than from a stranger. When buying a used car, you will ask the seller questions that help you assess the quality of the car, including information about the service history and its current condition. When answering, your relative will have to consider the impact of any misrepresentations on your future relationship, something that the stranger—even an honest one—will be less compelled to do. As a result, the representations made by your relative are more credible, and you are better off buying from the relative than from a stranger.

In contrast, consider that you are selling your used car. You must reasonably expect that the buyer will inquire about the quality of the car, and you know you will have to be more forthcoming with your relative than with a stranger. In fact, even when you believe that there is nothing wrong with the car, a future, unforeseen problem could have adverse consequences for your relationship with your relative; but with a stranger the situation is different, since you do not expect to have any long-term relation with him.[12]

Paradoxically, this means that you want to buy from a relative rather than a stranger but always prefer to sell to a stranger rather than to a relative. But, given this principle, after all, why would your relative choose you as the prospective buyer for her car?[13]

As a further example, consider the earlier example of Margaret buying a horse. Because horse sellers as a group have a reputation for dishonesty (even more than used car dealers), Margaret looked first to her friend for a recommendation. Although she might never purchase another horse from the seller, Margaret is very likely to have continued interactions with her friend. Because of this ongoing relationship, Margaret had more confidence in the reliability of this seller because her friend made the recommendation. In addition, she made sure that the prospective seller knew of her ongoing relation with her friend, thus leveraging the relation between the friend who recommended the seller and the seller to get more honest answers.

Relationships are much more diverse than just the distinction between relative and stranger. The type of relationship between you and your counterpart influences the choices that you perceive as options, the type of information that you will disclose, and the interaction itself. For example, spouses exchange information that often reveals facts and information, as well as feelings, while strangers typically reveal only facts and information.[14] Negotiators who have a bargaining history with their counterparts are more knowledgeable about what arguments will be most convincing, their counterparts' preferences, alternatives, and favored negotiating strategies. Yet, these same relationships may, in some situations, limit your ability to pursue value claiming, particularly if that value is denominated in dollars or wealth because you may favor relationship over *wealth maximization* in choosing your strategies.

Consider the negotiation behaviors and relative emphasis on the relationship of individuals who are strangers, acquaintances (e.g., friends or colleagues), or in long-term relationships (e.g., married couples). In a research study, acquaintances achieved solutions with higher joint benefits than those achieved by strangers or married couples when faced with the demand of a negotiation with integrative potential.[15] These findings suggest that there may be an inverted U-shaped relationship between the strength of the relational tie between the negotiating partners and the level of joint gain achieved in the negotiation.

As these results make clear, friends or colleagues and married partners have an advantage over strangers in negotiations because they possess information about the other party's preferences. However, married partners may be so concerned about the possible damage to the relationship, that they avoid potential conflicts rather than confront them. When comparing friends and colleagues with strangers in negotiation, on the other hand, these more casual relations proved much better at negotiating. Friends and colleagues had higher aspirations for their own outcomes than did the married couples and made more concessions than negotiators who were strangers. As a result, friends and colleagues, especially those with high aspirations for the deal, were better than either strangers or married couples at sharing the information necessary to create value. Finally, because of these offsetting differences, married partners were no more likely than strangers to reach agreements of high joint gain by logrolling or finding congruent issues.[16]

It would be easy to infer from the last few of paragraphs that no reasonable negotiator should favor relationships over the potential economic value of the well-negotiated exchange. From our perspective, however, reducing the complexity of negotiated interactions to such an either-or decision is short sighted and unnecessary. Our goal here is simply to emphasize that the quality of the relationship may be a metric by which you evaluate how well you have done in the negotiation. Having a relationship with your counterpart can systematically influence your aspirations, expectations, the type of information you seek, and the choices you make in service of that relationship.

A great example of the dominance of relationship over wealth is the choice made by the young couple in O. Henry's classic tale "The Gift of the Magi." A young couple facing a bleak Christmas decide, independently, to sell the only thing of value that each has to buy a special gift for the other. The wife cuts and sells her hair, her most valuable possession, to purchase a gold chain for the heirloom pocket watch that is her husband's most prized possession; the husband sells his pocket watch to buy a set of combs and mirrors for his wife.

The denouement of the story is that each gift is made useless by the sacrifice of the other—so objectively value was destroyed. Or was it? When discovered, the gifts with no economic value to the recipient and the sacrifice made by the counterpart were transformed into symbols of great value by conveying the importance of the relationship to each party.

Although you may never experience a sacrifice in your negotiations on the level of "The Gift of the Magi," think about the value of a carefully selected gift versus a check for an equal amount of money from a dear friend. From an economic perspective, the check is a better option because it allows you more choices—you can spend the money on anything you want. Yet, the choosing of a gift requires more effort by the giver, and as such, can add another type of value to the exchange.

In negotiation, those who focus on relationships typically reach agreements of less economic gain, set lower reservation prices, and make more concessions.[17] But lower economic value does not guarantee greater relational value. Relational outcomes have more to do with perceptions of respect and fairness, and the perceptions of "face," than with instrumental outcomes. Just as in the earlier discussion of concession behavior, here we aim to show the way your counterpart interprets your behavior can have more impact than the instrumental results. In general, positive relationships among parties are not the result of instrumental concessions but result from a satisfying social interaction.[18]

The notion of *face* is borrowed from the Chinese notion of *mienzi* or the positive social value you claim for yourself based, in large measure, on the way others treat you in the interactions.[19] Thus, a successful interaction needs to reflect consistency between how you are treated and the status you have claimed. (Note that you do not need to have the instrumental outcomes of the negotiation reflect your status; rather, it is how you are *treated* that reflects your status.)

How you are treated in a negotiation seems to affect your assessment of how well you did. A recent study investigated the impact of the assessment of subjective value (i.e., the feelings about the instrumental value of the deal, the self in the deal, the negotiation process, and the relationship between the parties) that employees experienced during their job negotiations. The subjective value of their outcomes predicted their compensation satisfaction, job satisfaction, and turnover intention after their first year on the job. As a point of interest, the actual compensation that resulted from the negotiation had no impact on any of the job attitudes measured, including turnover intention.[20] This disconnect between subjective value and actual value suggests that you can, by your behaviors, maximize the subjective value of the deal for your counterparts without necessarily sacrificing your objective value (and vice versa). Careful attention to the relationship that exists between you and your counterpart need not come at the cost of your individual wealth.

The type of relationships you have with your negotiating counterparts can be instructive as to the ways they expect to be treated. In addition, relationships can give you an informational edge (because of your knowledge of your counterparts) in your negotiations as well as creating additional barriers to getting more of what you want because you may privilege the relationship over the quality of the agreement.

Besides limiting your negotiating counterparts to friends or relatives, is there another way to improve how you gather, verify, and supplement the information necessary for successfully negotiated outcomes? One skill that may substitute for the informational advantages and burdens that relationships provide is your ability to consider the perspective of your counterpart. As it turns out, there are advantages to being able to put yourself in the cognitive and emotional shoes of your counterparts—but there are also costs.

The ability to consider the perspective of your counterparts allows you to anticipate their behaviors and reactions.[21] Although some are able to take their counterparts' perspective more easily than others, it is always a skill worth developing. The challenge is to understand and leverage your counterpart's perspective without becoming seduced by that perspective to your ultimate disadvantage.

While early research on perspective taking found that those high in this dimension were more empathic and better able to understand their counterparts' interests,[22] higher perspective takers were found to claim more value in the negotiation.[23] When asked how much of a scarce resource they should receive, those who had taken the perspective of their counterparts reported that they were entitled to significantly less of this resource as compared to those who were not asked to take their counterparts' perspective. However, those who had taken the perspective of their counterparts actually took 25 percent more than those who had not considered it. But the benefits of taking your counterpart's perspective don't stop at the amount of value you claim. Those who can take their counterparts' perspective are effective at identifying creative solutions, coordinating social goals, creating social bonds, and countering the anchoring effects of the opponent's first offer.[24]

People who are naturally inclined to adopt another's perspective are also more likely to gain strategic advantage from this inclination. But what should you do if you are not naturally inclined to take the perspective of your counterpart? You can enhance your perspective-taking capability by actively considering the interests, goals, and preferences of your counterparts:[25] exactly the information you need to complete the planning matrix that we described in Chapter 5.

The equivalent of a shared perspective-taking exercise is the prenegotiation discussion about what is important and how you and your counterpart will know a good deal. By engaging in this sort of dialogue, you increase your active perspective taking by trying to understand your counterparts' interests and purposes for engaging in this negotiation. When you do this, you improve your potential to get more of what you—and, interestingly, your counterpart—want in the interaction.

SUMMARY

In this chapter, we have explored strategies in using the negotiation itself to verify and supplement the information search that is necessary to identify opportunities for you to get more of what you want.

- Before you begin negotiating, consider scheduling a prenegotiation session with your counterpart to set the tone for the negotiation. In this session, focus on understanding the characteristics of a good deal for both of you, including what aspects of the negotiation are of particular importance to each of you.
- Carefully attend to the way in which you and your counterpart make concessions, both the timing and the amount, as concessions provide cues to how each of you value the issues.
- There are other filters that can enhance your ability to predict and interpret your counterpart's behavior. As you prepare for your negotiation, consider
  - Your counterparts' reputation, including their bargaining history
  - The potential for future interaction
  - If there were a future, the type of relationship that is likely to exist
- Take the perspective of your counterparts in considering how they will respond to your strategies. Doing so not only increases your ability to create value but also increases your ability to claim that value.
- Use a prenegotiation conversation as an opportunity to set the tone of the negotiation and exchange information about what is important and to assess your perspective-taking ability to understand your counterpart and as a way to mitigate cynical attributions that you and they might make.

CHAPTER NINE

CONCEDE OR ELSE!

The Influence of Promises and Threats

Negotiators often attempt to influence their counterparts by issuing threats or making promises. For example, they might threaten to walk away if their counterpart does not concede on an issue, or even threaten to take an action that is outside the negotiation; for example, unions typically threaten to strike, thereby imposing costs on management if they don't concede. On the other hand, negotiators also may promise to take an action that is outside the temporal frame of your current negotiation, such as: "If you concede on this issue, I will make sure that everyone knows what a great product you sell."

In this chapter, we focus on promises and threats of actions that occur after the negotiation has concluded as forms of influence. Thus, when the target of the threat or promise concedes, he does not know if the issuer will actually carry out the threat or honor the promise.

Obviously, to be effective at influencing the target, promises and threats have to be credible; that is the target must believe that, if he concedes, the issuer will make good on the promise—or carry out the threat, if he does not. Conversely, if the target believes that the threat or the promise is not credible (i.e., that it will not be carried out), then he should simply ignore that threat or promise. Of course, it also follows that issuers should only threaten or promise when those actions are perceived as credible by the target and thus likely to have the desired influence.

We'll begin by discussing the differences and the similarities between threats and promises. Then we focus on what makes promises and threats credible. We start with the assumption that both issuer and target act reasonably (or in Thomas's view, rationally). We will then expand our analysis to include the psychological perspective.

PROMISES VERSUS THREATS

Both threats and promises are used to influence your behavior. For example, airlines routinely promise their best customers access to seats with more legroom and upgrades to first class. Those promises are contingent on availability and, thus, not really enforceable—yet these benefits are effective in influencing customers' behavior only if they believe that the airline will make good on that promise. It is the same in a negotiation; promises are useful to the extent that you believe that your counterpart will honor her promises.

Just as in the case of promises where your counterpart can offer attractive inducements, she may threaten some other action that is costly to you if you do not concede. However, from your perspective (as the target of the action), an obvious difference between threats and promises is that if carried out, threats impose costs on you while promises offer benefits.

Carrying out either a threat or a promise, however, is costly to the issuer. Indeed, although it seems natural to focus on the costs and benefits from the perspective of the target of these attempts to influence, as we discuss next, what matters most for the credibility of the threats and promises themselves are actually the costs from the perspective of the issuer. After all, from a purely rational perspective, once a threat or promise is issued, there are real costs associated both with carrying out the threat or promise and also with failing to carry it out. In the first instance, the issuer must actually bear the cost of carrying out the action; in the second instance, failing to carry out the action will negatively affect the reputation of the issuer.

A second difference between threats and promises is that promises can be made contractually binding (at which point they become part of the settlement), thereby increasing their credibility. For example, promises can be made more credible if they are in the forms of warranties, which are typically legally enforceable. In contrast, threats generally cannot be made legally binding. For example, one cannot sign a legally binding contract to end the negotiation if you do not concede. Thus, making threats credible is a more challenging task—but there are ways to make threats more binding to the issuer and, thus, more credible.

A third difference between threats and promises lies in the target's actions. In the case of threats, the target has no incentive to induce the issuer to carry out the threat, if the issuer were to back down. However, in the case of promises, the target wants the issuer to honor the promise. Because a promise can be carried out at a future date, the target may issue its own threat, for example to publicize the issuer's failure to keep the promise.

Although the previous distinctions mainly focused on the economic aspect, from a psychological perspective, there is another important distinction. Promises and threats differ in that promises are associated with gains while threats are associated with losses, and there is a big difference in how people respond to potential gains and how they respond to potential losses. Therefore, framing your influence attempt as a threat or promise affects the amount of risk that your counterpart may be willing to accept.

To illustrate this psychological effect, consider the classic dread-disease example:[1]

The United States is preparing for the outbreak of an unusual Asian disease that is expected to kill up to 600 people. Participants in this experiment were randomly assigned to two groups. Group I was presented with the following two alternative programs and asked to select the one they favored:

1. If Program A is adopted, 200 people will be saved.
2. If Program B is adopted, there is a one-third probably that all will be saved and a two-thirds probability that none will be saved.

When presented with these two options, 76 percent of Group I participants chose Program A, while 24 percent chose Program B. Thus, it seems that Group I participants valued the prospect of saving two hundred lives for certain more than they valued the risky prospect, even though both programs were expected to save the same number of people.

Participants in Group II were presented with the following options:

1. If Program a is adopted, 400 people will die.
2. If Program b is adopted, there is a one-third probability that no one will die and a two-thirds probability that all will die.

13 percent chose Program a, while 87 percent chose Program b. Thus Group II participants expressed a strong preference for the riskier Program b,

rather than the certain Program a. The prospect of 400 people dying for certain was less attractive than a lottery of equal expected value for Group II participants.

Note that from a rational perspective, both groups saw identical alternatives. For example, if 200 of 600 will be saved (Group I), then 400 will die (Group II). Similarly, if all are saved (Group I), then none will die (Group II). So from a purely rational perspective, both sets of participants should have ranked the two proposals equally. But they did not!

What these results show is that framing a choice as a potential gain (saving lives) makes the certain option more attractive, while framing a choice as a potential loss (people will die) makes the risky option more attractive.

To translate this effect into the language of negotiation: the risky choice is to resist accepting a proposal, not agreeing and hoping for a better alternative in the future. That this future option may not materialize is the risk here. Framing a choice as a gain results in your being more risk averse and increasing the probability that you will agree to the proposal. The risk-averse choice is to accept what is currently being proposed—what is certain.

In the same way, threats focus on what the target has to lose and, thus, invoke a loss frame that encourages resistance. In contrast, a promise focuses on what the recipient of the promise can gain and, thus, frames the interaction as a potential gain and encourages acceptance of the proposal. Thus, the way you frame your proposals can significantly alter your counterpart's response.

THE POWER OF THREATS AND THE ALLURE OF PROMISES

The uncertainty about whether a threat or promise will be carried out stems from the temporal separation of issuing the threat or promise and its potential effect on the target. Once a threat is issued, the target must choose to concede or not, not knowing whether the issuer will actually follow through.

If the target were not to concede, the issuer then must decide whether to carry out the threat. But here lies the dilemma: the target has not conceded. His failure to concede has already happened. The threat has proved ineffective. Will the threat be implemented?

A similar dilemma exists for promises—just in the opposite direction. The target concedes: The promise has been effective. Now the issuer has to decide if it is worth honoring that promise. This is a problem particularly when the promise involves actions that are chronologically distant from the negotiation. Although the target might be able to make the issuer's failure to honor his promise public, the target may not be able to reverse her concession if the issuer ultimately does not honor the promise.

So what is a target to do? Following our advice from Chapter 6 to look ahead and reason back, begin your analysis in reverse chronological order. Will the issuer carry out the threat or make good on the promise? Let's first consider the one-time negotiation where there is little chance of future interaction. For example, you may negotiate a purchase while on vacation in a city where future interaction with the seller is unlikely. But even locally, some purchases are simply not repeated with sufficient frequency to make the chance of future interaction a relevant consideration for either party. For example, the car dealer may not attach much weight to the possibility of your purchasing future vehicles from him.

So the issuer of the threat or promise makes a calculation: Is there a reasonable risk that the target will make the issuer's bad behavior public? If the parties do not expect to interact in the future, from a rational perspective the target is not likely to make the bad behavior of the issuer public by advertising that a threat was ignored or a promise not honored. The reason for this inaction is that advertising such behavior requires the target to engage in costly activity such as holding up a sign in front of the dealer's showroom advertising that promises were not honored. That action is costly to the target and has little potential for offsetting economic benefit that would justify that effort.

To illustrate, consider the following scenario: A start-up is considering entering a market dominated by an incumbent firm. Anticipating the start-up's entry into its market, the incumbent firm privately issues a threat to fight a price war if the start-up goes through with its plans.[2]

If the start-up does not enter the market, the present value of the incumbent firm's profits is $300 million, and the present value of the start-up's profits is $0 (since it does not conduct business). However, if the start-up were to enter the market, the incumbent firm can either accommodate (ignore the threat it issued and simply accept the presence of the start-up) or carry out its threat and wage a price war. If it were to accommodate, the present value of the profits to the incumbent firm and the start-up are $100 million each. In contrast, if the incumbent firm were to decide to fight a price war, the incumbent stands to lose $100 million and the start-up stands to lose $200 million.

If you were an advisor to the start-up, how seriously would you take the incumbent's threat of a price war? At issue is the potential for your client to lose $200 million if the incumbent were to fight a price war and a $100 million profit if it did not.

In this scenario, the threat of a price war is not credible, and you should advise your client to proceed with its plans to enter the market. To arrive at this answer, consider first the profits and losses from the incumbent firm's perspective. What are the alternatives available to the incumbent once your client entered the market? The incumbent firm will earn $100 million by accommodating or lose $100 million by fighting a price war. Hence, once your client entered the market, it is more advantageous for the incumbent firm to accommodate than to carry out its threat. Thus, if you believe that the incumbent firm will act rationally, the threat of a price war is not in the incumbent firm's best interest once the start-up has entered the market and, hence, not credible.

So from the start-up's perspective the options are (a) not to enter the market and earn zero or (b) to enter the market and earn $100 million. Obviously the best alternative is to ignore the threat (since it is not likely to be carried out) and enter the market.

Of course, the situation is more complex if there were multiple potential start-ups who could enter the incumbent's market. In that case, the incumbent firm may issue the threat publicly and, if your client were to enter, fight a price war to establish a reputation of being tough in defending its market—with the primary goal of dissuading other potential entrants.

The situation is simpler when it involves promises, rather than threats. The issuer will compare the costs of making good on the promise to the reputational costs of reneging. If no future interaction with the target is expected, those reputational costs will arise only if the recipient decides to make the issuer's bad behavior public. But is that likely to occur?

So long as the issuer believes that the recipient is not willing to incur the costs to advertise the issuer's bad behavior, he will not honor his promise. But then, knowing that the issuer is unlikely to honor his promise, the recipient is not likely to be influenced by the promise of the promise. Without the opportunity for future interactions, the issuer will rationally renege on the promise, and the rational recipient will not be influenced by promises. Thus, when future interactions are not likely, threats and promises should typically not be issued; and, if issued, they are likely to have little influence on the target.

So in a rational world—and in a one-and-done situation—neither promises nor threats are going to be particularly effective in influencing the target. In turn, because threats and promises are not going to be effective forms of influencing the target, it is not rational to issue them in the first place.

But threats and promises are routinely issued in such situations, and they have influence on negotiators even when there is likely to be no future interaction. So what psychological factors make threats and promises effective in influencing the behavior of targets and honored by their issuers when rational actors would ignore them? If you were trying to predict the actual behavior of a target or an issuer, you will need to consider more than just a rational analysis.

THE PSYCHOLOGICAL ASPECTS OF THREATS AND PROMISES

What may surprise you is that implementing some threats may actually be a positive psychological experience. The term "schadenfreude" refers to the pleasure derived from seeing the misfortunes of others. In the context of threats, the issuer may actually enjoy implementing the threat. If you threaten to key your competitor's car, particularly if his car is very nice, you might actually take pleasure from his misfortune (at your hands). While schadenfreude is admittedly a primitive urge, it is real and, as such, must be taken seriously. But even with the benefit that the issuer gets from schadenfreude, executing a threat is still costly. Therefore, the enjoyment of schadenfreude has to exceed the costs of carrying out the threat for the threat to be credible. As such, a threat that is of low cost to the issuer to implement (keying the target's car) is much more credible than a threat that is costly for the issuer to implement. You have to take a threat to key your car much more seriously than you would take a threat to steal your car.

Psychological benefit can also be experienced when you publicize a wrong that you experienced or acknowledge exemplary behavior. Have you ever gone out of your way to do so, even when you were reasonably sure that you would never interact with that person or organization again? Why did you bother?

One reason may be your belief in a just world: that people get what they deserve.[3] The psychological cost to you of letting bad behavior go unpunished or good behavior go unnoticed could exceed the economic cost of the resources (for example, your time) of taking action. What if a person gains benefits in exchange for a promised future behavior—and then reneges on her promise? Getting undeserved benefits may challenge your belief that the world is a just place. So you may be motivated to take action to alter the situation to reestablish the balance.[4] You might expose the person's behavior in social media, write reviews of their business, share the information with your friends or classmates, or picket the establishment to publicize your counterpart's private failure. Take the case of many online sellers on eBay or Amazon. It might be very difficult to hold such multiple, virtual sellers to reasonable standards of honest and good behavior in their one-and-done transactions. To counteract this, sellers agree to be publicly rated by their customers. Thus, the cost to customers to advertise the bad behavior of sellers is minimal: a few keystrokes; and the potential damage to a seller's reputation is large because the dissemination of this information is public and easily accessible by others. As a result, promises by sellers on eBay's or Amazon's networks (such as speedy delivery, merchandise as advertised, or hassle-free returns) are more credible because of the public feedback about the sellers' reputations.

The extent to which you, as an individual, are willing to go out of your way to make public the bad (and good) behavior of your counterpart is associated with how strongly your beliefs in a just world have been violated, even when there is likely to be no future interaction. Of course, not all individuals are equally influenced by a just-world belief. When negotiating, it may be useful to convince your counterpart that you are a fierce believer in a just world and that behaviors—good or bad—will be made public. Then, concede in response to her promises only if you reasonably believe that you have convinced her of your sincerity.

Although the threat of making bad behavior public may deter your counterpart from behaving badly in the first place, the power of threats made in public is that they are more credible than threats made privately. The public nature of both threats and promises allows future partners to learn about the reputation of a counterpart. In essence, the issuer puts his global reputation (as opposed to the reputation with an individual counterpart) on the line for all to see. In turn, if that reputation is valuable, then the target must reasonably expect the issuer to follow through to preserve this valuable asset.

Even the public nature of threats, however, does not always result in costly threats being implemented. Take President Obama's now infamous "red line" remark in 2012 regarding use of chemical weapons by Bashar al-

Assad's regime in Syria.[5] President Obama publicly drew that red line. However, after it became clear that Assad's regime did use chemical weapons on its own people, no action followed (unless one calls the request that Congress consider authorizing an action a decisive act—but most would not). As a result, President Obama's reputation was tarnished. Not following through on this threat not only may have reduced his credibility with Assad but also may have encouraged others to question what other threats or promises he might also ignore. Thus, issuing of a threat or promise publicly increases its credibility precisely because it makes the costs of reneging so high.

While the public nature of a threat or promise is an important consideration in determining its credibility, other characteristics can affect how influential threats or promises are in extracting concessions from a counterpart. As a start, size does matter! Selecting the right size has two dimensions, the costs to the issuer and the cost/benefit to target.

Let's begin with promises. The size of the promise is an important determinant for both the issuer and the recipient. From the perspective of the issuer, the lower the cost of living up to the promise and the higher the reputational costs of reneging, the more credible the promise.

Given that the issuer is weighing the cost of the reputational damage against the cost of fulfilling the promise, the best promises from the issuer's perspective are those that are cheap to carry out, have high reputational costs of reneging, and have large benefits to the target. A good example is for a car dealer to promise superior service to customers who bought the car at the dealership (putting them ahead of those who bought their cars elsewhere or providing complimentary car detailing after service) and hiring an independent agency that will advertise the service experiences of its customers. The costs to the dealer are low relative to the reputational costs of reneging, and the benefits to the customers may be sufficiently high that they would be willing to pay more for the car in their negotiations.

A similar approach can be used to determine the optimal size of a threat. The issuer can make threats more credible by choosing threats that are cheap for the issuer to carry out, perhaps because they provide a large amount of schadenfreude, while inflicting relatively large costs on the target. For example, the threat to key your car (a small threat, typically a misdemeanor if caught) is more likely to be carried out than the threat to kill you (a really large threat that may result in life imprisonment). Thus from the perspective of both the issuer and the target, threatening to key the target's car is more credible than threatening to kill him. In contrast, in the case of the incumbent firm that tries to dissuade potential entrants, issuing the threat and fighting a price war in a very public manner, while costly, may be effective at deterring future start-ups from entering their market. Thus, what may be viewed as a crazy decision in isolation may actually be a very rational course of action when considered in a broader context.

In addition to size, two additional factors have been investigated: the form of the threat and the timing. You can issue an explicit threat or an implicit threat. An example of an explicit threat is "If you don't concede, I will inform your superior about your aggressiveness." An implicit or vague threat does not suggest a specific action; rather it implies that something bad will happen. "If you don't agree to my request, you will regret it."

How effective implicit or explicit threats are depends on when they are issued. Explicit threats are much more effective if they are issued late in the negotiation. Vague threats are more effective if they are issued earlier. Conversely, issuing an explicit threat early in the negotiation or a vague threat late has a worse impact on your counterpart's willingness to concede than their response would have been if you had issued no threat at all! Issuing the wrong type of threats at the wrong time is not only ineffective, but it also makes you appear much weaker or more aggressive than you'd probably like.[6]

Up until now, we have been discussing the credibility of promises and threats when no further interactions among the negotiating parties are likely. Changing the scenario by adding the possibility of future interaction does not change any of those conclusions, but it does make threats and promises more credible. The reason is simple: the presence of a future makes reputation a much more important consideration.

When there is a future, the situation is more complex. First, the very fact of issuing a threat may negatively affect your future interactions. Having a future favors promises when both promises and threats are an option. In addition, the possibility of future interactions increases both the likelihood of carrying out the threat if the target does not concede and the likelihood of making good on the promise if it does, because failing to follow through ruins your reputation in future interactions. Conversely, if you carry out the threat or honor the promise, you gain a reputational benefit of being tough (in the case of a threat) or trustworthy (in the case of a promise).

But the prospect of future interactions also has implications for the target. If the target yields to a threat, then the issuer gains a benefit in future interactions with the target because she knows about the target's willingness to concede when threatened. In the case of threats, the costs to the target's reputation are likely to reduce her willingness to yield because by not yielding, she establishes her own reputation for toughness. Of course, she is also likely to suffer the consequences of the threat and the issuer's enhanced reputation for toughness as he implements the threat. Therefore, when issuing a threat when there is future interaction, you must expect an increased probability of the target not yielding, and hence should seriously consider the situation you will face: not only will you not get the hoped-for concession, but you also may have to carry out the threat—or suffer reputational costs—if you do not.

Consider how the challenge of a future influenced the unsuccessful strategy of one of our colleagues. He received an offer from a prestigious east coast business school and proceeded to go to the dean with a threat: either match the offer, or I will leave. Given that our faculty colleague had a competing offer, his threat appeared credible; the dean, the target of the threat, could have complied. However, doing so—especially when he knew that his behavior would become known to other faculty members—would set a costly precedent by indicating to the rest of the faculty that the dean would raise their salaries when threatened. So the dean simply responded by wishing our colleague well in his new job. Although the dean valued the individual contributions of our colleague, the cost of complying with the threat would have been not only the cost of the additional compensation to this faculty member, but also the compensation of all the other faculty members who would inevitably have lined up outside his office with their new offers in hand.

In the case of threats like this, the issuer must also consider the reputational costs of not following through with a threat. When our colleague stayed at Kellogg, despite the dean's not matching his offer, no one, especially the dean, took his subsequent threats to leave seriously. Therefore, especially when future interactions are likely, the issuer should first consider whether to issue a threat in the first place because just issuing that threat may have negative consequences.

But as it turns out, there was a better strategy than issuing a threat. In negotiations with that same dean, a more skillful faculty member brought her competing offer to the dean and simply asked if the dean could let her know what her next year's compensation would be. This approach differed in two important aspects from the first one. First, because it was not formulated as a threat but rather as a request for information, it did not provoke a natural concern that the dean would get a reputation of yielding to threats. More importantly, it reduced (even though it did not completely eliminate) the pressure on her to accept the outside offer or risk losing face. What if the dean were to counter with an offer for the next year's compensation that was significantly lower than her competing offer and our faculty member were to remain at Kellogg? While the faculty member would have to make a choice, her behavior would not have painted her into so obvious a corner. But in this case, the dean matched the outside offer, and the faculty member happily remained at Kellogg. The whole negotiation took less than ten minutes.

THE POWER OF PRECOMMITMENTS

Consider the car dealer's promise to provide you with superior service after the purchase service. In general, you might not take that promise seriously if it were issued privately. But the dealership can make this promise more credible not only by making it publicly but also by hiring an independent marketing firm to follow up with customers, polling and publishing their after-the-sale service experiences. By entering in such an arrangement—a precommitment—the dealership effectively increases its reputational costs of reneging and hence makes the promises more credible. In turn, customers rationally will view such promises as more credible and be willing to make larger concessions, for example to pay more for the cars.

A similar precommitment can be used to make threats more credible. One example occurred during World War II. Switzerland was surrounded by Germany and its allies. It realized that it had a strategic importance to Germany because its passes over the Alps provided efficient routes to transport men and equipment between Germany and Italy, Germany's major ally. Of course, Germany could make that transport even more effective by occupying Switzerland. Although the Swiss Army was a moderate deterrent, realistically it could not have withstood a serious attack by the Wehrmacht.

To deter a German invasion, the Swiss mined all (both in the interior and on the border) their country's passes, tunnels, and bridges with explosives. Yet, on its own, the threat to blow up those passes and bridges would not have been credible. Once Germany invaded, after all, what would be the point of blowing up all the passes, tunnels, and bridges in the country? To give their threat credibility, the Swiss command assigned each bridge, tunnel, or pass a small military unit that had an irrevocable order to blow it up at the first sign of a German invasion anywhere in the country. If the officer in charge refused to obey the order, the men of the unit had the order to shoot the officer and detonate the object. Then the Swiss commanders made it easier for the unit to follow its orders. They assigned to each object troops who were not local. That is, units from the German part of Switzerland were assigned to the bridges, tunnels, and passes in the Italian part; while those from the Italian part of Switzerland were assigned to guard the French part; and so on. In this way, the army took advantage of Switzerland's cultural diversity to make it easier to follow the order because, in the sense, each unit would be blowing up somebody else's property.

Of course, the "secret" plan was then leaked to Berlin. In effect, what the Swiss strategy did was to put the decision to detonate the passes, bridges, and tunnels in the hands of the Germans. If they invaded Switzerland, they would lose what they wanted most. If they did not invade, they could still transport men and equipment more efficiently through a Switzerland with bridges, tunnels and passes than through a Switzerland without them! What both of these stories have in common is that a precommitment removes the decision that the issuer must make to actually implement the threat. When the commitment is irrevocable, it is more credible.

SUMMARY

When you and your counterpart have a future together, issuing threats exposes you to two negative consequences. First, there is the negative consequence of issuing the threat. Second, not carrying out that threat will damage your reputation. In such situations, therefore, you should only issue threats that you are ready to carry out. But again, big threats (ones that impose large costs on the issuer) may still not be credible if the reputational costs are less than the costs of carrying them out. Thus, our recommendation still holds: issue the smallest threat that is large enough to get your counterpart to concede.

The same is true for promises. Although issuing promises per se does not negatively affect future relations, the prospect of future negotiations makes it less likely that the issuer will renege and thus makes promises more credible. Of course, the issuer might still renege if implementing the promise is costly. Thus, for promises to be credible, the cost of making good on them to the issuer must be less than the reputational cost of reneging. So, consider making the smallest possible promise that is enough to make your counterpart concede. These smaller promises and the prospect of future dealings will make the promises more credible and thus more influential.

What emerges is the following decision pattern:

- Without the expectation of future interactions, privately issued threats or promises are not credible, should be ignored, and hence should not be issued. However, threats may be used by the target to retaliate (schadenfreude!) by making them public (even if they have not been carried out). Therefore, threats are not only unlikely to be effective without any future interactions, but they can also impose significant costs on the issuer.

- Without the expectation of future interactions, the issuer can increase the credibility of threats or promises by issuing them publicly or committing to make their fulfillment public. This may be sufficient to make them credible when the reputational costs to the issuer of not following through are high and/or the costs to the issuer of following through are low. Therefore, threats that are minor relative to the reputational loss of carrying out the threat, issued by a party with a high reputation, should be taken seriously while large threats or promises issued by parties with a low reputation should be ignored.

- With the expectation of future interactions, threats or promises may be credible when the reputational costs for future interaction to the issuer of not following through are high and/or the costs to the issuer of following through are low. Therefore, little threats or promises issued by parties with a high reputational capital should be taken seriously, while large threats or promises relative to the reputational costs of reneging should be ignored. Again, the issuer can make both threats and promises more credible by making them publicly and also committing to make it public that they have been carried out. Finally, issuing threats per se—even credible ones—may negatively impact on future interactions.

- Before yielding to a credible threat or promise, you still have to assess whether the concession is more costly to you than suffering the cost of the threat or benefiting from the promise.

To assist your assessment of your actions, regardless of whether you are potentially the issuer or the target of a threat or promise, we have created Matrix 9.1, which summarizes how effective a particular action might be.

MATRIX 9.1 COST/ BENEFIT ANALYSIS OF THREATS AND PROMISES BEING CARRIED OUT (MORE LIKELY WITH FUTURE INTERACTION)		Cost of fulfilling versus reneging to the issuer			
		Costs of reneging are likely to dominate		Costs of fulfilling are likely to dominate	
		By a little	By a lot	By a little	By a lot
Cost of threat or benefit of promise to the target	L	Moderate effectiveness	High effectiveness	Low effectiveness	Not effective
	H	High effectiveness	Moderate effectiveness	Moderate effectiveness	Low effectiveness

The conclusion is quite straightforward: threats and promises will not be effective unless the target expects them to be fulfilled. How likely they are to be fulfilled rests on the relative cost to the issuer compared to the cost of reneging. So clearly both issuer and target need to consider when a threat or promise is credible and when it is simply cheap talk!

SHOULD YOU LET THEM SEE YOU SWEAT (OR CRY)?

Emotions in Negotiation

E motions such as anger, happiness, sadness, surprise, and fear can play an important role in negotiations. However, the consequences to the parties displaying the emotion are mixed, sometimes enhancing and sometimes reducing their outcomes. Both the expression and experience of emotions can influence how you think and interpret information in the negotiation; they can also influence how your counterpart behaves, and ultimately can help or hinder your ability to get more of what you want.

As a negotiator, you can express your real feelings, or you can chose to display emotions you do not actually experience. Thus, emotions can be uncontrolled reflections of a negotiator's true feelings, or they can reflect a strategic choice to express a true feeling or to act as if you are experiencing a particular emotion when, in fact, you are not.

For example, you may be angry and express that anger, either because you choose to do so or because you simply cannot control your anger. Alternatively, you may be angry but express warmth or sympathy—emotions you don't actually feel. You could also be angry but suppress your emotions and appear neutral. Finally, you may not have an emotional response to the situation but act as if you were angry in an attempt to influence your counterpart.

For most people, it is not difficult to recall a negotiation when your emotions or those of your counterpart got in the way of getting what you wanted. Perhaps the expression of emotions was so extreme that your counterpart walked away because of words spoken in the heat of the moment or perhaps you blurted out information that should have been left

CONFLICT SPIRALS

Some readers will undoubtedly be old enough to remember the student demonstrations in the United States in the late 1960s and early 1970s. Often demonstrations would start with a few students staging a protest or a sit-in around some issue. The campus administration would call in security to disperse the student scofflaws, resulting in arrests, increased resistance, and media attention. As a result, other students would join into the melee, which led administrators to bring in more security or outside police or even, in some extreme cases, the National Guard. This action would then result in the involvement of even more students, provoked by the aggressive response of the administration rather than by the issue that originally generated the demonstration.

While the most common form of spiral in negotiation is such a conflict spiral, these spirals may be positive (generative spirals) or negative (degenerative spirals). They are typically a function of responding to others' behavior in kind or an intensifying of the counterpart's response. So responses may vary from relatively benign strategies such as ingratiation or implied threats to more aggressive strategies such as emotional outbursts, explicit threats, or irrevocable commitments—all of which could lead to impasses that are emotional rather than calculative.

unshared; or because—again at that moment—winning that particular point or getting back at your counterpart was the only thing you cared about. This experience is often associated with conflict spirals. If emotions, especially negative emotions get out of hand, the ensuing damage to the relationship and escalation of conflict that results can have long-lasting, negative effects on your relationships as well as the outcomes you achieve in your negotiations.

Thomas has experienced firsthand how emotions can actually destroy value. When Thomas was six years old, his family was preparing to emigrate from their native Poland to Israel. In preparation, they were selling most of their possessions, particularly those that were of little value in the Middle East. Thomas's father had a pair of high-quality winter boots—a prized possession in wintery Poland, but of no use in the Middle East. In 1957, boots of such high quality were very expensive in Poland, and few people could afford them. A few days before their scheduled departure, a prospective buyer showed up, offering half of his father's (considerable) asking price. Enraged by what he perceived to be a low-ball offer, his father, a typically rational nuclear engineer, took a heavy kitchen knife and cut the boots in half, exclaiming: "for half the money you can have half the boots!" Now obviously the offer exceeded his father's reservation price since the boots were useless in the Middle East (his father had made them useless anyway by cutting them in half). So unless he valued the satisfaction of destroying his prized boots by more than half of his asking price, this emotional outburst clearly got him *less* of what he wanted.

Emotions can also limit your ability to think and act strategically, and, especially when these emotions are negative, your emotional outbursts can be contagious, creating a cascade of emotional responses from your counterpart.[1] Because of the cognitive downside of these negative emotions, negotiators often attempt to suppress or hide their emotions—particularly negative ones such as anger. For instance, the prescriptive advice of Howard Raiffa in *The Art and Science of Negotiation* touts the importance of self-control, especially of emotions and their visibility. Similarly, Gerald Nierenberg in *The Art of Negotiating* states that "people in an emotional state do not want to think, and they are particularly susceptible to the power of suggestion from a clever opponent."[2]

There are different methods that you might employ to avoid strong emotions. First, you might avoid a situation that is likely to generate a strong emotional response. For example, you may avoid a colleague because you have information that might make her angry at you. Second, you might modify the situation to reduce the likelihood of a strong emotional response. You might avoid the topic that is likely to generate the negative emotion or sugar-coat provocative information. Third, if you find yourself getting angry with your counterpart, you might count to ten before responding or mentally go to your "happy place." Finally, you might simply suppress the expression of the emotion you are experiencing—that is, keep a poker face. These options are all ways to avoid or minimize your emotional response.

In contrast, you might reframe the outcome or reorient the personal meaning you ascribe to the situation. For example, the anger that your counterpart is expressing may be completely reasonable given the situation from her perspective. That is, the information is the stimulus for the anger and not you. Regulating your emotion before it is experienced is a *reappraisal* strategy. The reappraisal occurs early in a process that is expected to generate the emotion, and it involves cognitive efforts designed specifically to neutralize or reframe the experience. Reappraisal strategies change the experience of the emotions, reframing how you interpret the experience. This is a strategy that requires you to think carefully about your counterparts and their likely behavior—an aspect of negotiation preparation that presents a continual challenge for most negotiators.[3]

However, these prescriptions, while intuitive, all have some systematic disadvantages, because ignoring or suppressing your emotions in a negotiation can sometimes make you worse off. After all, inhibiting the expression of the emotion takes a lot of mental effort—effort that cannot be applied to the difficult thinking that is necessary for successful negotiations. Therefore, suppressing the expression of emotions may actually hinder your ability to think, specifically your ability to process and recall information.[4] In addition, suppression efforts have physiological implications—both for you (your blood pressure increases when you attempt to suppress emotions) and surprisingly, for your counterpart in the negotiation. Even when you are successful in suppressing your emotional response, not only does your blood pressure rise but the blood pressure of your counterpart rises as well, and he perceives you as less likable because you end up suppressing more than just your negative emotions![5] What's more, maintaining a poker face can reduce your ability to reach creative, negotiated outcomes because emotions provide unique information to both you and your counterpart.

THE RELATION BETWEEN THINKING AND FEELING

Humans have a limited amount of cognitive resources. Although there is a connection between how you feel and how you think, the resources that are allocated to your emotional experience are not simply deducted from those that are allocated to thinking. In some situations, emotions can enhance your thought processes, and at other times, they can make clear thinking difficult.

Although emotional and cognitive functions are under the control of separate and partially independent brain systems, your emotions can affect the choices you make by providing a form of information that can help you make decisions.[6] To demonstrate this, researchers asked people to rate how humorous they found a set of cartoons.[7] Before they rated the cartoons, half the participants in the study were asked to hold a pencil in their teeth such that the pencil stuck out like a straw. The other half of the participants were asked to hold a pencil in their mouth such that the pencil was horizontal with the point close to one ear and the eraser close to the other ear. You might be skeptical about believing that how you hold a pencil in your mouth would affect how funny you thought a set of cartoons were. But it did. Those who held the pencil like a straw were using muscles that are typically associated with a frown, while those holding the pencil horizontally were using muscles typically associated with a smile. Indeed, those in the horizontal condition rated the cartoon as funnier than did those in the straw condition. It was as if the participants were thinking, "This feels like frowning [first group] so these cartoons cannot be that funny." Or, "this feels like smiling [second group] so these cartoons must be funny."

Clearly, the participants were not aware of the effect of stimulating various muscles to mimic the expression of emotions had on their assessments of the cartoons. But just because you are not aware of a particular effect does not mean that it cannot influence your perceptions. While admittedly this research was done in the controlled environment of the laboratory, it shed light on just how interconnected our emotions and perceptions are.

For a real-world example of the interplay between emotions and perception, consider the powerful effect of audiences in influencing how you interpret your experience at a play or at a concert. And it doesn't even have to be a live audience: Hollywood, for instance, has long known the power of laugh tracks.

Emotions also affect your choices. Low or moderate levels of emotions can prepare you to respond to challenges and opportunities by providing information about what is important and how you are faring with respect to your goals. Recent research has explored another avenue by which emotions influence your thinking. In the past, it was generally accepted that positive moods were associated with increased creativity, breadth of thought, and flexibility while negative mood generated disagreement and conflict.[8] Now, there is a growing consensus that different emotions are associated with heuristic processing of information while others, with systematic processing of information.

What most people expect is that more thoughtful assessments or systematic processing occurs with positive emotions and this short-cut or heuristic type of thinking occurs with negative emotions. But as it turns out, this is not true! It is not the valence (positive or negative) that determines how deep or how superficial is your thinking. It turns out that both angry and happy people tend to engage in heuristic thinking. Happy people have been found to increase their reliance on stereotypes as did angry people.[9] In both these emotional states, individuals paid more attention to the visible characteristics of speakers than they did to the persuasive nature of their arguments.[10] In contrast, individuals experiencing sadness (often viewed as a negative emotion) or surprise (either a positive or a negative emotion, depending on the nature of the surprise) were likely to consider more alternatives and process information in a more careful and thoughtful way.[11]

As it turns out, happiness and anger influence our thinking differently from emotions such as surprise or sadness. These latter emotions produce a more systematic processing of information. The type of thinking in which negotiators engage is critical because heuristic thinking is associated with compromise and a focus on who gets what, while systematic thinking is associated with increased value creation.

But what is it about these emotions that change how you think? The more emotions are associated with feelings of certainty, the more experiencing these emotions encourages negotiators to think heuristically; In contrast, the more emotions are associated with feelings of uncertainty, the more systematically negotiators process information.[12] But emotions such as happiness and anger—while polar opposites—have more in common than just being associated with certainty and heuristic processing. Probably the most surprising similarity is that both happiness and anger are optimistic emotions.[13]

Now, most negotiators would not typically think of anger as being an optimistic emotion. However, it turns out that anger is optimistic if you consider the angry person's thinking and planning for future actions. When thinking about the future, angry people often feel as if they can change the future, influence the source of their anger, or find a way around the barriers that are thwarting them.[14]

In addition, anger can energize us to action, and many of us can relate to the exhilaration felt when wreaking revenge on a tormentor or watching with suppressed amusement as unfortunate events conspire against your enemies. Further, those who study anger have discovered that there is also a large difference between how anger is experienced in the moment and the memory of anger. In the moment, the experience of anger is positive; in memory, the experience of anger is negative![15]

So if anger were an optimistic emotion, then you would expect there to be some real benefits to being angry in a negotiation—not the least of which is that your optimism might be reflected in higher aspirations. Happiness is also an optimistic emotion. So, from a perspective of your own outcomes in a negotiation, are you better off when you are angry or when you are happy in the negotiation? That is, do angry or happy negotiators create more value, let alone claim more of that value?

IS IT BETTER TO BE ANGRY OR HAPPY IN A NEGOTIATION?

Historically, research on the impact of emotions on negotiation has indicated that happier negotiators—or at least those in a positive mood—are more likely to create value, while angry negotiators have typically dominated value claiming.[16] But consider the difference you could make with optimistic, angry (i.e., certain and heuristically inclined) negotiators if you could invoke in them a sense that the negotiation was not a routine experience. Could you create angry, but uncertain negotiators who experienced both the optimism of their anger coupled with the systematic thinking that accompanies uncertainty?

In a first study, researchers induced one member of a negotiating dyad to feel angry. Further, half of these angry negotiators were certain that their counterparts behaved unreasonably and became angry while the other half, while angry at the behavior, were not certain that this unfortunate outcome was the result of their specific counterpart's behavior.[17]

In a second study, researchers suggested to half the participants that the negotiation process was a predictable and routine interaction instead of being unpredictable and uncertain.[18] The results of both of these studies showed that anger—when accompanied by feelings of uncertainty—led to *greater value creation* in negotiations. In fact, angry but uncertain negotiators created more value than emotionally neutral negotiators, who in turn did better than angry, but certain, negotiators.[19] However, angry negotiators, in general, were able to claim a larger percentage of the resource than their counterparts. And as you would suspect, the reason that uncertain, angry negotiators did so much better was because they engaged in more systematic strategic thinking about the negotiation than did angry but certain negotiators.

But all of this occurred with a counterpart who was not angry. What if both parties were experiencing anger or happiness and either thought that their counterpart was responsible for behaviors that led to these emotions or was uncertain? It turns out that success in value claiming is enhanced by emotion, while success in value creating is enhanced by uncertainty.[20]

Let's first take the effect of value claiming or the decision of how to divide up the resources. Angry negotiators were able to claim more value than were their happy counterparts. However, whether you were happy or angry made little difference to the amount of value you and your counterpart were able to create. What mattered was how certain or uncertain you were about the situation, the interaction, or the event. In the study, the more the negotiators were uncertain about how the negotiation would unfold and the more negotiators who were uncertain (no negotiators uncertain < one negotiator uncertain < two negotiators uncertain), the more value those dyads created.

But there was another interesting finding regarding the value-creating capacity of angry/certain and angry/uncertain negotiators. It turns out that the greatest amount of value created of all possible combinations was when one negotiator was angry and uncertain; and the *least* amount of value created occurred in negotiations with a counterpart who was angry and certain! The value created by happy negotiators fell between the values created by the two types of angry negotiators.

Thus, anger can be a useful emotion for value claiming, and it can also facilitate value creation, especially when the situation is uncertain. In addition, there is a difference in the effects between the optimism that anger produces and the optimism that happiness produces. Although there were no differences in how angry or happy negotiators rated their optimism in the negotiated outcome and their confidence that they could achieve that outcome, the initial offers that the angry negotiators presented were significantly more extreme than those of the happy negotiators. This lack of aggressive action on the part of happy negotiators is consistent with their not wanting to "kill the buzz." Individuals who are happy tend to avoid actions or situations that they believe would dampen their good feelings—and so often fail to get more of what they actually entered the negotiation to get.

EXPERIENCED VERSUS EXPRESSED EMOTIONS

Expressions of emotions communicate important social information such as danger (fear expressions) or opportunity (happiness expressions). When you experience such expressions during a negotiation, they can convey information about your likely actions and behaviors to your counterpart.[21] Of course, this assumes that your expressed emotions are truthful representations of your experienced emotions. You can express emotions that you do not feel—or feel emotions that you do not express.

What is the impact of each of these types of expressions on your ability to negotiate? To answer that question, let's consider two aspects of emotions: what function they serve for you (the intrapersonal aspect of emotions) and what function they serve for your counterpart (the interpersonal aspect of emotions).

First, emotions can be intrapersonal, impacting your assessment of your environment and your counterpart. For example, anger is associated with blaming others, experiencing a violation or offense, and feeling certain. Anger influences the angry individual's perceptions, the decision he makes, and the behaviors he implements. That is, anger motivates you to change the situation, remove barriers, and re-establish a previous status quo.[22] A negotiator experiencing anger is likely to become more aggressive and more optimistic—perhaps by expressing an increased resistance to making concessions or escalating the concessions demanded from the counterparts.[23]

However, negotiators who become angry may get distracted by their anger, and their thinking may become impaired.[24] At that point, negotiators tend to focus on issues related to the anger rather than issues related to the negotiation, losing sight of their primary goals—to get more of what they want![25] If experiencing anger diffuses your focus, even if it makes you optimistic, the likelihood of reaching value-creating integrative agreements is reduced. You are more likely to reach an impasse, especially when your anger reduces your motivation and, indeed, your capacity to process complex information and thereby to find an outcome that makes you better off.

Happiness, on the other hand, is associated with the expectation of positive future states as well as a sense of certainty or predictability. You assess the situation as moving toward a positive outcome—and conclude that you simply need to stay the course and are not particularly motivated to extract further value from your counterpart.[26] Specifically, negotiators in a positive mood were found to be more cooperative and less competitive, while increasing their reliance on simple heuristics that, in the context of negotiation, could lead to quick and cooperative, but inefficient, agreements.[27]

Now consider the other impact that the expression of emotion has—not just on you, but also on those around you. Expressions of emotions such as anger can have interpersonal effects far different from the subjective experience of anger to the angry person, just as expressions of happiness may have different effects from feelings of happiness.

First and foremost, the simple expression of an emotion is likely to have little impact on how you think. Acting happy is unlikely to encourage heuristic thinking just as acting sad or surprised is unlikely to encourage systematic thinking. You must feel these emotions for them to have their effect. But what expressing emotions can do is change the way those around you respond to you. Negotiators are more willing to concede when facing counterparts who expressed anger.[28] Thus, expressing anger benefited the expressers by allowing them to claim more value, but it had no effect on their ability to create value. This suggests that the mechanisms that effect emotional expressions may differ from those of emotional experience. In line with this, negotiators conceded less to counterparts who expressed happiness than they did to those who expressed anger.[29]

Clearly, expressing emotions can have different effects from experiencing those emotions. For example, expressing surprise may be a very different cognitive experience from experiencing surprise. Expressing surprise that you do not feel actually changes how your counterpart responds to you.[30] The emotions that you express seem to have a much greater impact on your counterpart than on yourself; hence, the expression of emotions is an interpersonal phenomenon.

Expressing anger in a negotiation has worked to Thomas's benefit on one occasion. In 2013, he decided to sell his home in a suburb of Chicago. The real estate market was strong, and Thomas received two offers within the first week of listing his house. He informed both bidders that there was competition, and both submitted revised bids that exceeded the original listing price.

Naturally, Thomas picked the higher of the second round offers and signed a sales contract with the couple making the winning bid. The sales contract stipulated that the price would be adjusted if an inspection revealed undisclosed problems. Following the inspections, the buyers demanded a price adjustment of $32,000, producing a list of items that, they claimed, needed to be remedied. For example, the inspection revealed that the furnace was old and likely needed replacement soon. However, the age of the furnace had been disclosed to the buyers, and, from Thomas's perspective it could not be legitimately characterized as undisclosed. After an initial negotiation through his real estate agent produced no agreement, Thomas expressed anger (again through his real estate agent) and threatened to put the house back on the market. At first, the buyers did not respond, so Thomas reactivated the listing and annulled the sales contract.

Within a few days, the prospective buyers conceded, and the house was sold for the contracted price minus a small adjustment for one item that was, indeed, unknown to Thomas and, therefore, undisclosed.

Not only does the expression of emotion have more impact on your counterparts but also there is an impact on you. Expressing emotions that you don't experience requires consistent cognitive effort. Remember that earlier we noted that suppressing emotion requires cognitive energy that is then unavailable for meeting the informational demands of the negotiation. As such, the more the expressed emotion is at odds with your experienced emotional state, the more cognitive effort it will require to maintain the ruse required to express that emotion. The more cognitive effort it will require, the fewer cognitive resources will be left for solving the negotiating challenges you face. Thus, to the extent that expressed and experienced emotions are the same, there is both an interpersonal and an intrapersonal component to that emotion—and the cognitive effort is less. If on the other hand expressed and experienced emotions are different—that is, one does not express the emotion one feels—then the expression and the experience can activate two different effects, but the cognitive demands of this situation may result in significantly diminished success in creating value.

In the next section, we consider a third problem with expressing emotions that you do not experience—you actually begin to experience the emotions that you express strategically; they often become real.

EMOTIONAL CONTAGION

It may be in your best interest, particularly for value claiming, for your counterpart to experience positive emotions, independent of your emotional state. This is because happy people come to agreement more quickly and, in general, see the world as more friendly and more positive—and so they demand less. Thus, putting your counterpart in a happy state of mind may be very useful. Just how can you get your counterpart to be more positive?

Emotions are contagious, as negotiator Joe Girard knows all too well. Girard is probably one of the best negotiators on the planet: he is listed in the *Guinness Book of World Records* as the greatest car salesman. Part of this surely has to do with the emotional signals he sends to clients. He is reported to have sent out thirteen thousand greeting cards each month to past and potential customers. Although the greetings on each of these cards differed, the message was clear: "I like you." While there are likely many additional reasons why Joe Girard was so successful, it is likely that he conveyed a positive, friendly face to his customers, and there is ample research to show that such positive emotions spread to the people who observe them.[31]

Emotions may be transmitted from one person to another, typically through subconscious mimicry of facial expressions, body language, speech patterns, and vocal tones of others. If the expression of positive emotion can make an individual more attractive and influence subsequent performance, then the success of people like Joe Girard may be in large measure the result of their ability to infect those in their environment with a positive, friendly attitude—and to do so at a level that is often unconscious to even the most cynical of counterparts. Thus, by expressing positive emotions, you may infect others with that positivism. Of course, the inverse is true. If you express anger, those around you may also experience anger.

Surprisingly, this contagion works on you as well. If you strategically express anger, you will—over time—become angrier. That is, you can escalate yourself into an angry state of mind. So thinking back to the earlier discussion of the cognitive effort required to maintain an emotional expression you do not experience, that effort is likely to be less effective over time because of the increasing consistency of your expressed and experienced emotional states. To maintain such a discrepant state requires constant vigilance and, as such, creates huge demands of self-control.

So while expressing emotions, particularly negative ones can influence both you and your counterpart, are there better alternatives? For example, is it better to express anger or to issue a threat? It turns out that, from a psychological perspective (as opposed to the economic perspective discussed in Chapter 9), when the impact of threats and the impact of anger are directly compared, threats are more effective than anger. So while the implementation of threats can be problematic and expressing anger does have advantages, expressing either of them has differential costs and benefits that you should carefully consider.

SUMMARY

When it comes to judging the impact of emotions on negotiator performance, much of the common anecdotal advice does not hold up under scientific scrutiny. So rather than going with your gut—and being guided by your emotions—during a negotiation, keep the following tips in mind:

- Research shows that, rather than suppressing emotion and trying to maintain a poker face, a better strategy is to engage in emotional reappraisal. In other words, if you believe that you may be subject to strong emotional experiences, a good strategy is to reappraise the situation prior to experiencing the emotion. Because suppression occurs after the emotional experience is present, it is a much less effective negotiation strategy—both because of how it affects your ability to problem-solve and because of the affective response it generates in your counterpart—than is reappraisal. Unlike suppression, reappraisal occurs prior to the initiation of the emotion and focuses on the meaning of the situation and the information that may be obtained from your counterpart's emotional reactions to that situation. For example, you can attempt to suppress your emotional choice to escalate in response to your counterpart's threats during the negotiation; alternatively, you can proactively view threats as information about what your counterpart values in the negotiation—and use that information to adjust aspects of future proposals.
- Emotional responses or states can provide wise negotiators with another source of information about their own preferences and choices and the relative importance of various options. Further, emotions that give rise to or are associated with uncertainty can ultimately improve value creation. In addition, other emotional states such as anger can facilitate value claiming. The trick is to get the best of both worlds.
- Be sensitive to the emotional state of your counterpart and to ways in which it can influence the emotions that you experience. The contagion that may result from expressing positive emotions may increase the willingness of your counterpart to agree to your proposals and view you and the situation in much more positive and cooperative terms.
- Because positive emotions have been shown to enhance the creation of joint outcomes but is typically associated with less effective value claiming, you should consider expressing emotions strategically that you do not necessarily experience. For example, you may wish to encourage positive emotions in your counterpart early in the negotiation (when value creating is most likely to occur); in later stages of the negotiation, you may wish to express more negative emotions such as anger and the

resulting perception of toughness to facilitate one's own ability to claim value.

While you would be clearly worse off without the information available to you from your emotional responses, you should explicitly consider the influence those emotions (yours and your counterparts) have on your ability to create and to claim value. Your emotions can serve as a resource in your interaction or as a powerful magnet, drawing your attention and cognitive effort away from the demands of the negotiated interaction.

CHAPTER ELEVEN

POWER

Having It—or Not—and Getting More

I f you had three wishes in an important negotiation, one of them might well be to have a power advantage over your counterpart. In Chapter 2, we discussed how your alternatives create a potent source of power in the negotiation—the ability to walk away. In this chapter, we now focus on the systematic effect of power on your thoughts, emotions, and strategic choices—regardless of whether that power flows from your personal or organizational status, the alternatives available to you, or your ability to control valuable resources.

Power is typically defined as the inverse of dependence.[1] That is, you are in a more powerful position when you are less dependent on others (or your counterparts are more dependent on you) for valued resources. For example, the better your alternatives, the less dependent you are on reaching a deal.

Of course, any time you negotiate, there is interdependency because for a deal to be reached, all parties must agree. But even in this interdependence, you might be relatively more or less interdependent compared to your counterpart. The better and more numerous your alternatives to the current negotiation, the more you can and will demand—and the more successful you will be at getting what you want. So, if your alternatives are better than your counterpart, you are relatively more powerful.

Yet being more powerful does not ensure a better outcome. Most negotiators have, at some point, had great alternatives yet agreed to outcomes that made them worse off. But having great alternatives is just one source of power. There are many others that can influence your ability to get more of what you want.

Another source of power that can be consciously adjusted independent of your particular alternative is your mind-set. You can experience power or be perceived as powerful by your counterparts because of your verbal and nonverbal behavior—consequences that can flow directly from a powerful mind-set. This mind-set can be the result of a powerful position in your organization, your view of your situation, or—surprisingly—from just thinking about times when you were powerful and in control of your experience or destiny and how that felt and how others treated you! Throughout this chapter, we will examine different forms of power and the systematic effects that they have on how you and your counterparts behave.

THE EFFECTS OF POWER

Recent research has suggested that the experience of having power activates different action orientations in powerful or powerless individuals.[2] When experiencing power, the behavioral approach system (BAS) is activated. This behavioral system is typically related to actions that are designed to achieve rewards and opportunities. In contrast, when experiencing powerlessness, the behavioral inhibition system (BIS) is activated, resulting in heightened vigilance and awareness of the risks and challenges inherent in the environment and in social interactions.

Powerful individuals, for example, typically experience reward-rich environments as compared to less powerful individuals. Thus, when the BAS is activated, those in power are more able to act on their immediate desires and goals without incurring serious social sanctions. In contrast, when the BIS is activated, those powerless individuals will have less access to resources and are targets for social control and punishment. As a result people in relatively powerful positions are assessing situations in terms of rewards and opportunities, while those in relatively powerless positions are assessing their environment (including those same situations) in terms of threats and punishments.

POWER CHANGES HOW YOU SEE THE WORLD

While it may be difficult for you to notice, the way in which you respond to social situations is systematically and dramatically influenced by your relative power. Not only do you behave differently when you have power, but those around you also behave differently in response to your power. Recent research has demonstrated three major ways in which power affects the actions of the powerful: a bias to action, a loss of sensitivity to subtle social nuance, and seeing others as a means to your ends.

Individuals who are more powerful are more likely to initiate action. For example, consider Captain Jean-Luc Picard of *Star Trek: The Next*

Generation. Readers who are old enough will remember that his commands were variants of "Engage!" or "Make it so!" In a more traditional organizational setting, Picard would be the CEO who barks: "Just make the numbers!" They both want action, but it is others' responsibility to figure out how to meet their expectations. This emphasis on action results in a much quicker response between experiencing a desire and acting to achieve that desire. In a negotiation, we have a great example of this: more powerful negotiators are likely to make the first offer to initiate the negotiation. Their willingness to make the first offer may be related more to their relative power than to a thoughtful analysis of the costs and benefits of making a first offer.[3]

Powerful people also tend to ignore social conventions. Given the behavior of some powerful individuals, indeed, you might easily assume that to be powerful one must ignore social norms and rituals! A colleague of ours tells a story about Jann Wenner, the long-time editor and publisher of *Rolling Stone* magazine, who, in meetings with her, would reach into the small refrigerator near his desk, take out a bottle of vodka and a large raw onion. During these meetings, he would often proceed to take a big bite of the onion and wash it down with a swig of vodka directly from the bottle, never asking if she wanted to share his snack. Margaret and Thomas experienced another example of this when they saw a very senior law professor colleague take off her shoe in the middle of a panel session in which she was a presenter and put it on the table to examine the heel. A third example appears in the scene Bob Woodward paints in *State of Denial* (2006) of President Bush's behavior at a Pentagon briefing. Each participant had a small number of peppermint candies. After President Bush finished his peppermints, he eyed and accepted the peppermints of others at the meeting including General Hugh Shelton, the chairman of the Joint Chiefs.[4] Actions such as these clearly fly in the face of social norms, and this sort of behavior may seem to be the purview of the powerful—but of course it is not this insensitivity to social nuance that is the reason for their power. Rather, it is the result of their power; the more powerful people are, the more insensitive they are to social norms, politeness rituals, and everyday courtesies. Nor does this mean that all powerful people engage in this bull-in-a-china-shop behavior. However socially astute you were in a power-neutral situation, you will become increasingly insensitive as you gain more power. But your starting point makes a difference! Thus, this insensitivity to social nuance—as the *bias to action*—is not just a trait of the individual; rather, it is greatly affected by the state or the situation in which that individual is involved.

Individuals with power are also much more likely to objectify others—that is, to view others as means to accomplishing their own ends; rather than considering others as independent actors, those with power view them agents of their wishes. Research demonstrates that executives report emphasis on what others can do for them in their hierarchical relations as compared to their peer relations; and that as one's power increases, the more the high-power person is attracted to others based on how useful they are in facilitating the achievement of his or her goals.[5] Power also enables decision makers to choose actions that further positive social or organizational goals so long as those goals are the goals of the powerful actor.

In the setting of a negotiation, although these findings imply that powerful people often get more, there is much more to this story. Powerful people get more of the pie—but how do they impact value creation? The experience of power influences more than just the who-gets-what aspect of negotiation; and here is where the story gets more surprising—and interesting.

Recall that value creation results from taking advantage of the differences in how you and your counterpart value issues. It turns out that it is the powerless (and not the powerful) party that does the hard work necessary to figure out where those value-creating opportunities are. In contrast, the powerful party predominately focuses on value claiming and not on value creating.

Now let's switch the focus: you are the less powerful party. If you were not in a particularly powerful position (e.g., you do not have great options, you do not control valued resources: you do not bring much to the table), you are in no position to claim a large portion of the value in the negotiation. To offset your lack of control of valuable resources, your only option is to work harder to figure out where the nonobvious sources of value are—those synergistic combinations of issues that enlarge the resources available to both you and your counterpart.

This motivation to create value is more typically associated with negotiators who are in relatively low-power positions than with negotiators who are in high-power positions. When researchers closely monitored the negotiations of high- and low-power negotiators, they found that it was the low-power parties who were most likely to introduce packages that took advantage of the asymmetrical interests and preferences of the parties.[6]

One likely reason is that low-powered negotiators know that the only way they are going to get any reasonable outcome is to make sure that the high-powered folks get what they expect. So those with less power have to be more creative and are motivated to think harder about innovative ways to enlarge the size of the real pool of resources that they were splitting with their powerful counterparts.

Another telling example of the way in which power drives behavior appears in the planning documents of students in our negotiation courses. When they are placed in high-power roles, even their planning documents reflect their lack of motivation to think systematically about the opportunities presented by the negotiation. This focus on value claiming is visible even in the length of their planning documents. There is a huge difference in the number of words that comprise the typical high-power player's planning document (I am powerful; I want a lot; I will get a lot) as compared to the multipage, single-spaced works of low-power players, outlining multiple strategies contingent on what the high-power party does.

If all negotiators cared about were value creation, then low-power negotiators would win this competition. However, value claiming is really the focus of getting more. So what options would exist for you if you were in a situation where you had poorer alternatives than your counterpart? Is there a way for you to take advantage of the benefits of having power without actually have power?

THE IMPORTANCE OF A POWERFUL MIND-SET

Consider a situation in which two individuals are negotiating, and in which each of them has only modestly positive alternatives. Although their objective level of power is approximately equal, one of them has a powerful mind-set while the other does not. What differences might we expect to see between these two negotiators?

In a study that was conducted with exactly these characteristics (both parties have approximately equal objective levels of power, but one party was manipulated to have a more powerful mind-set than the other), the results illustrated that the negotiators with powerful mind-sets were able to claim more value than their counterparts with less powerful mind-sets.

Creating a powerful mind-set is a lot easier than you might think. A powerful mind-set can be created in at least three ways. The first is by simply recalling a time when you had power over another person. The second way is by recalling a time when you felt physically attractive. The third way leverages the connection between your mind and your body through the use of power poses. Let's look at each of these separately.

First, think about a time when you had power over another; when you were in a position to evaluate another person or you controlled the ability of other people to get something they wanted. Now focus on what happened, how you felt, what that experience was like. You may be thinking that it cannot be that simple.[7] But recall Chapter 1 and the discussion of the impact of expectations. If you can be influenced by others' expectations about you, then your expectations about yourself may also influence your behavior. And the results of research manipulating people's mind-set of their powerfulness (or powerlessness) demonstrate that this self-talk creates the three effects of power: bias to action, insensitivity to social nuance, and objectification of those around you.[8]

Second, think back to a time when you felt physically attractive. Although it may surprise you, research shows that recalling a time when you felt physically attractive influences your ability to claim value in the negotiation, but had no impact on your ability to create value. In addition, negotiators who remembered a time when they felt physically attractive did no better than negotiators who remembered a time when they felt physically unattractive when they had better alternatives than their counterparts. However, negotiators who had worse alternatives than their counterparts achieved better outcomes in their negotiations than did their more-powerful counterparts when they felt attractive.[9] Interestingly, their counterparts who had better alternatives rated them as significantly more powerful and influential in the negotiation.

Third, consider your physical stance in the negotiation. Your posture influences both your physiological responses as well as your mental state. In a series of studies, researchers have demonstrated that your posture can influence your levels of cortisol (the stress hormone) and testosterone (the power hormone) as well as your willingness to take risks.[10] On entering the experiment, participants were asked to give a saliva sample. Then they were escorted into a small room where they were either asked to sit in an expansive posture or in a constricted posture. After a short time, they were asked to give another saliva sample. Your mother was right when she told you that it matters how you stand and sit! The participants who were sitting in the expansive posture showed lower levels of cortisol and higher

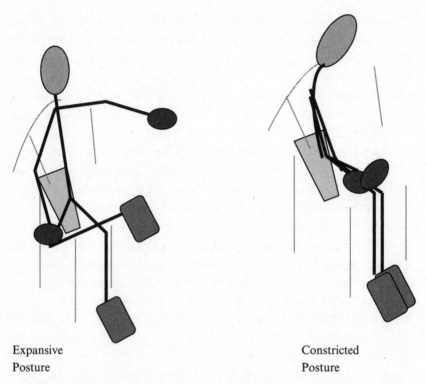

Expansive   Constricted
Posture   Posture

FIGURE 11.1

L. Z. Tiedens, M. M. Unzueta, and M. J. Young, "An Unconscious Desire for Hierarchy? The Motivated Perception of Dominance Complementarity in Task Partners," *Journal of Personality and Social Psychology* 93, no. 3 (2007): 402.

levels of testosterone. Those sitting in the constricted posture had higher levels of cortisol and lower levels of testosterone. In addition, those in the expansive posture condition were more likely to take a risky bet while those in the constricted posture were more likely to take a certain outcome. If you are wondering what an expansive or a constricted posture looks like, have a look at Figure 11.1.

Of course, these mind-sets and postures effects do not inoculate you from feelings of powerlessness. They are, however, simple but apparently effective short-term tactics to get yourself thinking—and acting—more powerfully. And if you initiate a social situation in that powerful mind-set, your counterpart is likely to respond in ways that reinforce your sense of power—thus creating a positive feedback loop.

As with many other aspects of human social interaction, power does not exist in a vacuum. Rather, power is a relative phenomenon. You have power to the extent that others view you as powerful or the situation provides you with the cues or attributes of power—which are typically socially constructed. How you behave is a combination of your internal assessment and of how others respond to you. Thus, to the extent that you have a powerful mind-set and engage in behaviors that are consistent with that mind-set, you increase the chance that your counterpart will defer to you.

Think about your social interactions—negotiations included—as taking place on two dimensions: the horizontal dimension is affiliation, while the vertical dimension is control.[11] People generally match behavior for behavior on the affiliation dimension: for example, folks are more likely to behave agreeably with those who are agreeable and by quarreling with those who are quarrelsome. In contrast, people are more comfortable complementing the behavior of others on the control dimension; your behaving deferentially is likely to trigger your counterpart to behave dominantly, or your dominance behavior is likely to trigger a deferent response on her part.[12]

Understanding the different effects that displays of power have on negotiations is the first step to using them to your advantage. In the next section, we explore the surprising effect of complementarity on negotiators' performance—and show why acting deferentially in some situations may result in your achieving higher-quality outcomes than if you were to act dominantly.

Complementarity

Displays of dominance by one party can result in a similar display of dominance by another party. You probably have experienced or witnessed situations where one party's dominant behavior was matched (or exceeded) by his or her counterpart's dominance. So we see matching rather than complementing.

For the most part, when people respond to a dominant behavior with dominance, they are likely to be in a competitive situation. It turns out that when individuals are engaged in a cooperative endeavor, they are more likely to respond to dominant behaviors with deference; and the deference of one party encourages a dominant response by his or her counterpart.[13]

Research suggests that negotiators interpret and respond to the same set of dominant behaviors in very different ways, depending on the way they frame the interaction.[14] When participants believed that a negotiation was essentially cooperative, they perceived their counterpart's dominant behavior as instrumental in completing the assigned task; when the same set of behaviors were expressed by their counterpart but the negotiation was framed as competitive, these very same behavior were seen as aggressive and negative, obstructing their ability to reach a deal!

Negotiations are social interactions that require individuals to coordinate through information sharing to achieve mutually beneficial outcomes.[15] Complementarity can enhance performance on tasks that require coordination and resource allocation. However, on tasks that have few coordination demands (e.g., proofreading a report), complementary dyads don't have a distinct advantage.[16] But complementarity does create hierarchy—and hierarchies (even hierarchies of two) facilitate coordination. Having a clear, even if not explicit, idea of who is directing and who is following makes coordination of information exchange and allocation of resources much more efficient.[17]

You might be wondering just how dominating behavior can encourage coordination. The study examined specific verbal and nonverbal behaviors associated with dominance that included displaying heightened facial expressiveness, demonstrating an expansive posture, reducing interpersonal distances (i.e. standing or sitting close to the counterpart), speaking in a loud voice, speaking slowly and in a relaxed tone, looking away when others are speaking to you, and interrupting others.[18]

Given the benefits of coordination that come from complementarity, negotiators in complementary dyads should be better able to coordinate reciprocal information exchange that can lead them to discover sources of joint value, and those in the dominant role were able to claim more of that value. What was unexpected was that those in the deferent role were actually better off negotiating with a dominant counterpart than they were when negotiating with another, equally deferent counterpart. The pool of resources created by the complementary dyad was significantly larger than the pool of resources created by the two deferent negotiators. In contrast, negotiators in interactions that were framed as competitive were more likely to meet dominance with dominance. In this case, it turns out that the dominant member of the complementary dyad was also significantly better off as well. This dominant-dominant dyad created significantly less value and, thus, each had less value to claim. And, as you might expect, this competitive situation was perceived to be even more competitive when both parties displayed the same dominance behaviors as compared to the negotiators in the cooperative situation where the same dominance behavior by one party led to greater coordination and subsequent value creation.

The implication is clear: you should complement your counterpart's dominance behavior while framing (or reframing) the negotiation as cooperative because you are concerned about value claiming. But doing this will likely take a great deal of discipline on your part. If your counterpart is displaying dominant behaviors, you should respond with deferent behaviors; and if she is expressing deference, you should respond with dominance. Doing so will increase the amount of value that will be created in the negotiation—and if you are fortunate enough to be displaying the dominant behavior, you will also claim a significantly greater share of the resources as compared to what you would claim if both of you were dominant or both of you were deferent. Even if you need to display deference in response to your counterpart's dominance, you will still be significantly better off in the value that you ultimately claim compared to what you would achieve by matching his dominance with yours.

Mimicry

In contrast to complementarity in the control or power dimension, one effective way to enhance the affiliation or relationship between yourself and others is through mimicry. Humans tend to mimic or subtly imitate others' behaviors including their speech patterns, facial expressions, and mannerisms.[19] And you get positive responses when you mimic. Romantic couples feel more in sync with each other the greater the amount of mimicking they do;[20] food servers were found to get larger tips when they verbally mimicked their customers than when they did not;[21] and those being mimicked are more likely to engage in a subsequent altruistic behavior directed at the mimicker.[22]

Although the evidence suggests that humans unconsciously tend to mimic the mannerisms of people who are important to them, some are more likely to mimic than others. Those who have a strong motivation to get along with others have been observed to mimic their social partners more.[23] It is one thing to synchronize your behavior to that of those in your social environment without intention. However, it is altogether different to employ mimicry to persuade or seduce.

Successful, intentional mimicry involves reflecting your counterpart's behavior—but with a little delay. If he sits up in his chair, then wait a beat or two and do the same. If she crosses her legs, then again, delay for a while, then respond. Mimic your counterpart, but imperfectly and with a delay. Mimic too closely and folks will perceive they are being mocked—and their response to such a perception is typically negative. This effect can be seen even if the mimic was a computer-generated figure, an avatar. And the avatar was more likely to come across as warm and genuine to the extent that the avatar mimicked the person's behavior with a slight delay.[24]

If done tactfully, mimicry can help you get a better outcome in negotiation. Negotiators who mimicked their opponents' mannerisms were more likely to create more value, and the mimicker claimed more of the value that was created. Interestingly, the person being mimicked was not worse off than he would have been with a counterpart who was not strategically mimicking; but the excess value that was created by the dyad went to the party who mimicked. Further, when negotiators who were being mimicked did not recognize that they were being manipulated in this way, they expressed greater trust in their counterparts.[25]

Complementarity versus Mimicry

Complementarity and mimicry may at first seem to be contradictory concepts. When we discussed complementarity, our advice was to complement your counterpart—act deferent to his or her dominance or dominant to his or her deference. Then, we advised you to mimic, or match, the behavior of your counterpart. Clearly both pieces of advice cannot be true—or can they?

Margaret and a coauthor designed a study to find out whether mimicry or complementarity was the better negotiating tactic.[26] Some participants were instructed to behave dominantly while their counterparts were instructed to behave deferentially to create complementarity. Another set of participants were directed to mirror the behaviors of their counterparts during the negotiation to see what effect mimicry would have.

It turns out that mimicry is a very effective way of enhancing liking and trust between negotiating counterparts. Having one negotiator mimic the behaviors of another often made for rather quick and relatively cooperative agreements. However, the effect of mimicry depends on what you are mimicking. For example, if your counterpart is behaving dominantly, your individual and joint outcomes are systematically worse if you mimic this behavior. If your counterpart is behaving in a more submissive manner, mimicking that behavior also reduces the value that the two of you create.

In contrast, there are other behaviors that you can mimic that will enhance your counterparts' liking and trusting of you—and, thus, their willingness to share information. For example, you might mimic the accents, speech patterns, or facial expressions of your counterparts—and there is considerable evidence that you mimic the behaviors of those around you all the time.[27] And the more motivated you are to get along with others, the more you mimic their behavior. For example, researchers have found a very strong relationship between the amount of rapport between romantic couples and the amount of mimicking that takes place in their social interactions.[28]

When told to mimic the mannerisms of their partners, including mirroring their posture and body movement, while making sure that their mimicry was sufficiently subtle so as not to attract the explicit attention of their counterparts, negotiators were more successful in getting an agreement—and the negotiation in this case involved a negative bargaining zone! So not only were agreements more likely to occur, in general, but they were also more likely to occur even when an agreement made the party that was being mimicked worse off. Further, buyers who mimicked sellers in this negotiation were perceived by the seller as more trustworthy—and it was this increase in perceived trustworthiness that accounted for the increased willingness to reach a deal by the sellers.[29]

To decide when to mimic and when to complement during a negotiation, it is important to first frame the interaction as cooperative. Then, engage in complementary behavior in terms of the expression of dominance and deference: express nonverbal dominance when your counterparts are acting in a submissive manner and express nonverbal deference when they are expressing dominant behaviors). Third, mimic your counterpart in other, non-status-oriented behaviors including accents, speech cadence, emotional tone, posture, body positioning, and the like—just make sure that your mimicry is sufficiently subtle to escape their attention. In doing so you will be combining the benefits of complementarity in value creation with the relational benefits of mimicry to enhance trust, liking, and willingness to reach agreements. You will be able to maximize the value created by you and your negotiating counterpart while claiming a larger share of the value for yourself.

ANGER: THE EMOTION OF THE POWERFUL

Power doesn't only influence how you act; it also affects the emotions you express. Certain emotions are more likely to be expressed by powerful or powerless individuals. Consider the situation in which a powerful person and a powerless person have had their progress on a project blocked. The powerful person is more likely to respond with anger. In contrast, when the powerless—or less powerful—person is blocked, the modal emotional experience is one of sadness, guilt, or frustration; but not anger.

Most people generally believe that anger is a negative emotion and happiness is positive. Yet in a recent review of research on anger, anger was more strongly associated with the desire to change the situation than was happiness.[30] In fact when researchers studied the brain pattern activity associated with anger, they found a pattern that was similar to the pattern observed when individuals were acting on desires.[31] Further, individuals who were angry experienced increased perceptions of control and certainty; they made more optimistic assessments of the risks they faced. In contrast, those who were fearful experienced a decrease in their sense of control or certainty.[32]

As with powerful individuals, those who were angry were not deluded by their anger into thinking that they were going to experience only good outcomes. In fact, they fully expected to face negative outcomes or challenges in the future; the difference was that although angry, those individuals expected that their preferred outcome would prevail. Anger appears to stimulate a sense of the self as powerful and capable. In addition, angry individuals are more likely to hold optimistic expectations about the future.[33]

The effects of anger are not limited to an individual's predictions about the future. Angry, powerful negotiators are more likely to process information heuristically, not stopping to consider the more subtle nuances or alternative perspectives of their social interactions.[34] They are quick to take action and slow (if at all) to consider the implications of their actions or demands. They approach challenges confidently, optimistic that they can control the outcomes. So it quickly becomes clear that anger is an emotion associated with power—and contributes to the positive feedback loop described earlier: if you are powerful, you are more likely to experience anger. In anger, you feel more in control, more optimistic about the future, quicker to take action to change the status quo, and more certain about your ability to prevail. All of these feelings result in an increased experience of power.

These descriptions of anger may run counter to what you may have experienced. When we consider the emotion of anger, it is not the explosive, violent or even chronic state of "being angry" associated with increased stress-related disorders such as coronary heart disease.[35] In contrast, the anger that was the subject of study is a low-intensity, controlled emotional expression that is situation specific. It is steely rather than hot. It is certainly not the out-of-control, so-angry-I-could-cry, having-a-hissy-fit, throwing-things type of emotion. In fact, that type of emotion is typically associated with frustration rather than with power. The associations others are likely to make to such an emotional display are not those typically associated with power or control.

Those in power are more likely to feel "steely," rather than "hot," anger—and they are also more likely to express anger. Does it follow then that if you express anger in negotiation that others will perceive you as more powerful? It turns out that expressing anger does typically increase the amount of status or power that others attribute to you.[36] However, expressing anger when you are clearly a powerless person will not lead your evaluators to rate you as more powerful. If you are moderately powerful, however, such expressions will enhance the power others give to you; if you are relatively powerless, such expressions of anger are likely to generate a backlash from your more powerful counterparts.

As you might expect, there are differences in others' responses and attributions to individuals expressing anger if the anger expression is done by a male or female. Men who express anger are perceived as more powerful. However, for women to get this same attribution of power, anger expression must be coupled with a justification for the anger. That is, while a man can express his anger and be perceived as powerful, a woman who simply expresses her anger will be perceived as less powerful. In displaying anger, being explicit about why you are angry will significantly reduce the likelihood of others' making an out-of-control attribution and increase the attribution of power if you are female.[37]

POWER, ANGER, AND NEGOTIATIONS

In Chapter 10, we talked about the importance of emotions in predicting value claiming. We also emphasized the importance of perceiving uncertainty in the interaction as a precursor to the systematic thinking necessary for value creation. Now, let's integrate these concepts to understand just how power (or the lack of it) and anger expression affect negotiators.

In a recent study, the high-power party was angry in half the pairs; in the other half, the low-power party was angry.[38] The results for the high-power negotiator should not surprise you: the high-power parties demanded and received more of the value that was created in the exchange. When high power was coupled with anger, these negotiators become more effective and, as a consequence, were able to claim even more value. The reason for this effect is that low-power negotiators were negatively affected by an angry (and high-power) counterpart; they lost focus and were more likely to make concessions that favored their opponent.

Because of the optimistic effect of anger coupled with the uncertainty experienced by the low-power party of what the high-power party might do, the presence of angry high-power negotiators also increased the value creation capability of the dyad. For low-power negotiators, anger expressed by their high-power counterparts increased their uncertainty and seemed to motivate them to achieve a higher level of value creation. As you might expect, the majority of the value created was claimed by the high-power player. Note that *both parties* achieved better outcomes when at least one party was angry. Even the anger of negotiators who are low in power benefitted both themselves and their high-power counterparts by creating more value than would have been created by neutral negotiators.

SUMMARY

In this chapter, we have focused on the consequences of being powerful, and those of being powerless on negotiation strategy and outcomes. Research indicates that negotiators who are powerful have a bias for action (e.g., are more likely to make the first offer), are less likely to explore opportunities to create value, are less sensitive to social nuance, and more likely to see their negotiating counterpart as a means to their own ends rather than as an opportunity for solving the problem at hand.

Although these tendencies may be beneficial in some situations, in other situations they do not help high-power parties get more of what they want—and might even work against that outcome. For example, combine our suggestions from Chapter 7 on first offers with what you now know about the likely behavior of the powerful. Powerful folks are likely to make the first offer. This is beneficial for them *if* the benefit of anchoring their counterpart dominates the value of the information they might receive if their counterpart were to make the first offer. However, because of the powerful parties' bias to action, they are unlikely to take the time to consider whether a first offer would be beneficial or not; they will simply get the ball rolling by making the first offer.

Negotiating dyads with a combination of high- and low-power players (or, as research discovered later, dominant and deferent counterparts) were able to achieve a higher level of value creation within the negotiation as compared to negotiating dyads with two high-power/dominant or two low-power/deferent counterparts, particularly when the negotiations are framed as cooperative. As such, power has both its downsides and a silver lining for both high- and low-power negotiators.

- By seeking out counterparts who have less power, you increase the likelihood of creating significant value in the interaction, and you will be able to claim most of that created value.
- If your goal is simply to get an agreement, nonverbal mimicry of the affiliative behaviors of your counterpart is a useful strategy.
- If your goal is to claim value, then you should complement the control-oriented nonverbal behavior of your counterparts. If they are behaving in a neutral or deferent way, respond with nonverbal dominance; if they are behaving dominantly, respond with nonverbal deference.
- If you believe that your alternatives are not that attractive, try to engage that powerful mind-set which, if successful, may provide the catalyst necessary to create the complementary benefits described above, by thinking about other situations in which you had power and were in control or felt physically attractive.
- Use your anger judiciously and strategically. Individuals who are angry are typically conferred more status or are perceived as more powerful than are individuals who express sadness, guilt, or frustration.
- If you are female, make sure that your expressions of anger are accompanied by an explicit rationale for why you are angry.

CHAPTER TWELVE

MULTIPARTY NEGOTIATIONS

The More the Merrier?

U p to this point, we have focused on negotiations that take place between two individuals. Although many of your negotiations take place between you and a single counterpart, even negotiations with only two sets of interests can have a side composed of an individual or of a team with multiple members. Negotiating as part of or across the table from a team is really not that unusual. For example, your family is meeting with the families of your siblings to select a residential facility for your aging parents. Or you are trying to get a permit to build a barn, and you need the approval of the zoning board, which consists of several members. Or you and your team are presenting a proposal for a new project to the executive team of your company or the management team of your newly formed start-up is meeting with partners of a venture capital firm to discuss their willingness to fund your new venture.

In some of these situations, you are negotiating as an individual facing a multiperson counterpart. And in others, there are team-on-team negotiations. Although these are still two-party negotiations (there are only two sides) having multiple individuals represent one side greatly increases the complexity of the negotiation.[1]

Specifically, it becomes necessary to coordinate the planning process, understand and integrate the preferences or interests among the members of your team, and develop and implement a cohesive negotiating strategy. Of course, the complexity increases when there are more than two perspectives represented in the negotiation. If negotiating among two teams seems complicated, imagine the difficulty of three or more sides when you are negotiating with multiple individuals or teams, each with a different set of interests. For the sake of simplicity, we first consider the basics of team negotiating, and toward the end of the chapter we will describe some of the more complex scenarios you might face in multiteam negotiations.

THE CHALLENGE OF NEGOTIATING IN A TEAM

I n contrast to the planning an individual should do in advance of a negotiation, a team faces additional hurdles such as whose voice is heard and how the individual interests will be considered. To negotiate successfully, the team must identify and integrate the preferences and priorities of its members in a process of intrateam negotiation. In addition, during the actual negotiation, team members must coordinate their behavior to maximize the team's potential for value claiming. Finally, since teams are typically more competitive than individuals, they often have the unintended effect of making negotiations more adversarial—something that teammates must plan for before they reach the negotiating table.[2]

Team members may not be aware of the extent to which their interests and preferences differ, particularly since some team members may be reluctant to voice their conflicting preferences. Psychologically, team members generally believe that there is more similarity among themselves than with others who are not members of the team. If unverified, this assumption can lead to trouble. Although the criteria for membership may create similarity on some dimensions, such as organizational affiliation, team membership alone does not automatically lead to a common set of preferences and interests.

Failing to recognize and resolve internal disagreements and conflict among team members before the negotiation can have a number of damaging repercussions. Team members may develop reduced identification with the team, and because of their inability to resolve the internal conflict, members may be unable to reach an internal consensus on what they want to achieve or the strategies and tactics they want to implement in service of their goals in the upcoming negotiation. The challenge is for team members to fashion an agreement with their team counterparts who are on the same side of the dispute but may bring very different expectations about the issues, strategies, and outcomes that constitute an acceptable agreement.

In the preparation phase, it is important to understand just how aligned the team members are in terms of their preferences. It might be the case that all members have exactly the same preferences, priorities, and perspectives on their alternatives, reservation prices, and aspiration prices. If so, then there is likely to be little internal conflict among the team members—and the preparation process, with possibly the exception of the difficulty of scheduling meeting times, would, to a large extent, resemble the preparation of an individual.

But what if team members have very different—and perhaps conflicting—views of what a good deal should be? What if there were internal conflicts about what members expect to achieve in the negotiation—their aspirations, reservation prices, and their preferences and priorities? In this case, achieving internal agreement may be quite difficult. Although there has been little research in the negotiation domain that explicitly examines the challenges of intrateam negotiations, we can draw from team-based research to inform negotiators in teams of the challenges and opportunities that await them.[3]

On occasion, you may have the opportunity to pick a team for a negotiation. In most cases, it is more likely that you will be a member of an already existing team who has been assigned the task to negotiate. This distinction is important, because team members often naively assume that because they are on the same side of the table in a dispute their interests are aligned—regardless of how similar the team members are in terms of their social demographics (such as age, race, ethnicity, tenure within the organization, gender, and other such markers) or their backgrounds (such as education, expertise, experience, or status). Because they expect greater similarity of viewpoints and opinions among themselves and other group members,[4] they may be less willing to voice disagreement when it, in fact, occurs. Research on groupthink demonstrates that homogeneity can decrease individuals' sensitivity to disagreement—but not because there is no disagreement; rather, members may be voluntarily censoring their expression of their disagreements.[5]

When groups are homogenous or similar in dimensions important to the team, members are likely to believe that their views are more similar than those of diverse groups, even when the views of both groups are identical.[6] More importantly, research shows that individuals in a team believe that they are more likely to agree with a member of their team even when the basis for the team membership is unrelated to the issue on which agreement is being sought.[7]

This selective perception of similarity leads to what researchers have labeled the delusion of homogeneity or the belief that team members are more similar in their beliefs, aspirations, and goals than an objective assessment indicates.[8] A delusion of homogeneity is reflected in the team's belief about its internal consensus. The resulting, but illusory, consensus leads to proposals that are inconsistent with the true preferences and priorities of some (or even all) of the team members. This mismatch may sometimes become evident only during the external negotiation.

The more visible or surface-level similarities (demographic category membership or professional background and expertise) there are among team members, the more members will expect consensus in their goals and preferences (deep-level dimensions). But surface-level similarity can conceal deep divides in what team members are trying to achieve and the outcomes they find desirable or acceptable. Individuals normally expect congruency between surface- and deep-level distinctions such that people who are similar are assumed to have the same preferences, and people who are different are assumed to have different preferences. When team members extrapolate from surface-level to deep-level similarity, they expect little conflict and more agreement. In contrast, the mere presence of surface-level difference increases perceptions of uncertainty, raises the expectation of conflict, and motivates a more elaborated and systematic search for unique or discriminating information.[9]

Because the surface-level differences between teammates can change how confident team members are in their predictions of others' interests and preferences, researchers found that individuals who expected to interact with those who were different from them were more likely to engage in more systematic information processing in attempting to understand others' perspectives.[10] This expectation resulted in more elaborate and detailed plans of action. Indeed, those who expect to work with dissimilar others are more likely to seek out unique information, while those who face similar others are more likely to discuss information that they and their counterparts have in common.[11] This additional elaboration of information and planning resulted in members' coming to meetings better prepared and able to articulate their preferences and the bases for those preferences.

When a team's internal conflicts are not resolved before the negotiation begins, members experience a difficult choice: whether to maximize their individual interests or subjugate their individual interests in the service of the team's interests. Having this conflict remain unresolved and playing out at the same time as the interteam negotiation itself reduces the team's ability to develop a shared identity and discourages information sharing within the team.[12] Further, teams that experience this internal conflict are less able to carry out organized, collective action to implement the team's strategy in the negotiation.[13] Finally, teams whose members experience internal conflict are less satisfied with the outcomes of the negotiation and with their fellow team members. So, from the perspective of the team, it is clear that you want to ensure that your team's interests are aligned as much as possible with the interests of the members. Allocating the time and effort necessary to prepare, plan, and implement a successful negotiation process is a critical precondition for effective team performance.

Individuals start favoring members of their team (and disfavoring non-team members) even if they were assigned to a team based on trivial or random differences.[14] In one study, participants were shown a slide that contained a large number of dots, and they were asked individually to estimate the number of dots on the slide. The experimenter then randomly assigned individuals to teams of "high-dot estimators" and "low-dot estimators." Even though the assignment was random, people quickly began identifying differences between the two groups. Just as soon as these boundaries were identified, there was a clear development of an us-versus-them divide—and the way in which members of one group behaved toward members of the other group changed.

Members of a group not only favor other members of their own group (in-group) but also punish members of other groups (out-group).[15] Thus, the presence of in-group and out-group members increases the competitiveness of the overall interaction.[16] This is called the discontinuity effect.[17] So the first thing you can bet on is that when teams are present, the negotiation will be more competitive.

Part of a team's tendency toward competitiveness may result from the presence of the other team. Unlike the members of your team who are likely to assume a similarity of goals, interests, and preferences, the negotiators across the table are the out-group. Your team is more likely to make the reverse assumption and to expect incompatibility among negotiators.

The strength with which your team makes and persists in this assumption of interteam incompatibility makes the negotiation more adversarial (as opposed to solving a problem) and may be as damaging to effective negotiations as is your team's expectation of intrateam homogeneity.

As the size of the team increases, so too do the likely number of issues, the perspectives on those issues, and the sheer amount of information the parties need to consider. Keeping track of the factual information, as well as the values, attitudes, and perceptions of each member of the team is a major challenge. Integrating this massive amount of information into an optimal solution can be a highly demanding task as the bargaining zone changes from two dimensions to three, four, five, or more.

Thus, negotiators facing team counterparts are often victims of information overload. Because of negotiators' efforts to deal with this complicated information, they may become concerned about feeling regret over accepting an agreement that they might later judge to be suboptimal.[18] The less that negotiators know about their counterparts and the landscape of potential deals, the more second guessing and doubt they may experience. This increased doubt can easily lead to more impasses in a negotiation.

THE ADVANTAGES OF TEAM NEGOTIATIONS

Although negotiating with teams creates a host of challenges, it's also true that teams—particularly those that function well—are often better able than individuals to generate ideas and develop creative alternatives. Because members of a team can pool their information and identify and correct misguided assumptions and errors of judgment within the team, they may be more adept at fashioning proposals that create value than are individuals.[19] The likelihood that teams can devise a creative solution to the problems facing both sets of negotiators is facilitated by attacking the problem with the different perspectives that the individual team members may generate.

Second, having multiple members can help a team allocate the necessary negotiating tasks more effectively. Think about the communication demands for a negotiator acting alone. She must be able to convey proposals, listen to the other's proposals, evaluate the veracity of the information that is being presented by the other side, consider and choose what information to share and what information to withhold from the counterpart, figure out how to incorporate new information and adjust the current proposal, and know when to say yes. Having multiple members of the team available to take responsibility for these various tasks (e.g., parts of the information processing and communication demands) can make the team much more effective at gathering and processing information. Realizing this potential, however, requires additional planning that draws on the unique advantages of a team.

LEVERAGING TEAM NEGOTIATIONS

As with many aspects of negotiating, there is not one best way to negotiate with a team. Teams have the potential to increase value creation if they are able to overcome the challenges of coordination and the intensity of an us-versus-them mentality. To see negotiation as an opportunity for value creation and to have the ability to propose value-enhancing outcomes requires more than just a group of people getting together on one side or the other of the negotiating table. Rather, team members must engage in systematic assessment of their own and their counterparts' preferences as well as develop strategies to maximize their ability to create and claim value by taking advantage of the increased cognitive resources that teams provide.

The challenges of team negotiating loom particularly large if team members are not particularly skilled negotiators or have little experience in working together. What is likely to happen is that the challenges of coordination will prove too much for team members to overcome and they will, in effect, trip over each other in their attempts to negotiate. In the case of inexperienced teams, they are likely to be perceived by their counterparts as less reliable, behave in ways that increase their counterparts' distrust, and be perceived as more competitive and less cooperative as compared either to individual negotiators or experienced teams.[20]

Teams with negotiating expertise were viewed (both by their counterparts and by themselves) as more powerful and generated higher-quality solutions when compared to counterparts who were also trained but negotiating as individuals. So teams composed of trained negotiators were able to create more value, claim more of the value created, and do so while being perceived as cooperative and trustworthy.

Expert negotiators are better able to enlarge the pool of available resources and claim a greater portion of those resources, and expert teams have the same advantage compared to novice teams. When competing with expert individual negotiators, expert team negotiators were able to claim more of the available value. Of course, if one were to assess the team's ability to claim value on a per member basis, then the synergy would not be so impressive. That is, an expert team of three does not do, on average, three times better than their expert individual counterpart.

Even considering a team's increased value-claiming potential, each group still needs to coordinate their strategies and actions to achieve these superior results. Perhaps one of the major ways in which teams run into trouble, particularly in negotiation, is their lack of explicit coordination on the "who's," the "how's," and the "what's" required for the implementation of their strategic plan once the negotiation starts. Although researchers over the last six decades have repeatedly emphasized the importance of intragroup preparation, very few negotiating teams plan and prepare ways in which to coordinate their actions.[21] This failure is not simply the specific failure of negotiating teams. Teams, in general, are often superior in analyzing and dissecting tasks but often fail to consider how to coordinate the pieces of their solutions into an organized whole.[22]

To take advantage of the benefits of team negotiation, teams should engage in a three-step preparation process.[23] In the first step, team members should convene well before the negotiation to discuss the substance of the negotiation. At a minimum, this discussion should include a brainstorming process to identify the issues to raise in the negotiation.

Team members should then assess the priorities of these issues and potential trades among these issues. At this point, it is critical for members to be heard on what issues they believe to be more—and less—important contributors to a high-quality agreement. Some members of the team should also be assigned to take the counterpart's (team or individual) perspective—in effect, mirroring the planning process from a different perspective. What issues are they going to want discussed? How will the counterpart set priorities on these issues? Once the issues have been identified, these two subgroups should identify alternatives, set reservation prices, and set aspirations.

The final aspect of this first phase is to identify the team's assumptions about their counterparts—what they want and how they will likely behave. Then the team should set up ways to test those assumptions—for example, by tapping into their social networks to verify their expectations with knowledgeable others—as well as gain clarity on the information that needs to be supplemented and verified.

The second phase is unique to team preparation. The team should assess the skills of its members and assign specific roles in the negotiation. Who is most technically fluent in the issues under consideration? What past negotiating experience do members have? Are there members who have well developed listening skills or acting ability? Is there someone who is skilled at facilitating and directing conversation?

Once their skills have been identified, members should be assigned specific roles. Much as in a theatrical play, team members should have their parts to play in the negotiation. Who will take on the role of team leader, chief negotiator, relationship analyst, time manager, data czar, or the bad cop to another member's good cop?

The third phase requires that the team plan how the negotiation will unfold. From the decision to make or receive the first offer, members need to know how concessions will unfold, who will monitor the information being shared by the other side, how to unobtrusively call for a caucus when new or disparate information is revealed or intrateam disagreements arise. In addition, attention must be directed to maintaining the proposal as a package rather than devolving to an issue-by-issue negotiation process, all this while keeping accurate records of the progress made.

Even within the most motivated and expert teams, all members may not be able to reach complete agreement on a particular proposal because the team members may not agree about the rank ordering of the issues and the strategies to achieve their preferred outcomes. As a result, teams must establish a method of agreement, such as majority rule or consensus. Absent such a mechanism, individual members from one or both sides of a team negotiation may revert to another way to maximize their unique interests within the context of an intrateam negotiation: they may join a subgroup by forming a coalition that has the political power to move the larger team or set of disputants to accept a specific proposal or outcome.

Coalition Formation: Who's In and Who's Out?

A coalition is a subgroup composed of multiple parties who cooperate to obtain an outcome that satisfies the interests of the coalition members rather than those not in the coalition. Through the formation of a coalition, individual members of a team can create a dominant subgroup that can cooperate to obtain an outcome that satisfies the interests of its members rather than those of the larger group or team.[24] Coalitions are possible whenever there are more than two negotiators, even if those individuals represent sides of the deal. That is, while coalitions may be formed within the boundary of a particular team, coalitions can also be formed by members of different teams who may be negotiating with each other. In either situation, members of the winning coalition are likely to get more of what they specifically want rather than what might be in the best interest of their teammates or the other side.

Coalitions typically begin with one founder who initiates the coalition by enlisting others with promises and commitments of resources. Initiating or joining a coalition early in its development involves some risk, because the initiators and early joiners are uncertain whether the coalition will garner enough critical mass to win. Because of the uncertainty, the founder typically has to offer a disproportionate share of the resources to induce early potential partners to join, at least until the coalition is well established.[25]

Note the interesting aspect here of coalitions—they are relationships that are built through the process of negotiating cooperative agreements among allies or disrupting the negotiating process of potential adversaries. Potential coalition partners are those who have compatible interests and who are open to relationships that foster trust and mutual obligation; what's more, each of these potential coalition partners will be attracted to a particular coalition because membership offers benefits that cannot be realized in other coalitions or by individual action.

Coalitions gain power because of the resources that their members control. One reflection of that power is the exclusivity of the coalition. The more people are attracted to joining the coalition and the fewer opportunities for joining, the more powerful it and its members are.

Coalitions are not simply about exclusivity. They exist because they have the potential to achieve the goals of their members. They might block a more powerful counterpart, or control critical resources (votes, dollars, solutions) to achieve a common goal (as is often the case in parliamentary forms of government).[26]

An individual's power within a coalition can be strategic, normative, or relational.[27] Strategic power is the classic form of power that emerges from the availability of alternative coalition partners; those who are invited to join alternative coalitions are perceived as more powerful by their colleagues. Normative power is based on what parties consider just or fair mechanisms to allocate the resources the coalition can command. Normative power also can serve a strategic function because the party that proposes the principle of what constitutes a fair distribution often proposes an allocation norm that favors their particular interests. Finally, relationship-based power comes from the compatibility of preferences among coalition members. Parties who see each other as having compatible interests, values, or preferences are likely to maintain a relationship over time that can influence or block other possible coalitions.

In an empirical test, relationship power was most effective for negotiators seeking to be included in final deals and to claim more value, as it affected both the formation and stability of coalitions. Resistance from parties outside the coalition tended to strengthen the bond among the coalition members, making it more likely for them to continue to identify and cooperate with each other and to compete with the non–coalition members. Therefore, when coalitions initially formed because of relationship power, they were likely to be broadly effective, influencing even those issues for which the coalition members did not have compatible preferences. In essence, this sort of power lowered uncertainty about future exclusion.

Strategic Considerations That Enhance Effective Coalitions

Research on teams has demonstrated the importance of the "first advocacy effect," which is vital to understand when confronting a team negotiation. A form of anchoring, this effect occurs when an early position is offered by a team member on a contentious issue. In hearing this early position statement, undecided team members are influenced in the direction of the position. Those who hold opposing positions, speaking later, must not only make their arguments but also neutralize the influence of this early advocate. This makes their task more difficult. In much the same way, motivated negotiators who see the benefit of a coalitional strategy are more likely to found a coalition the earlier they identify their potential partners and begin to secure their commitment. Once that initial tie is secured, then both members of this coalition can identify and enlist additional members until the necessary size or level of influence is achieved. The strategic lesson is to meet early and often with potential coalition partners, to identify valuable partners—and begin building a strong coalition—as soon as possible.

The most powerful member in a coalition is the marginal member of the winning coalition—that is, the person whose participation expands the coalition to a size that allows it to achieve its goals. Consider the power of the small political party, in coalition governments, that with its few seats, brings the not-quite-majority party to the necessary 50 percent to allow it to govern. In these political contexts, it is clear that this minority party can extract considerable resources for its alignment relative to the number of voters it might represent.

Securing coalition membership is not unique; it, too, is a negotiation. Consider the interests of potential members and what aspects of your coalition would make their alignment more attractive. Much like individual coalition members, after all, coalitions themselves have two forms of power: how attractive a coalition is to potential members and the coalition's ability to block competing coalitions. What makes a coalition attractive is its ability to control resources. Thus, think about how attractive coalition membership is to weaker parties; if they are members, they can rely on the stronger coalition partners to fight their battles.

Strategically, members of a coalition would do well to consider how competing coalitions can be blocked or which members of competing coalitions are most subject to defection. Because coalitions are often seen as transitory, less powerful members may be attracted to coalitions that have a history and a future, or to coalitions where stability among members is valued. As you consider new members, focus as well on ways to divide and conquer competing coalitions.

To make your coalition more attractive to new members, take advantage of potential relationships and create the perception of a future. Coalitions are often viewed as transitory relationships that dissipate once the decision or allocation is made.[28] This seems completely understandable if the basis for the coalition were simply issues. You resolve the dispute, allocate the resulting resources, and dissolve the coalition (and your obligations). However, if the coalition were formed not as the result of a transitory issue but as the result of a real or potential relationship and the commonality that these relationships imply, then the coalition might easily survive beyond the particular issue or when the challenge gets resolved.

SUMMARY

Negotiating in teams presents unique opportunities for value creation and value claiming—if for no other reason than that teams have more cognitive resources that can be directed towards these goals. To realize their team's potential, however, negotiators must also be sensitive to some unusual challenges, primarily because of the way in which individuals view themselves in the context of teams.

- Being a member of a team increases the perception and salience of similarity among members. Although this similarity often includes similar goals, individual members may be more dissimilar in their preferences and their priorities than their common group membership might reflect.
- Emphasizing similarity that is expected within a team may result in teams misperceiving the actual preferences and priorities of their members as they plan and prepare for a negotiation. This delusion of homogeneity may result in team members having to choose between submerging their own interests in service of the team or to stay true to their interests and surface the intrateam disagreement in the negotiation. Such disagreement may take the form of disputes among team members, implementing behaviors that openly or unintentionally sabotage the team's strategies, or aligning with counterparts in ways that diminish the ability of the team to achieve its goals.
- Team members are often motivated to agree with their team members in ways that do not extend to the interteam interactions. Having a team as a counterpart also often reinforces the adversarial notion of opposition in goals, values, priorities, and preferences. Rather than seeing a team counterpart as having interests that are both in opposition to and in concert with your interests, you are much more likely to see a team counterpart as a monolith with preferences that are in pure opposition to you.
- Having an exaggerated sense of commonality within your own team is as potentially destructive as expecting unfettered opposition. In both situations, proposals are not likely to reflect the parties' interests, and behaviors are likely to be viewed through a lens that interprets actions in their most adversarial light.
- Negotiations can take place between two sides of a table (interteam), but can also occur on one side of the table (intrateam). The latter scenario presents the possibility of coalitions. Coalitions offer parties the opportunity to combine to create value for themselves—often at the expense of the excluded parties. As such, the attractiveness of a coalition is based on its ability to secure the commitment of a minimum number of individuals necessary to achieve influence as well as its ability to block the formation of competing coalitions.

- Although the coalition is the mechanism for value creating, the members of the coalition must compete with one another to claim that value. As such, the order of membership can be critical. The member who is the difference between a winning and a losing coalition—the marginal member—is often able to extract dramatically more value than her commitment would command if she were the founder or a subsequent member (but not the marginal member that guaranteed influence).
- Negotiating within and between teams creates both considerable challenges and opportunities for the value creating that can enhance the eventual value claiming, both by the team and by the team's individual members. But beware! Failing to take into consideration the systematic challenges that negotiating in teams creates is a recipe for both individual and team-level value destruction.

Chapter Thirteen

AUCTIONS

Lots More than Two

Negotiations, as we've stated repeatedly, are a special form of exchange. In this chapter, we consider another form of exchange: the auction. An auction brings potential buyers and sellers together. For example, you can advertise an item for sale and negotiate with a potential buyer(s) who responds, or you can put that item up for auction (e.g., at eBay, or any other auction outlet). Thus, auctions are an alternative to negotiating a purchase or a sale. The difference between auctions and a for-sale listing is that auctions set a fixed transaction date, thereby increasing the competition among potential buyers or sellers. Another difference is that, contrary to a for-sale listing, auctions do not involve any direct interaction between the parties, which some may find attractive—particularly those who are uncomfortable with negotiations. But there are more issues to consider than just your level of comfort with negotiating.

In this chapter, you will learn when an auction is likely to offer advantages over a negotiation and when it does not. Understanding the potential benefits and limitations of auctions is important, especially as negotiators often have the choice of negotiating with a particular individual or engaging in an auction as a way to exchange resources.

Auctions have been around for centuries. For example, early Roman texts document the auction of war spoils, food, and household goods.[1]

To function properly, auctions require that items under consideration can either be fully described or inspected by prospective bidders. Think of an art auction catalogue that is distributed in advance with descriptions of the artwork and certification of their authenticity. In an auction of residential

AUCTIONS

Auctions are an alternative mechanism to negotiation for exchanging goods, services, or commodities. Auctions can be open bid or sealed bid. As discussed in this chapter, there are advantages and disadvantages to each type of auction.

The most common form of auction is the open ascending first-price (or English) auction, where buyers bid openly against one another (either in person, electronically, or through the facilitation of an auctioneer), with each subsequent bid higher than the previous bid. The highest bidder wins and pays the price she bids. In a variant, the second-price auction, the highest bidder wins but pays the value bid by the second highest bidder.

In a first-price sealed-bid auction all buyers simultaneously submit sealed bids so that no bidder knows the bid of any other participant.

In an open bid declining-price (or Dutch) auction, the auctioneer begins the auction with the high asking price and moves down until a buyer accepts the price.

real estate, you would have the opportunity to inspect a house before bidding. Participants' willingness to bid depends on the information about the item and the terms of sale (e.g., quantity, delivery terms, etc.) they have.

The behavior of bidders in auctions has been extensively studied by economists and psychologists. For example, auctions are likely to result in higher average selling prices than negotiations when the costs of disclosing information are the same for buyers and sellers, when critical information is known by both parties, when parties are risk neutral, and when there are no costs to enter an auction.[2] The basic reason for this effect is that auctions are an efficient mechanism to identify the counterpart with the most extreme reservation price—those sellers with the lowest reservation price when you are buying and those buyers with the highest reservation price when you are selling. Finding multiple counterparts strengthens your position, whether that interaction is a negotiation, an auction, or securing a date to the prom! In the case of an auction, the process is designed to attract as many interested parties—buyers or sellers—as possible and to get them to compete against one another.

And it works, sometimes even better than it should! Consider the behavior of bidders in one of the common auction opportunities: eBay. On this website, some goods are available to be purchased either through a buy-it-now price or by winning an auction. The availability of a buy-it-now (BIN) option offers an interesting insight into bidders' behavior in auctions. From a rational perspective the BIN price should represent the reservation prices for bidders. There is clearly no reason to pay more in an auction than you could pay for that same item on the same site by simply clicking the BIN button.

Yet, when researchers compared the auction prices to the BIN price for the same item on the same webpage, they found some pretty crazy behavior. In 42 percent of the auctions, the winning bid exceeded the BIN price. And the overbidding was considerable: 27 percent of bidders exceeded the BIN price by more than 8 percent, and 16 percent, by 16 percent. In fact, the average net overbidding was 10 percent over the BIN price of the item.[3]

To illustrate how crazy auction bidding can become, consider the case of the Chicago Cows. In 1999, the city of Chicago sponsored a public art event and auction (some live and some online) of life-sized fiberglass cows decorated by local artists. The famous auction house Sotheby's estimated that the cows would sell for $2000–$4000 each. To everyone's surprise, including the experts, the average winning bid for the online auctioned cows was 575 percent above Sotheby's estimate and for the live auction it was 788 percent above that estimate.[4]

One explanation for this behavior is the psychological process of competitive arousal—the desire to beat your competitive counterpart, even when it means exceeding your reservation price.[5] This competitive emotional state, which is stronger in live auctions than in online auctions where your competitors are typically not so salient, can lead to very expensive mistakes for bidders as they vie for corporate acquisitions, managerial talent, or even life-sized fiberglass cows.

There seems to be at least three drivers of this arousal: the presence of rivals, time pressure, and audience. In the case of rival bidders, people increase their willingness to bid more when there are more potential bidders, often violating their reservation prices in the process. From an economic perspective, this is exactly the wrong strategy. We will go into more details as to why when we discuss the winner's curse later in the chapter, but for now, consider the fallacy involved in such behavior: your reservation price is determined by your alternatives, and there is no rational reason to assume that it would be influenced by the number of rivals or your ability to identity them. When the bidding winds down to just a few individuals, having a few but salient number of rivals increases peoples' competitive arousal even further. Now you know exactly who it is you want to beat!

To avoid these effects, you need to be vigilant throughout the auction. Early on, large numbers of competing bidders are likely to encourage you to increase your reservation price. Late in the auction, the presence of a small number of rivals is likely to fuel your desire to win, resulting in your violating your reservation price and, as a result, getting less of what you want (of course, unless what you want is simply beating your rivals).[6]

A second factor in competitive arousal is time pressure. Deadlines, whether set by the auctioneer or by you, can narrow your willingness or perceived capacity to gather the necessary information you need to set your reservation price and map out your bidding behavior. There is often precious little time available between bids for you to assess the reasonableness of your next move. This pressure becomes stronger the closer you are to the (preset) end of the auction. If you have ever been involved in an online auction, you can sometimes physically experience the increased intensity of your emotional response as the seconds tick down to the end of the auction. The more the time pressure, the more aroused you become. The more aroused you become, the more likely you are to rely on past decision strategies that you have used—regardless of whether that strategy is appropriate in this particular situation.[7] Thus, when time pressure is highest as an auction comes to a close, you are again more likely to violate your reservation price to insure that you do not lose the item to a rival.

Competitive arousal also increases in the presence of an audience. When there is an audience, even if they are not directly observing you, research has found that your performance on well-learned tasks improves and your performance on novel tasks declines. This is called social facilitation.[8] So your competitive arousal would be higher at in-person auctions than at online auctions—just as was found in comparing the two auctions of the Chicago Cows. Knowing this effect, online auctions have often been designed to let you, the bidder, know how many people are following the auction. This is the virtual equivalent of creating an audience—and auction sites like it because it pushes you to keep raising your bid.

To control—or at least mitigate—excessive competitive arousal when you find yourself in an auction, consider these strategies:

- Redefine rivals as simply other parties who have similar interests and goals. This is not a war.
- Consider having an agent who is less emotionally invested than you serve as your bidder. Set clear parameters for the agent (or for yourself) in advance of the auction.

- Assess the appropriateness of your bidding strategy throughout the auction—if necessary by engaging a competent and trustworthy consultant—and stick to the strategy she outlines.
- Assess whether the time pressure you experience is because of a real deadline or an arbitrary one that you have set for yourself.
- Give serious consideration to whether you need to take this action now. Is it the case that there may be future opportunities and that the time between now and then may help you improve your preparation to insure a good deal?
- Rely on members of your team to help you diffuse the arousal that comes from being the one leading the charge.
- Throughout the auction, reaffirm the importance of your actual objective—getting more of what you want and reinforce what is a good deal for you.

WHY AUCTIONS?

What are the benefits that are unique to an auction? What advantages do auctions offer that negotiating may not? In addition to the psychological effects just discussed, the main reason to choose an auction is as a means to identify counterparts with the highest reservation price. Throughout the book we have assumed that you know with whom you are negotiating. But what if that were not the case? Reasonably, you want to identify the counterpart who has the most extreme reservation price. However, when considering potential counterparts one at a time, it is difficult to identify the one with the most extreme reservation price. After all, potential counterparts don't go around advertising their bottom lines! In effect, this is exactly what auctions do.

But let's explore exactly how this works. Assume for simplicity, that bidders (let's make them buyers) are disciplined and willing to pay up to their reservation price (this is an important assumption, and we will revisit the implications of this assumption later).[9] As a result, the winning bidder will be the buyer who has the highest reservation price: The auction process will automatically result in the buyers' bidding against each other until the point is reached where the buyers with lower reservation prices drop out, leaving only the bidder with the higher reservation price still bidding. Once the bidding has exceeded the reservation price of the second-to-last bidder, the bidding stops, and the winner is the bidder with the most extreme reservation price. Notice that this bidder does not have to bid her reservation price; rather, the winning bid will be just a bit more than the reservation price of the second-highest bidder.

In contrast, in the negotiation situation, because the counterparts' reservation prices are not common knowledge, you are unlikely to identify the one counterpart who has the most extreme reservation price. Thus, when negotiating the sale of an item, you might be able to push the buyer to his or her reservation price. However, you would have done even better if you had a buyer with a more favorable (to you) reservation price—an outcome for which auctions are specifically designed to achieve.

One way in which auctions also encourage parties to participate is that the auction process does not require the same level of preparation as a negotiation. You do not know who your counterpart will be in an auction on eBay, so there is little to be gained by considering the potential preferences or interests of someone who is not knowable to you. What preparation you will and should do is mostly related to the quality of the item you want to purchase or sell, your reservation price, the security of the payment process (e.g., PayPal). However, you don't have to derive a negotiation strategy, identify the types of issues, your counterparts' negotiation strategies, and the like.

But if auctions are so great, why have you spent the last twelve chapters learning how to negotiate? It turns out that there are some real limitations to auctions. First, auctions are not well suited for transactions with multiple issues; rather, auctions are most effective for single-issue exchanges such as price. When there is more than one issue to be considered, you still need to convert those multiple issues into a single metric. For example, you may receive multiple offers (bids) when listing your house, differing on multiple dimensions such as price, closing date, contingencies, and so forth. Thus, you still need to construct an issue-value matrix, as described in Chapter 5, that allows you to compare such diverse bids. However, such multi-issue situations complicate the auction process and make the auctions themselves more challenging. Under ideal conditions, auctions may be the most efficient means to claim value, but there is little opportunity to exchange information and, as a result, auctions are ill suited for exchanges with value creation potential. As a result, for transactions where such potential is present, you may be able to claim more through negotiations than through auctions.

Third, auctions are not well suited to situations in which the value of the item is determined by proprietary information. To be successful, auctions must provide information to potential bidders by providing detailed descriptions of the item, allowing inspections such as due-diligence in the acquisition of corporate assets. The purpose of such information is to re-duce bidders' fear of overbidding—referred to as the winner's curse (the subject of the next section). Disclosing such information is generally in the best interest of the seller—but not always.

Consider buying a corporation—let's say Coca Cola. To facilitate bid-ding, Coca Cola might consider giving potential buyers access to its trade secrets. If there were multiple potential bidders, Coca Cola's trade secrets would no longer be secret. Thus, while providing access to its trade secrets—its primary source of value—might give bidders a better picture of the value of the company, doing so would reduce the value of Coca Cola to the eventual winner (as now many know the trade secrets), thus reducing the amount that bidders would be willing to bid.

You don't have to have a trade secret for this to be true. When the amount of proprietary or private information is large enough, auctions lose their advantages over negotiations even when the auction is about price. Indeed, one study reports that 52 percent of companies were sold through negotia-tions and those that were contained the most proprietary information.[10]

The problem the auction creates because of the presence of multiple bid-ders is that simply winning the auction can itself be informative. It could be that the item is simply more valuable to the winner than it is to the other bidders. Of course, this is not a problem. However, it could be that the win-ner overvalued the item more than any of the other bidders and thus he was willing to bid more—and he "won"! And that is why he won. The auction reveals that he was the biggest fool in the room. This is the winner's curse.

THE WINNER'S CURSE

The winner's curse refers to a situation where, after winning an auction, the bidder realizes that the true value of the item is substantially more (if he were the seller) or less (if he were the buyer) than the amount bid.

To see how easy it is to experience the winner's curse, consider a situa-tion where the item at auction is pure common value; that is, the item has the same value to all buyers. Private-value items are goods or services that

have value unique to an individual buyer or seller. The winner's curse is a
condition that occurs in common-value auctions because the differences in
bidders' reservation prices are affected by errors in estimating the true,
but common, value. Thus, in a common value auction—when the item has
the same value to all bidders—the winner may, in fact, be the biggest fool.

In contrast, when items with private value are auctioned differences in
valuations among bidders reflect both estimation errors and differences in
the underlying private values. Therefore, the buyer with the highest estimate is not necessarily the buyer who makes the highest error in estimating the value of the item. She may simply value the unique aspects of the
item in a way that is different from other bidders. In such a scenario, the
winner's curse is mitigated, and bidders can bid closer to their reservation
prices—confident that winning the auction does not necessarily mean
that they have bid poorly.

To illustrate this point, let's consider an extreme example, the auction-
ing of a sealed envelope containing cash: a pure common-value item. Obviously, before placing your bid, you would like to know how much cash
there is in the envelope. Assume that the seller provides each of the potential bidders with the following information: each bidder receives an individual note from the seller reflecting an amount equal to the sum of the
true dollar value plus a random number drawn from a uniform distribution with a mean of zero and a range of −3 to +3.[11] So obviously the information provided to each bidder reflects the true amount of cash (since the
average value added is zero), but a random error.

Your note says $6.60. What you know for sure is that the envelope con-
tains between $3.60 and $9.60. What is the most you would bid—that is,
what is your reservation price? Is it $6.60?

If bidders were to set their reservation prices equal to what their respective information says the expected value of the item is, the winner would
be the one whose estimate had the most positive error. Thus, the winner of
the auction is most likely to be the person whose individual report had the
highest random number. In more day-to-day terms, the winner is likely to
be the person with the most optimistic assessment of the value of the item,
regardless of whether that item is an envelope, a piece of real estate, a company, or a fiberglass cow).

To avoid this problem, you should set your reservation price lower than
your information suggests it is. But by how much? Well, if you want to be
absolutely sure never to lose money, you could set your reservation price at

$3.60 (that is the expected value minus the maximum potential error contained in your information). Although this strategy will avoid losses, it also is unlikely that you will win the auction. So realistically you may want to set your reservation price somewhere between $3.60 and $6.60. But where? The mathematical computation is quite involved, but we can give you some intuition about how to think about this.

First, consider that you were to set it at $4.50. Would that number change if the number of potential bidders were different? In other words, if you were to set the reservation at $4.50 with 40 bidders, would you set it higher, lower or the same if there were 4,000 bidders? Intuitively, most would either set their reservation price the same or higher, as the number of bidders increases. As it turns out, that intuition is leading you astray. The correct answer is that you should set your reservation price *lower* as the number of bidders increases.

Consider what appears to be an unrelated question. Who is taller: the tallest Chinese male or the tallest Swiss male? Well, what do we know about the relative height of the average Swiss as compared to the average Chinese? As it turns out, the average Swiss male is 5'9" while the average Chinese male is 5'6". So, you might be tempted to choose the Swiss option to our question. But you would be wrong. Think about the population of Switzerland (about 7.6 million) compared to the population of China (about 1.3 billion). Now, we are not interested in the height of the average male but in the most extreme (i.e., tallest) male in each of these countries. If we sample 7.6 million times compared to sampling 1.3 billion times, in which would we be more likely to find the more extreme? Clearly, we would find the tallest male among the Chinese even though as a population, they are shorter. In fact, Yao Ming who plays basketball for the Houston Rockets is reported to be 7'5", and a man from the inner Mongolia region of China, is nearly 7'9" and has been confirmed by the *Guinness Book of World Records* as the tallest naturally growing person in the world.[12]

This analogy is useful for understanding the auction of the envelope containing cash because it shows that, in that scenario, the expected value of the error of the bidder receiving the highest feedback increases with the number of bidders. So if there are only 40 of you, it is unlikely that anybody got the +3.00. After all, there are only 40 possible draws on the random numbers between +3 and −3. However, if there were 4000 draws, the likelihood that somebody got a +3.00 is much higher, approaching certainty as the number of draws from the −3.00 to +3.00 distribution increases. Thus, to avoid this problem, you should reduce your reservation price as the number of potential bidders increases. Yet, in practice, bidders expect to have to pay more—and thus set their reservation prices higher—as the number of bidders increases. And, because of competitive arousal, they actually bid more if they know that there are many other bidders.

Note that the winner's curse is a problem no matter how relatively big or small the winning bid. Not only do people on eBay risk suffering from the winner's curse, so do CEOs of large corporations who acquire other companies. In a study of eighty-two mergers that occurred between 1985 and 2009 that had at least two concurrent bids, the performance of the eventual winners and the eventual losers was compared in the months and years prior to and after the acquisition. There was no difference in stock-market performance prior to acquisition; however, after the acquisition, those companies that did not win the acquisition clearly outperformed the companies that won the merger contest. The most likely explanation for this result is that the winners won by paying too much. They suffered the winner's curse, and their relatively lower stock price in subsequent months and years reflected their overpayment. In fact, over the next three years after the acquisition, losers outperformed winners by 50 percent.[13]

The existence of the winner's curse makes it critical for each party to consider the insight about the value of their bid if they were to win the auction. Each party should estimate the value of the item if they were to win. For example, buyers should estimate the value of the item if the sellers were to accept their offer; and the sellers should estimate the value of the item if the buyers were to accept theirs. Remember our earlier mention of the Groucho Marx remark: "I don't want to belong to any club that will accept people like me as a member." If a club were to accept him as a member, it obviously accepted all sorts of riff-raff, and who would want to belong to a club that had such low standards?

In addition to those economic effects, powerful psychological effects also contribute to the winner's curse. In Chapter 7, we discussed first offers. In general, we suggested that making an extreme first offer was a beneficial strategy. In contrast, in some situations—and auctions may clearly be one of those, it may be best to make a modest first offer.

While, on average, you gain a strategic advantage in making an extreme first offer, there are times when you can gain considerable strategic advantage by making a more modest initial offer. Probably the most common example of when you might want to make an offer that is perceived by your potential counterparts as reasonable—or even low—is when you are trying to start an auction.[14] A low asking price is likely to lure in more bidders, increasing the likelihood that bidders with the most extreme reservation prices will be in the auction.

This was a strategy that many real estate agents used during the height of the dotcom mania in Silicon Valley. The residential real estate market in Silicon Valley was very hot. There were lots of buyers and very little available inventory. So, one strategy might be to list the available houses at very aggressive levels. Certainly some agents and sellers followed this strategy. In contrast, a number of other agents and sellers offered their homes at what appeared to be relatively reasonable prices. The intent of these more reasonable listing prices was to induce many buyers to make an offer.

In addition to the artificially low asking price, it was also common practice for the seller to demand that buyers submit their bids in a relatively short time horizon. Sellers would often set a specific time and date when they would consider offers and make their decisions. As a potential buyer, you were under considerable pressure to get your offer to the seller by the deadline—and to make an offer that would attract the attention of the seller. Often that offer would include not only a bid that exceeded the seller's listing price but also such other inducements as offering the seller full-cash offers, stock options, automobiles, computers—anything that might make the bid unique and attractive to the seller. At the appointed time, some of the sellers would simply accept the most attractive offer while others would inform the buyers of where their bid stood and the numbers of bidders in contention. Then the sellers would invite the bidders to make another offer for a final round. Although some of the bidders might drop out after the first round, there were many others who improved their very generous initial offers. Those who stayed were either those with higher reservation prices, or those most affected by competitive arousal. Either way, this was good for the sellers.

While perhaps not consciously—or, more likely, with great intention—sellers were systematically lowering the barriers to entry for bidders by setting low listing prices.[15] Then, they took advantage of buyers' desire to finish what they started. That is, once a buyer made an initial bid, making the second bid was much easier. Also, given that the buyer had already indicated interest by making the first bid, a second bid seemed a much more reasonable strategy to justify the time and effort that had already been expended in making the first bid. This tendency was exacerbated by knowing that others were bidding for the same property. Not only did this arouse the buyers' competitive juices; it also reaffirmed that other people found the property attractive.

You are considering participating in an auction. What *should* you do? When should you avoid getting into an auction? You should avoid an auction when there are many bidders on your end of the deal, when there are multiple issues that you and your counterparts can value differently (a large integrative potential), or when your desire to win is extreme. On the other hand, when should you consider an auction? When there is only a single issue—particularly price; when there is little risk of disclosing information to potential bidders that will affect their assessment of the value of the item, when preparation time is extremely limited (allowing you to only focus on your reservation price), when there are a large number of parties on the other side, and when the identity of the ideal counterpart is unknown. In such scenarios, auctions can be extremely beneficial to you.

SUMMARY

Under specific conditions, auctions can get you more of what you want. First and foremost, you should consider auctions if you have a particularly strong aversion to negotiation, cannot identify counterparts that are likely to have a high reservation price (if you are the seller) or a low reservation price (if you are the buyer), or simply do not have the time to prepare adequately and go through the negotiation process. But still, auctions have their limitations.

- Auctions are very effective in negotiations when there is only a single issue such as price, the product or service is fairly standardized, or the product or service has broad appeal. In those circumstances, both the economics and the psychology of the auction process work to your favor: consider attracting multiple bidders with a low opening price (you can specify a reserve to mitigate the downside if too few bidders show up), set a reasonably tight deadline, and favor an open outcry auction process to maximize the psychological factors to maximize competitive arousal.

- Auctions are less well suited to situations that have a large (and complex) value-creation potential, and when the due diligence that bidders require involves proprietary information that if made broadly available would reduce the value of the object to the eventual winner. In those situations, negotiations are likely to get you more of what you want.
- When participating in an auction, beware of competitive arousal. Just as in any negotiation, set and respect your bidding limits. As a general rule, such limit should only be revised if you learn something that you could not have known when preparing for the auction.

CHAPTER FOURTEEN

BRINGING IT HOME

Making the Deal Real

How well am I doing? This is a question that is hard to answer with certainty, even at the end of any negotiation. You can never be sure of how much potential value there was in a negotiation, or how effective you were in claiming that value. (The obvious exception, of course, is for students in negotiation courses like ours. One of the benefits of such a course is the opportunity to know exactly how well you did in comparison not only to your counterpart but also to other negotiators who faced the same facts.)

But if you cannot attend one of our courses, there are two other ways in which you can improve the odds that you are creating and claiming as much value as you can: leverage your counterpart's subjective value of the negotiation, the deal, and you as well; also engage in a discussion of the settlement after the negotiation is over. The former sets up the future with your counterpart so as to improve your chances of getting more of what you want tomorrow. The latter allows you to engage them in a discussion of what you and they can do now to enhance the ultimate outcome.

LEVERAGING THE DEAL'S SUBJECTIVE VALUE

As you consider your negotiated outcome, think about how your counterpart's assessment of the subjective value he has created in this negotiation will likely influence his future behavior. The subjective value of a negotiated outcome has four dimensions: the instrumental value of the deal, including perceptions of how desirable and effective the negotiator was in getting what he wanted; how competent he felt as a negotiator and how satisfied he was with the way he behaved in the negotiation; how fairly he was treated in the negotiation process; and his assessment of the status of his relationship with you, including his willingness to work with you in the future.[1]

How your counterparts experience both the negotiation and their respective outcomes is important. They may not be able to be as precise as they would like in determining the objective value of the outcome to which they have agreed. Thus, they are likely to rely on how they feel about the negotiation process and outcome to assess how well they did. How satisfied are they with their performance? How proud are they of what they were able to achieve? Negotiators routinely use their feelings about the negotiation process as a surrogate for how successful they were. This is more likely to occur when the information to which they have access is imprecise or ambiguous.

Consider counterparts who are not as disciplined in their planning and preparation as you. Rather than rationally assessing their outcome, they are likely to judge it against their assessment of the subjective value that was created by the interaction. How successful they feel in subjective value has implications not only for their willingness to engage in future negotiations with you but also for your future value claiming. Having a better rapport in one negotiation is likely to increase a negotiator's willingness to share more information in a subsequent negotiation with the same counterpart.[2]

It turns out that negotiators' subjective assessment of the value that was created in their negotiation is only weakly correlated with the actual value that was created in that same interaction.[3] For this reason, creating in your counterpart a positive subjective assessment of the interaction can have clear economic benefits for you in subsequent negotiations. Not only does this positive halo extend from one negotiation to another with the same counterpart, it also generalizes across different negotiations. That is, the more your counterparts experience an increased sense of accomplishment and satisfaction when negotiating with you, the greater your reputation as a reasonable and fair negotiator.[4] For example, when subjective value was high on an initial job-offer negotiation, the satisfaction with the compensation and the job was also high (and intent to turnover, low) even one year later. In fact, negotiators' assessment of subjective value was a better predictor of job satisfaction one year later than was the actual economic value of the compensation that was negotiated.[5]

Based on this, it seems that a final consideration is how good your counterpart feels about the interaction. This is especially important when there is a future, and you want to leverage the rapport that you have created in the current negotiation to improve the quality of your outcomes in future negotiations. What you want to do is to get high levels of your objective value while providing your counterparts with high levels of their subjective value. Interestingly, this is a trade to which many of your counterparts will enthusiastically agree. Thus, to the extent you are strategic in identifying and leveraging intangible issues such as perceptions of control, fairness, and competency that may be highly important to your counterparts, you can increase their sense of the value of the deal, independent of the objective value that is available to be claimed.

So how is subjective value assessed? Think about how your counterpart might answer the following questions:[6]

- How satisfied are you with your outcome (the extent to which the terms of the agreement benefited you)?
- Did you feel as though you "lost" in this negotiation? Did this negotiation make you feel more or less competent as a negotiator?
- Did you behave according to your own principles and values? Was the negotiation process fair?
- Did your counterpart consider your wishes, opinions, or needs? Do you trust your counterpart?
- Did the negotiation build a good foundation for a future relationship with your counterpart?

These questions are some of the ones that your counterparts are probably asking themselves after the negotiation has ended. Keeping them in mind yourself will help you be more cognizant of the subjective value your counterpart is taking from the negotiation—and will also allow you to maximize that subjective value, thereby laying the foundation for positive interactions in the future.

THE POSTSETTLEMENT SETTLEMENT:
A SECOND BITE AT THE APPLE

In Chapter 6, we explored the strategic implications of sharing information, noting that sharing information can harm value claiming. Trading information can be dangerous, however; the trick is to create value while still enhancing your ability to claim value. Depending on the complexity of the negotiation, it may be difficult, if not almost impossible, to reliably know that you have settled on the best outcome; in economic terms, achieve the deal that is the best one possible for both parties. Economists refer to this as a Pareto-optimal deal.[7]

Consider what happens as the number of potential deals increases. For example, if there are two negotiators with independent preferences (the issues are not distributive in nature—there is an opportunity for value creation), three of ten potential settlements (or 30 percent) might be Pareto optimal. If there were 100 potential agreements, those three potential Pareto-optimal solutions would account for only 3 percent of the potential agreements. What if there were 1000 potential agreements of which only 3 (i.e., 0.3 percent) were Pareto optimal? Think how difficult it would be to try to identify those increasingly rare Pareto-superior deals when the negotiations are very complex.[8]

If your negotiations were only modestly complex, it would be worthwhile to explore potential replacements for a deal. A postsettlement settlement (PSS) is an alternate deal that can replace an original agreement, but only if both parties prefer the new agreement over their original one. In economic terms, a PSS is a Pareto-improving deal.[9]

Often a PSS requires facilitation by a neutral third party to guide the discussion. Using a third party is likely to be successful, especially if the negotiations between the parties were particularly contentious. As such, the parties may be hesitant to re-initiate face-to-face discussions. The negotiating parties could meet with the third party privately, conducting a careful analysis of each party's interests, preferences, and values. With a confidentiality agreement in place, the third party is in a unique position to ferret out information about the parties' positions that could open up new, more preferred options to their dispute. Identifying those options and presenting them to the disputing parties may reveal solutions that are better for both parties than their current deal.

At this late date in the book, you can assume that the original agreement of the parties is one that exceeded their respective alternatives. Although the parties may not have achieved their aspirations, the current deal now becomes their safety net. With the original settlement as their new alternative, they can now engage in a process with the third party to identify agreements that make them better off. If not, they simply revert to their original agreement.

Parties themselves may serve as the PSS facilitators. Although the claiming-creating balancing act during the original negotiation is challenging, the situation changes once the first agreement is reached. Because the value that a negotiator claimed in the original deal is now the new alternative and both parties have a future (at least as long as it takes to implement the terms of the negotiation), they may be more willing to share information. This increased willingness to share information may enhance the success of engaging in a PSS discussion as well as highlighting to the other side the goal of realizing and capturing additional value for both the parties.

If you and your counterpart were to consider a PSS process, the first step is to reflect on the information that was exchanged in the negotiation. Were there unrealized opportunities for you and your counterpart to improve your respective outcomes? Were there any changes to the deal that would make you better off—and either leave your counterpart's outcome unchanged or improve it? Perhaps you noticed that there was an issue that you and your counterpart valued differently, but had you acknowledged that difference in the primary negotiation, you might have not been able to claim as much value. Now that you have established a new standard (the current deal), trading off this issue for something that you value more may increase the amount of value that you can claim in the interaction.

However, this is not the time to opt for a full disclosure of information. If there was considerable disparity between the amount of value that you were able to claim and the value claimed by your counterpart, the PSS could lead to considerable tension since you and your counterpart would gain insight into who "won" and who "lost." The loser would then focus on ways to offset the loss. In fact, we once observed executives in one of our negotiation seminars walk away from a perfectly reasonable deal (one that substantially exceeded their alternatives and improved on their status quo) because they discovered that they had claimed less than their counterparts, which they perceived as defeat. They preferred an impasse to the loss (mostly the loss was of face). Nevertheless, a PSS process is a useful tool to have. In fact, you may want to consider appending a PSS process as a formal milestone in important negotiations. Once negotiators reach an initial agreement, they can be more open about their interests and preferences.

What each party values in the negotiation may become clearer to them or to their counterparts, thus enhancing more value creation and subsequent claiming during a PSS process.

If your negotiations were especially acrimonious, you might have to rely on a third party to orchestrate the PSS. In addition, the more parties there are at the table, the less likely there are to be deals that are Pareto-improving compared to the one to which the parties initially agreed. For successful PSS discussions, there needs to be a reasonable amount of goodwill between the parties. This is most likely when you and your counterparts have a future—when you and they are likely to meet again in negotiations. Not only does the future enhance the potential of PSS discussion, but having a future also makes it more likely that information will be shared. The leveraging of this potential is the topic of our next post-deal consideration.

NEGOTIATION POSTMORTEM

Even if you can't be sure about your overall performance in a negotiation, the quality of your planning can affect your assessment of how well you did—not to mention how pleased you are with the deal. From a rational perspective, all you'd have to do is compare your outcome with your aspirational level on issues to assess how well you did. The more value you claimed and the closer you were to your aspirations, the better the deal.

There are significant psychological hurdles that negotiators face when attempting to assess the deal to which they have just agreed. Negotiators would need to know how they felt about the deal and why, how they will feel in the future about it, and how they felt about similar deals in the past. Humans are particularly inept at remembering and responding to what they wanted in the past, assessing what they value in the present, or predicting what their future selves will want tomorrow.[10] Even with a well-developed and updated negotiation strategy, there is still that uncertainty: how well did you *really* do? What negotiators typically do in trying to assess their performance in a negotiation is interpret clues from the behavior of their counterparts. In his 1981 book *The Art and Science of Negotiation*, Howard Raiffa suggests that, after closing a merger for $7 million, you do not tell your counterpart that you would have done the deal for $4 million.

In other words, you should refrain from doing the dance of joy in public. It really does not matter if the just-agreed-to proposal is exactly what you wanted; doing the dance of joy in public is likely to result in significant negative consequences in future negotiations, and in fact may even jeopardize the deal that you believe you just closed. This is because most people view negotiation as the allocation of a fixed amount of resources, the myth of the fixed pie (see Chapter 5). If your counterparts subscribe to this myth, then seeing you so happy will convince them that they have done particularly poorly. At a minimum, you need to continue to manage your emotional expression, even after you have a deal. If you must dance for joy, resist the temptation to express your happiness until you are alone—or at least out of sight and hearing of your counterpart.

Using the behavior or the performance of the other party as a metric to figure out how well you did is not limited to the emotions displayed by the parties once they have reached an agreement. Think about how your assessment of your performance is affected by comparing what you got with what your counterpart got versus the outcomes you received and those of others who are in the same situation as you. These are just a few of the comparisons you could use to decide how well you did. Think back to our discussion in Chapter 2 of how your performance in the negotiation differs when you focus on your aspirations compared to when you focus on your alternatives. The particular reference point that you choose can influence not only an objective assessment of your performance (how much you claimed in the negotiation) but also the subjective assessment of your performance (how satisfied you are with your outcome). You might be very satisfied with a $100 discount on your new cell phone right up to the moment when you find that your friend got a $150 discount from the same carrier.[11]

Picking your comparisons, it turns out, has a big impact on how you evaluate a particular outcome. Imagine that you have reached an agreement with your counterpart. What is the impact of learning that you did better than your counterpart? You might think that knowing that you got more than your counterpart would increase your satisfaction with the outcome. Actually, research suggests that it does not really matter whether you did better or worse than your counterpart; both comparisons result in your being less satisfied with your performance than you would be if you had no comparative information.[12] Of course, getting more is better than getting less; ironically, however, discovering that you got more or less than your counterpart only reduces your satisfaction with your outcome.

In contrast, doing better than someone in your same position is different. If you are a seller, comparing your deal to that received by other sellers in the same market—well, now the comparison reflects the objective value; that is, doing better than this external comparison increases your satisfaction, while doing worse decreases your satisfaction.

You are most satisfied, it seems, when you take all rather than an equal or most of the available surplus in the negotiation. Learning how well or how poorly your counterpart did in the negotiation will make you feel worse about your performance because it shows you that your counterpart managed to claim at least some value that you did not. When your comparisons are others in your position but not a part of your negotiation, on the other hand, you are satisfied with simply taking more.

Perhaps feeling good is not your ultimate goal. For the serious negotiator, learning to adjust and improve your negotiation performance may be the primary motivation of your self-evaluation. Discovering the accuracy of your assessment of the interests, preferences, and priorities of your counterpart is an important component of that process. Although you may not be able to get the full picture, you may be able to do considerable reconnaissance once the deal is done.

Even once handshakes have been exchanged and contracts signed, after all, the negotiation is still not over; the deal must still be implemented. Having your counterpart feel good about the outcome and how that outcome was reached can have far-reaching implications for how the deal becomes a reality—and whether you have the opportunity to make similar deals in the future.

SUMMARY

For many negotiations, finding a deal is just one stop on a long journey. Having completed a negotiation, there are new opportunities for learning for future negotiations and surprising opportunities for additional value claiming in this negotiation. Even if you were not likely to interact with a particular counterpart in the future, how you bring a specific negotiation to a close can have both direct and indirect impact on the implementation of your agreement and on future negotiations with others who may have access to your bargaining history.

- One of the basic assumptions of this book is that you need to consider both the economic and psychological aspects of a negotiation. No clearer example of this exists than the distinction between objective and subjective valuation. Negotiators place considerable weight on how they feel about the negotiation process—how they were treated. Maximizing the subjective valuation of a deal and the intangibles associated with it— respect, legitimacy, control, and fairness—can go a long way to insure that your counterpart feels satisfaction with the negotiation process, the outcome, and with you. And these intangibles are likely to be outcomes that benefit your counterpart much more than they cost you to give.

- Consider conducting a postsettlement settlement conference with your counterpart. Once the deal is done, let that new deal serve as an alternative and see if you and your counterpart can identify solutions that you overlooked—solutions that might be as or more attractive than your current deal.

- Once the deal is done and the celebration is complete, set aside time to conduct a negotiation postmortem. This is an important, but often overlooked, opportunity to hone your negotiating skill. Assess your performance relative to your expectations. How well were you able to maintain a focus on your aspiration? Did you honor your reservation price? How accurate were you in judging the interests and preferences of your counterpart? Were there aspects of the interaction that you would do differently? Triaging your performance in this negotiation can help in identifying ways for you to adapt your planning process for future negotiations.

CONCLUSION

Before we leave, there are a couple of points that need to be emphasized. Getting (more of) what you want in business and in life requires focus. Many negotiators go boldly into a negotiation having neither mapped out a strategy nor developed a plan to accomplish their goals. Observing hundreds of individuals attempt to negotiate each year, we are struck by how many smart people act as if negotiation is simply improvisational theatre rather than an interdependent process that requires planning and preparation, making strategic choices, and maintaining discipline. Once they have been exposed to thinking systematically about how to negotiate, these same individuals embrace the discipline necessary to improve their negotiating outcomes. They now have the capacity to craft outcomes that get them more of what they want in their lives, and they have a basis for saying yes or for saying no to these potential deals and walking away.

Neither our journey nor yours is done, however. By integrating the insights from economics and psychology, we have learned how to be more effective in our own negotiations; and in writing this book, we have worked to translate these insights into practical advice that can make you a better negotiator. Consider what it is that you want more of . . . and what information you need and are willing to exchange. Most importantly, take to heart (and mind) our injunction to look ahead and reason back. Figure out the path that you need to take to get you where you want to be—and as you travel down that path, assess whether the strategies and tactics that you are using are moving you closer to your goal. If not, reassess and correct.

As you reassess, hold as your shining star the standard of economic rationality. Beware of and have a strategy to mitigate the multitude of psychological factors that are likely to systematically influence your actions. At the same time, realize that you can predict and influence the likely behavior of your counterpart such that you are able to get you more of what you want because of these same systematic effects.

There is no one best way to negotiate—but there are numerous bad ways to negotiate if you do not stay focused and disciplined.

Finally, if you seek them out, opportunities to negotiate—to get (more of) what you want—present themselves each day of your life. Actively search out these prospects to develop solutions to the problems of scarcity that you face. What is scarce can range from wealth to relations and reputation to time and autonomy in your life and work. Use the unique perspective and knowledge that you have to fashion proposals to the problems that you and your counterparts' face; outcomes that make you better off—ever mindful that negotiation is an interdependent process in which you cannot force an agreement but must fashion one that at least keeps your counterpart whole or makes them better off.

Now, get going on getting (more of) what you want in your life!

ACKNOWLEDGMENTS

Being an academic means embracing the concept of paying forward. No piece of research or idea, lecture, class, or book is written without the contributions of others who have broken the ground of the paths that we have chosen to take. Whether it is our mentors to whom we apprenticed, our colleagues, students, and coauthors who helped shape us over the years, or our universities that provided us with both haven and crucible for our ideas, we owe a debt that cannot—and perhaps should not—be repaid. What we can do is acknowledge our obligation and great good fortune.

Writing the book introduced us to members of another tribe—our agent, Giles Anderson; our editor, Alex Littlefield; and our publisher, Lara Heimert. Without their enthusiastic support, negotiating skills, editorial acumen, and sharp virtual editing pencils, who knows how many more decades this book would have taken.

Finally, to you—our readers; after all, you are the reason we sat down to write in the first place.

NOTES

PREFACE

1. All names and numbers have been modified not only to protect the privacy of our student and the confidentiality of the data we used but also for didactical reasons.

2. E. Tuncel, A. Mislin, S. Desebir, and R. Pinkley, "The Agreement Bias: Why Negotiators Prefer Bad Deals to No Deal at All" (working paper, Webster University, St. Louis, MO, 2013).

3. Many of our students ask us whether the doctor knew his patent would soon become worthless or whether this was sheer coincidence. They are somewhat disappointed when we tell them that we simply don't know (and we suspect our client was equally in the dark). But in the end, it is simply irrelevant for the point we are making whether the doctor did or did not know about the competing patent. The situation presented our student an opportunity to reassess, and doing so would have revealed the new patent and that buying the doctor's patent was not the right course of action.

CHAPTER ONE

1. Linda Babcock and Sara Laschever, *Women Don't Ask: Negotiation and the Gender Divide* (Princeton, NJ: Princeton University Press, 2003).

2. In 1970, American women were paid 59 cents for every dollar their male counterparts were paid; by 2010, the ratio was 77 cents to every dollar. A. Hegewisch, C. Williams, and A. Henderson, Institute for Women's Policy

Research Fact Sheet, The Gender Wage Gap 2010 (April 2011), http://www .iwpr.org/publications/pubs/the-gender-wage-gap-2010-updated-march -2011.

3. M. S. Schmidt, "Upon Further Review, Players Support Replay," *New York Times*, September 5, 2006, D2.

4. B. Shiv, H. Plassmann, A. Rangel, and J. O'Doherty, "Marketing Actions Can Modulate Neural Representations of Experienced Pleasantness," *Proceedings of the National Academy of Sciences* 104, no. 3 (2008): 1050–1054, http://www.pnas.org/content/105/3/1050.abstract.

5. Robert Rosenthal and Lenore Jacobson, *Pygmalion in the Classroom: Teacher Expectation and Pupils' Intellectual Development* (New York: Holt, Rinehart and Winston, 1968).

6. C. M. Steele and J. Aronson, "Stereotype Threat and the Intellectual Test Performance of African Americans," *Journal of Personality and Social Psychology* 69, no. 5 (1995): 797–811.

7. M. Shih, T. L. Pittinsky, and N. Ambady, "Stereotype Susceptibility: Identity Salience and Shifts in Quantitative Performance," *Psychological Science* 10 (1999): 81–84.

8. M. A. Belliveau, "Engendering Inequity? How Social Accounts Create Versus Merely Explain Unfavorable Pay Outcomes For Women," *Organizational Science* 23 (2012): 1154–1174.

9. H. B. Reilly, L. Babcock, and K. L. McGinn, "Constraints and Triggers: Situational Mechanisms of Gender in Negotiation," *Journal of Personality and Social Psychology* 89, no. 6 (2005): 951–965.

10. L. L. Kray, L. Thompson, and A. Galinsky, "Battle of the Sexes: Stereotype Confirmation and Reactance in Negotiations," *Journal of Personality and Social Psychology* 80, no. 6 (2001): 942–958; L. Kray, A. Galinksy, and L. Thompson, "Reversing the Gender Gap in Negotiation," *Organizational Behavior and Human Decision Process* 87 (2002): 386–410.

CHAPTER TWO

1. E. Tuncel, A. Mislin, S. Desebir, and R. Pinkley, "The Agreement Bias: Why Negotiators Prefer Bad Deals to No Deal at All" (working paper, Webster University, St. Louis, MO, 2013).

2. R. L. Pinkley, M. A. Neale, and R. J. Bennett, "The Impact of Alternatives to Settlement in Dyadic Negotiation," *Organizational Behavior and Human Decision Processes* 57, no. 1 (1994): 97–116.

3. M. W. Morris, R. P. Larrick, and S. K. Su, "Misperceiving Negotiation Counterparts: When Situationally Determined Bargaining Behaviors Are Attributed to Personality Traits," *Journal of Personality and Social Psychology* 77, no. 1 (1999): 52.

4. For a great example of this phenomenon, see chapter 1 in Daniel Ariely's book *Predictably Irrational: The Hidden Forces That Shape Our Decisions* (New York: HarperCollins, 2008).

5. Some may argue that there is uncertainty regarding one's reservation price. For example, what if the reservation price were $28 plus or minus $2? But all that this implies is the effective reservation price for the buyer is at most $30, not a penny more! We will continue the discussion of reservation prices in Chapter 3.

6. V. L. Huber and M. A. Neale, "Effects of Self-and Competitor Goals on Performance in an Interdependent Bargaining Task," *Journal of Applied Psychology* 72, no. 2 (1987): 197; V. L. Huber and M. A. Neale, "Effects of Cognitive Heuristics and Goals on Negotiator Performance and Subsequent Goal Setting," *Organizational Behavior and Human Decision Processes* 38, no. 3 (1986): 342–365.

7. R. L. Pinkley, M. A. Neale, and R. J. Bennett, "The Impact of Alternatives to Settlement in Dyadic Negotiation," *Organizational Behavior and Human Decision Processes* 57, no. 1 (1994): 97–116.

8. S. S. Wiltermuth and M. A. Neale, "Too Much Information: The Perils of Nondiagnostic Information in Negotiations," *Journal of Applied Psychology* 96, no. 1 (2011): 192.

9. A. Galinsky, T. Mussweiler, and V. Medvec, "Disconnecting Outcomes and Evaluations in Negotiation: The Role of Negotiator Focus," *Journal of Personality and Social Psychology* 83 (2002): 1131–1140.

CHAPTER THREE

1. D. G. Pruitt, *Negotiation Behavior* (New York: Academic Press, 1981).

2. At this point, we will act as if we have full information about the reservation prices of both parties, and that both parties know their individual reservation prices with certainty.

3. Of course, one of the parties could agree to a deal that violates their reservation price, allowing a deal to be struck.

4. E. Tuncel, A. Mislin, S. Desebir, and R. Pinkley, "The Agreement Bias: Why Negotiators Prefer Bad Deals to No Deal at All" (working paper, Webster University, St. Louis, MO, 2013).

CHAPTER FOUR

1. In economic terms, an action that makes at least one party better off without hurting the other party is referred to as weakly Pareto efficient. (A process that leaves both parties better off is referred to as strongly Pareto efficient.) The Italian economist Vilfredo Pareto (1848–1923) developed this concept to study economic efficiency and income distribution. You may have noticed that we have inserted the qualifier "has the benefit of potentially making at least one party better off without hurting the other." As we discuss in Chapter 6, the process of value creation can have a detrimental effect, leaving one party worse off than it would have been had less value been created.

2. S. Wiltermuth, L. Z. Tiedens, and M. A. Neale, "The Benefits of Dominance Complementarity in Negotiations," *Negotiations and Conflict Management Research* (in press).

3. Literarily, this assumption implies that Thomas would be indifferent between paying $160 if the tires were delivered in 45 days and $610 per tire ($160 + ($10 × 45)) if the tires were delivered instantly. We make this assumption for ease of exposition. In reality, Thomas's willingness to increase the price is likely to decrease as the delivery time is reduced, say $10 to reduce the time to delivery by one day, $8 for the next day, and so on. While such an assumption would be more realistic, it would only complicate what we are trying to establish for now without adding any additional insights.

4. D. M. Messick and C. G. McClintock, "Motivational Bases of Choice in Experimental Games," *Journal of Experimental Social Psychology* 4, no. 1, (1968): 1–25.

5. For more detail about this type of value-creating strategy, see M. H. Bazerman and J. J. Gillespie, "Betting on the Future: The Virtues of Contingent Contracts," *Harvard Business Review* (September–October 1999).

6. Of course, this is not the real name of the architectural firm!

CHAPTER FIVE

1. Jeffrey T. Polzer and Margaret A. Neale, "Constraints or Catalysts? Reexamining Goal Setting within the Context of Negotiation," *Human Performance* 8 (1995): 3–26.

2. G. Marks and N. Miller, "Ten Years of Research on the False-Consensus Effect: An Empirical and Theoretical Review," *Psychological Bulletin* 102, no. 1 (1987): 72.

3. J. Cao and K. W. Phillips, "Team Diversity and Information Acquisition: How Homogeneous Teams Set Themselves Up to Have Less Conflict" (working paper, Columbia Business School, 2013).

4. A. F. Stuhlmacher and A. E. Walters, "Gender Differences in Negotiation Outcome: A Meta-Analysis," *Personnel Psychology* 52, no. 3 (1999): 653–677; H. R. Bowles, L. Babcock, and K. L. McGinn, "Constraints and Triggers: Situational Mechanics of Gender in Negotiation," *Journal of Personality and Social Psychology* 89, no. 6 (2005): 951.

5. M. W. Morris, R. P. Larrick, and S. K. Su, "Misperceiving Negotiation Counterparts: When Situationally Determined Bargaining Behaviors Are Attributed to Personality Traits," *Journal of Personality and Social Psychology* 77, no. 1 (1999): 52.

6. The car dealer could attempt to get a higher price (distributive issue) for the upscale audio option (integrative issue), but there might be more value created if the upscale audio option was yoked to the financing rate (another integrative issue).

7. T. Wilson, D. Lisle, D. Kraft, and C. Wetzel, "Preferences as Expectations-Driven Inferences: Effects of Affective Expectations on Affective Experiences," *Journal of Personality and Social Psychology* 56 (1989): 519–530.

8. L. Lee, S. Frederick, and D. Ariely, "Try It, You'll Like It," *Psychological Science* 17 (2006): 1054–1058.

9. C. H. Tinsley, K. M. O'Connor, and B. A. Sullivan, "Tough Guys Finish Last: The Perils of a Distributive Reputation," *Organizational Behavior and Human Decision Processes* 88, no. 2 (2002): 621–642; M. A. Neale and A. R. Fragale, "Social Cognition, Attribution, and Perception in Negotiation: The Role of Uncertainty in Shaping Negotiation Processes and Outcomes," in *Negotiation Theory and Research*, ed. L. Thompson, 27–54 (New York: Psychology Press, 2006).

10. B. M. Staw, L. E. Sandelands, and J. E. Dutton, "Threat Rigidity Effects in Organizational Behavior: A Multilevel Analysis," *Administrative Science Quarterly* 26 (1981): 501–524; W. Ocasio, "The Enactment of Economic Adversity–A Reconciliation of Theories of Failure-Induced Change and Threat-Rigidity," *Research in Organizational Behavior: An Annual Series of Analytical Essays and Critical Reviews* 17 (1995): 287–331.

11. A. W. Kruglanski, "The Psychology of Being 'Right': The Problem of Accuracy in Social Perception and Cognition," *Psychological Bulletin* 106 (1989): 395–409.

12. A. W. Kruglanski and D. M. Webster, "Motivated Closing of the Mind: 'Seizing and freezing,' *Psychological Review* 103 (1996): 263–283; O. Mayseless

and A. W. Kruglanski, "What Makes You So Sure? Effects of Epistemic Motivations on Judgmental Confidence," *Organizational Behavior and Human Decision Processes* 39 (1987): 162–183; D. Webster and A. W. Kruglanski, "Individual Differences in Need for Cognitive Closure," *Journal of Personality and Social Psychology* 67 (1994): 1049–1062.

13. C. K. W. De Dreu, "Time Pressure and Closing of the Mind in Negotiation," *Organizational Behavior and Human Decision Processes* 91 (2003): 280–295.

14. S. Chaiken and Y. Trope, eds., *Dual-Process Theories in Social Psychology* (New York: Guilford Press, 1999).

15. J. S. Lerner and P. E. Tetlock, "Accounting for the Effects of Accountability," *Psychological Bulletin* 125 (1999): 255–275; P. E. Tetlock, "The Impact of Accountability on Judgment and Choice: Toward a Social Contingency Model," in *Advances in Experimental Social Psychology*, vol. 25, ed. L. Berkowitz, 331–376 (New York: Academic Press, 1992).

16. R. E. Petty and J. T. Cacioppo, "The Elaboration Likelihood Model of Persuasion," in *Advances in Experimental Social Psychology*, vol. 19, ed. L. Berkowitz, 123–205 (New York: Academic Press, 1986).

17. C. K. W. De Dreu, S. Koole, and W. Steinel, "Unfixing the Fixed-Pie: A Motivated Information Processing of Integrative Negotiation," *Journal of Personality and Social Psychology* 79 (2000): 975–987.

CHAPTER SIX

1. But even in this extreme case, research shows that dictators take the interests of their "subjects" at least partially into account. See, for example, T. N. Cason and V. L. Mui, "Social Influence in the Sequential Dictator Game," *Journal of Mathematical Psychology* 42, no. 2 (1998): 248–265; G. E. Bolton, E. Katok, and R. Zwick, "Dictator Game Giving: Rules of Fairness versus Acts of Kindness," *International Journal of Game Theory* 27, no. 2 (1998): 269–299.

2. One example of extending the rational approach to one which takes systematic irrationality into account can be found in Daniel Kahneman, *Thinking, Fast and Slow* (New York: Macmillan, 2011).

3. W. Güth and R. Tietz, "Ultimatum Bargaining Behavior: A Survey and Comparison of Experimental Results," *Journal of Economic Psychology* 11, no. 3 (1990): 417–449.

4. J. Henrich, "Does Culture Matter in Economic Behavior? Ultimatum Game Bargaining among the Machiguenga of the Peruvian Amazon," *American Economic Review*, 2000, 973–979; H. Oosterbeek, R. Sloof, and G. Van De

Kuilen, "Cultural Differences in Ultimatum Game Experiments: Evidence from a Meta-Analysis," *Experimental Economics* 7, no. 2 (2004): 171–188.

5. S. J. Solnick, "Gender Differences in the Ultimatum Game," *Economic Inquiry* 39, no. 2 (2001): 189–200.

6. S. B. Ball, M. H. Bazerman, and J. S. Carroll, "An Evaluation of Learning in the Bilateral Winner's Curse," *Organizational Behavior and Human Decision Processes* 48, no. 1 (1991): 1–22.

7. We often see such an affinity to the middle point between the two reservation prices—even though there is no reason why the middle point is any better or fairer than any other point between the two reservation prices. Even if you were to privilege the middle as more "fair," this would require that you know both reservation prices—an unlikely condition.

8. While such extreme differences in information are unusual (T knows for certain, while you only know the distribution), the result would be similar (although the mathematics would be much more complicated) as long as T has an informational advantage over you.

9. In fact, rational buyers will realize that no offer should be made in this case—the information asymmetry is simply too big to be offset by the 50% synergy. For example, if you were to offer $30, an accepted offer indicates that T has less than $30 worth of oil—or $15 on average. Adding a synergy of 50% leads to an expected loss of $7.50 if your $30 offer were accepted. Indeed, the expected synergies would have to be at least 100% for you to expect to at least break even on average.

10. Because you are indifferent between accepting or rejecting an offer at your reservation price, your counterpart is better off offering slightly more and "tipping" you over your reservation price.

11. Remember that in our example in Chapter 2, $30 was your reservation price for the theater ticket you were trying to purchase!

12. S. B. White and M. A. Neale, "The Role of Negotiator Aspirations and Settlement Expectancies in Bargaining Outcomes," *Organizational Behavior and Human Decision Processes* 57, no. 2 (1994): 303–317.

13. D. M. Messick and C. G. McClintock, "Motivational Bases of Choice in Experimental Games," *Journal of Experimental Social Psychology* 4, no. 1 (1968): 1–25.

CHAPTER SEVEN

1. For example, in Australia, residential real estate is typically not listed for sale as it is in the United States but auctioned off. Thus, sellers in Australia do

not make a "first offer." Rather, it is the prospective buyers who make first offers.

2. N. G. Miller and M. A. Sklarz, "Pricing Strategies and Residential Property Selling Prices," *Journal of Real Estate Research* 2, no. 1 (1987): 31–40.

3. P. Slovic and S. Lichtenstein, "Comparison of Bayesian and Regression Approaches to the Study of Information Processing in Judgment," *Organizational Behavior and Human Performance* 6, no. 6 (1971): 649–744.

4. A. Tversky and D. Kahneman, "Judgment under Uncertainty: Heuristics and Biases," *Science* 185 (1974): 1124–1131.

5. G. B. Northcraft and M. A. Neale, "Experts, Amateurs, and Real Estate: An Anchoring and Adjustment Perspective on Property Price Decisions," *Organizational Behavior and Human Decision Processes* 39 (1986): 228–241.

6. H. J. Einhorn and R. M. Hogarth, "Ambiguity and Uncertainty in Probabilistic Inference," *Psychological Review* 92 (1985): 433–461.

7. Adam D. Galinsky and Thomas Mussweiler, "First Offers as Anchors: The Role of Perspective-Taking and Negotiator Focus," *Journal of Personality and Social Psychology* 81, no. 4 (2001): 657; A. D. Galinsky, T. Mussweiler, and V. H. Medvec, "Disconnecting Outcomes and Evaluations: The Role of Negotiator Focus," *Journal of Personality and Social Psychology* 83 (2002): 1131–1140.

8. V. L. Huber and M. A. Neale, "Effects of Cognitive Heuristics and Goals on Negotiator Performance and Subsequent Goal Setting," *Organizational Behavior and Human Decision Processes* 38, no. 3 (1986): 342–365.

9. Galinsky and Musweiller, "First Offers as Anchors."

10. E. J. Langer, A. Blank, and B. Chanowitz, "The Mindlessness of Ostensibly Thoughtful Action: The Role of 'Placebic' Information in Interpersonal Interaction," *Journal of Personality and Social Psychology* 36, no. 6 (1978): 635; R. J. Bies and D. L. Shapiro, "Interactional Fairness Judgments: The Influence of Causal Accounts," *Social Justice Research* 1, no. 2 (1987): 199–218.

11. N. Epley and T. Gilovich, "Putting Adjustment Back in the Anchoring and Adjustment Heuristic: Differential Processing of Self-Generated and Experimenter-Provided Anchors," *Psychological Science* 12 (2001): 391–396. N. Epley and T. Gilovich, "When Effortful Thinking Influences Judgmental Anchoring: Differential Effects of Forewarning and Incentives on Self-Generated and Externally Provided Anchors," *Journal of Behavioral Decision Making* 18 (2005): 199–212; N. Epley and T. Gilovich, "The Anchoring-and-Adjustment Heuristic: Why the Adjustments Are Insufficient," *Psychological Science* 17 (2006): 311–318.

12. M. F. Mason, A. J. Lee, E. A. Wiley, and D. R. Ames, "Precise Offers Are Potent Anchors: Conciliatory Counteroffers and Attributions of Knowledge in Negotiations," *Journal of Experimental Social Psychology* 49, no. 4 (2013): 759–763; C. Janiszewski and Dan Uy, "Precision of the Anchor Influences the Amount of Adjustment," *Psychological Science* 19 (2008): 121–127.

13. A. D. Galinsky, V. Seiden, P. H. Kim, and V. H. Medvec, "The Dissatisfaction of Having Your First Offer Accepted: The Role of Counterfactual Thinking in Negotiations," Personality and Social Psychology Bulletin 28 (2002): 271–283.

14. U. Simonsohn and D. Ariely, "When Rational Sellers Face Nonrational Buyers: Evidence from Herding on eBay," *Management Science* 54, no. 9 (2008): 1624–1637.

CHAPTER EIGHT

1. C. K. W. De Dreu and T. L. Boles, "Share and Share Alike or Winner Take All? The Influence of Social Value Orientation upon Choice and Recall of Negotiation Heuristics," *Organizational Behavior and Human Decision Processes* 76 (1998): 253–276; G. A. van Kleef and C. K. W. De Dreu, "Social Value Orientation and Impression Formation: A Test of Two Competing Hypotheses about Information Search in Negotiation," *International Journal of Conflict Management* 13 (2002): 59–77.

2. J. R. Curhan, M. A. Neale, and L. Ross, "Dynamic Valuation: Preference Changes in the Context of a Face-to-Face Negotiation," *Journal of Experimental Social Psychology* 40 (2004): 142–151; I. Ma'oz, A. Ward, M. Katz, and L. Ross, "Reactive Devaluation of an 'Israeli' vs. 'Palestinian' Peace Proposal," *Journal of Conflict Resolution* 46 (2002): 515–546; L. Ross, "Reactive Devaluation in Negotiation and Conflict Resolution," in *Barriers to Conflict Resolution*, ed. K. Arrow, R. H. Mnookin, L. Ross, A. Tversky, and R. Wilson, 26–42 (New York: W. W. Norton, 1995); L. Ross and A. Ward, "Psychological Barriers to Dispute Resolution," in *Advances in Experimental Social Psychology*, vol. 27, ed. M. Zanna, 255–304 (San Diego, CA: Academic Press, 1995); Lee Ross and Constance Stillinger, "Barriers to Conflict Resolution," *Negotiation Journal* 8 (1991): 389–404.

3. S. Kwon and L. Weingart, "Unilateral Concession from the Other Party: Concession Behavior, Attributions and Negotiation Judgments," *Journal of Applied Psychology* 8 (2004): 263–278.

4. The U.S. tax code provides no taxes on the first $500,000 of capital gains on one's principal residence. That is, you owe no taxes if you bought

your principal residence of $1,000,000 and sold it for $1,500,000 or less. On the other hand, if you sold that principal residence for $1,600,000, your profit on the sale is $600,000 and, assuming a capital gains tax of 25 percent, you owe $25,000 since your profit in excess of $500,000 is $100,000.

5. D. G. Pruitt and J. Z. Rubin, *Social Conflict: Escalation, Stalemate, and Settlement* (New York: Random House, 1986).

6. O. Ben-Yoav and D. Pruitt, "Resistance to Yielding and the Expectation of Cooperative Future Interaction in Negotiation," *Journal of Experimental Social Psychology* 20 (1984): 323–353; O. Ben-Yoav and D. Pruitt, "Accountability to Constituents: A Two-Edged Sword," *Organizational Behavior and Human Decision Processes* 34 (1984): 282–295.

7. K. M. O'Connor, J. A. Arnold, and E. R. Burris, "Negotiators' Bargaining Histories and Their Effects on Future Negotiation Performance," *Journal of Applied Psychology* 90, no. 2 (2005): 350.

8. R. R. Vallacher and D. M. Wegner, "Levels of Personal Agency: Individual Variation in Action Identification," *Journal of Personality and Social Psychology* 57 (1989): 660–671.

9. C. H. Tinsley, K. M. O'Connor, and B. A. Sullivan, "Tough Guys Finish Last: The Perils of a Distributive Reputation," *Organizational Behavior and Human Decision Processes* 88 (2002): 621–642.

10. K. M. O'Connor and J. A. Arnold, "Distributive Spirals: Negotiation Impasses and the Moderating Effects of Disputant Self-Efficacy," *Organizational Behavior and Human Decision Processes* 84 (2001): 148–176.

11. K. M. O'Connor, J. A. Arnold, and E. R. Burris, "Negotiators' Bargaining Histories and Their Effects on Future Negotiation Performance," *Journal of Applied Psychology* 90 (2005): 350–362.

12. J. J. Halpern, "The Effect of Friendship on Personal Business Transactions," *Journal of Conflict Resolution* 38, no. 4 (1994): 647–664.

13. Ultimately, this paradox is at the center of George Akerlof's famous paper, see George A. Akerlof, "The Market for Lemons: Quality Uncertainty and the Market Mechanism," *Quarterly Journal of Economics,* 1970, 488–500.

14. T. L. Morton, "Intimacy and Reciprocity of Exchange: A Comparison of Spouses and Strangers," *Journal of Personality and Social Psychology* 36 (1978): 72–81.

15. K. L. Valley, M. A. Neale, and E. A. Mannix, "Friends, Lovers, Colleagues, Strangers: The Effects of Relationships on the Process and Outcome of Dyadic Negotiations," *Research on Negotiation in Organizations* 5 (1995): 65–94.

16. L. L. Thompson and T. DeHarpport, "Negotiation in Long-Term Relationships" (paper presented at the International Association for Conflict Management, Vancouver, Canada, 1990).

17. E. Amanatullah, M. Morris, and J. Curhan, "Negotiators Who Give Too Much: Unmitigated Communion, Relational Anxieties, and Economic Costs in Distributive and Integrative Bargaining," *Journal of Personality and Social Psychology* 95 (2008): 723–728; J. Curhan, M. Neale, L. Ross, and J. Rosencranz-Engelmann, "Relational Accommodation in Negotiation: Effects of Egalitarianism and Gender on Economic Efficiency and Relational Capital," *Organizational Behavior and Human Decision Processes* 107 (2008): 192–205.

18. J. B. White, "The Politeness Paradox: Getting the Terms You Want without Sacrificing the Relationship You Need" (paper presented at the annual meeting of the International Association for Conflict Management, Instanbul, July 2011).

19. E. Goffman, *The Presentation of Self in Everyday Life* (New York: Anchor Books, 1967).

20. J. R. Curhan, H. A. Elfenbein, and G. J. Kilduff, "Getting Off on the Right Foot: Subjective Value versus Economic Value in Predicting Longitudinal Job Outcomes from Job Offer Negotiations," *Journal of Applied Psychology* 94, no. 2 (2009): 524.

21. M. Davis, "Measuring Individual Differences in Empathy: Evidence for a Multidimensional Approach," *Journal of Personality and Social Psychology* 44 (1983): 113–126.

22. M. Neale and M. Bazerman, "The Role of Perspective Taking Ability in Negotiating under Different Forms of Arbitration," *Industrial and Labor Relations Review* 36 (1983): 378–388.

23. N. Epley and E. M. Caruso, "Egocentric Ethics," *Social Justice Research* 17, no. 2 (2004): 171–187.

24. A. Galinsky and T. Mussweiler, "First Offers as Anchors: The Role of Perspective Taking and Negotiator Focus," *Journal of Personality and Social Psychology* 81 (2001): 657–669; A. D. Galinsky, G. Ku, and C. S. Wang, "Perspective-Taking and Self–Other Overlap: Fostering Social Bonds and Facilitating Social Coordination," *Group Processes and Intergroup Relations* 8 (2005): 109–124.

25. A. Galinsky, W. Maddux, D. Gilin, and J. White, "Why It Pays to Get Inside the Head of Your Opponent," *Psychological Science* 19 (2008): 378–384.

CHAPTER NINE

1. A. Tversky and D. Kahneman, "The Framing of Decisions and the Psychology of Choice," *Science* 40 (1981): 453–463.

2. Example adapted from Avinash K. Dixit and Barry J. Nalebuff, *Thinking Strategically: The Competitive Edge in Business, Politics, and Everyday Life* (New York: W.W. Norton & Company, 1993).

3. M. J. Lerner, *The Belief in a Just World* (New York: Springer US, 1980), 9–30.

4. M. J. Lerner and D. T. Miller, "Just World Research and the Attribution Process: Looking Back and Ahead," *Psychological Bulletin* 85, no. 5 (1978): 1030.

5. On August 20, 2012, President Barack Obama is reported to have said: "We have been very clear to the Assad regime, but also to other players on the ground, that a red line for us is we start seeing a whole bunch of chemical weapons moving around or being utilized. That would change my calculus. That would change my equation." Statement to reporters at White House, http://www.washingtonpost.com/blogs/fact-checker/wp/2013/09/06 /president-obama-and-the-red-line-on-syrias-chemical-weapons/.

6. M. Sinaceur and M. A. Neale, "Not All Threats Are Created Equal: How Implicitness and Timing Affect the Effectiveness of Threats in Negotiations," *Group Decision and Negotiation* 14, no. 1 (2005): 63–85.

CHAPTER TEN

1. We are reminded of the Goethe's "Sorcerer's Apprentice," a poem written in 1797 which in summary suggests that "powerful spirits should only be called by the master himself."

2. G. I. Nierenberg, *The Art of Negotiating: Psychological Strategies for Gaining Advantageous Bargains* (Lyndhurst, NJ: Barnes & Noble Publishing, 1995), 46.

3. J. Gross, "Emotional Regulation in Adulthood: Timing Is Everything," *Current Directions in Psychological Science* 10 (2001): 214–219.

4. J. Gross, "Emotional Regulation: Affective, Cognitive and Social Consequences," *Psychophysiology* 39 (2003): 281–291.

5. E. A. Butler, B. Egloff, F. H. Wilhelm, N. C. Smith, and J. J. Gross, "The Social Consequences of Emotional Regulation," *Emotions* 3 (2003): 48–67.

6. R. B. Zajonc, "Feeling and Thinking: Preferences Need No Inferences," *American Psychologist* 35, no. 2 (1980): 151.

7. F. Strack, L. L. Martin, and S. Stepper, "Inhibiting and Facilitating Conditions of the Human Smile: A Nonobtrusive Test of the Facial Feedback Hypothesis," *Journal of Personality and Social Psychology* 54 (1998): 768.

8. A. M. Isen, K. A. Daubman, and G. P. Nowicki, "Positive Affect Facilitates Creative Problem Solving," *Journal of Personality and Social Psychology* 52, no. 6 (1987): 1122; B. L. Fredrickson, "The Role of Positive Emotions in Positive Psychology: The Broaden-and-Build Theory of Positive Emotions," *American Psychologist* 56, no. 3 (2001): 218; G. F. Loewenstein, L. Thompson, and M. H. Bazerman, "Social Utility and Decision Making in Interpersonal Contexts," *Journal of Personality and Social Psychology* 57, no. 3 (1989): 426; M. M. Pillutla and J. K. Murnighan, "Unfairness, Anger, and Spite: Emotional Rejections of Ultimatum Offers," *Organizational Behavior and Human Decision Processes* 68, no. 3 (1996): 208–224; K. G. Allred, J. S. Mallozzi, F. Matsui, and C. P. Raia, "The Influence of Anger and Compassion on Negotiation Performance," *Organizational Behavior and Human Decision Processes* 70, no. 3 (1997): 175–187.

9. G. V. Bodenhausen, G. P. Kramer, and K. Süsser, "Happiness and Stereotypic Thinking in Social Judgment," *Journal of Personality and Social Psychology* 66, no. 4 (1994): 621. See also H. Bless, G. L. Clore, N. Schwarz, V. Golisano, C. Rabe, and M. Wölk, "Mood and the Use of Scripts: Does a Happy Mood Really Lead to Mindlessness?" *Journal of Personality and Social Psychology* 71, no. 4 (1996): 665.

10. G. V. Bodenhausen, L. A. Sheppard, and G. P. Kramer, "Negative Affect and Social Judgment: The Differential Impact of Anger and Sadness," *European Journal of Social Psychology* 24, no. 1 (1994): 45–62.

11. J. P. Forgas, "Don't Worry, Be Sad! On the Cognitive, Motivational and Interpersonal Benefits of Negative Mood," *Current Directions in Psychological Science* 2, (2013): 225–232; L. Z. Tiedens and S. Linton, "Judgment under Emotional Certainty and Uncertainty: The Effects of Specific Emotions on Information Processing," *Journal of Personality and Social Psychology* 81, no. 6 (2001): 973.

12. L. Z. Tiedens and S. Linton, "Judgment under Emotional Certainty and Uncertainty: The Effects of Specific Emotions on Information Processing," *Journal of Personality and Social Psychology* 81, no. 6 (2001): 973.

13. J. S. Lerner and L. Z. Tiedens, "Portrait of the Angry Decision Maker: How Appraisal Tendencies Shape Anger's Influence on Cognition," *Journal of Behavioral Decision Making* 19, no. 2 (2006): 115–137.

14. J. S. Lerner and L. Z. Tiedens, "Portrait of the Angry Decision Maker: How Appraisal Tendencies Shape Anger's Influence on Cognition," *Journal of*

Behavioral Decision Making 19, no. 2 (2006): 115–137; J. S. Lerner and D. Keltner, "Fear, Anger, and Risk," *Journal of Personality and Social Psychology* 81, no. 1 (2001) 146; P. Shaver, J. Schwartz, D. Kirson, and C. O'Connor, "Emotion Knowledge: Further Exploration of a Prototype Approach," *Journal of Personality and Social Psychology* 52, no. 6 (1987): 1061.

15. J. S. Lerner and L. Z. Tiedens, "Portrait of the Angry Decision Maker: How Appraisal Tendencies Shape Anger's Influence on Cognition," *Journal of Behavioral Decision Making* 19, no. 2 (2006): 115–137.

16. P. J. Carnevale and A. M. Isen, "The Influence of Positive Affect and Visual Access on the Discovery of Integrative Solutions in Bilateral Negotiation," *Organizational Behavior and Human Decision Processes* 37, no. 1 (1986): 1–13.

17. N. R. Anderson and M. A. Neale, "All Fired Up but No One to Blame" (working paper, Stanford Psychology Department, Palo Alto, CA, 2006).

18. M. A. Neale, S. Wiltermuth, and C. Cargle, "Emotion and the Uncertainty Of Negotiation" (working paper, Stanford Graduate School of Business, Palo Alto, CA, 2009).

19. N. R. Anderson and M. A. Neale, "All Fired Up."

20. N. R. Anderson and M. A. Neale, "The Role of Emotions and Uncertainty in Negotiations" (working paper, Psychology Department, Stanford University, Palo Alto, CA, 2008).

21. E. J. Johnson and A. Tversky, "Representations of Perceptions of Risks," *Journal of Experimental Psychology: General* 113, no. 1 (1984): 55; A. M. Isen and B. Means, "The Influence of Positive Affect on Decision-Making Strategy," *Social Cognition* 2, no. 1 (1983): 18–31.

22. J. S. Lerner and L. Z. Tiedens, "Portrait of the Angry Decision Maker: How Appraisal Tendencies Shape Anger's Influence on Cognition," *Journal of Behavioral Decision Making* 19, no. 2 (2006): 115–137.

23. J. S. Lerner and D. Keltner, "Fear, Anger, and Risk," *Journal of Personality and Social Psychology* 81, no. 1 (2001): 146.

24. R. S. Adler, B. Rosen, and E. M. Silverstein, "Emotions in Negotiation: How to Manage Fear and Anger," *Negotiation Journal* 14, no. 2 (1998): 161–179; K. G. Allred, "Anger and Retaliation: Toward an Understanding of Impassioned Conflict in Organizations," *Research on Negotiation in Organizations* 7 (1999): 27–58; L. L. Thompson, *The Truth about Negotiations* (Upper Saddle River, NJ: Pearson Education, 2008).

25. J. P. Daly, "The Effects of Anger on Negotiations over Mergers and Acquisitions," *Negotiation Journal* 7, no. 1 (1991): 31–39.

26. P. J. Carnevale, "Positive Affect and Decision Frame in Negotiation," *Group Decision and Negotiation* 17, no. 1 (2008): 51–63.

27. S. G. Barsade, "The Ripple Effect: Emotional Contagion and Its Influence on Group Behavior," *Administrative Science Quarterly* 47, no. 4 (2002): 644–675; J. P. Forgas, "On Feeling Good and Getting Your Way: Mood Effects on Negotiator Cognition and Bargaining Strategies," *Journal of Personality and Social Psychology* 74, no. 3 (1998): 565; S. Lyubomirsky, L. King, and E. Diener, "The Benefits of Frequent Positive Affect: Does Happiness Lead to Success?" *Psychological Bulletin* 131, no. 6 (2005): 803.

28. M. Sinaceur and L. Z. Tiedens, "Get Mad and Get More than Even: The Benefits of Anger Expressions in Negotiations," *Journal of Experimental Social Psychology* 42 (2006): 314–322.

29. G. A. Van Kleef, C. K. W. De Dreu, and A. S. R. Manstead, "The Interpersonal Effects of Anger and Happiness in Negotiations," *Journal of Personality and Social Psychology* 86 (2004): 57–76.

30. M. Sinaceur, D. Vasiljevic, and M. Neale, "Surprise Expression in Group Decisions: When an Emotional Expression Affects the Quality of Group Members' Processing and Decision Accuracy" (working paper, INSEAD, Fountainbleau, France, 2014).

31. S. D. Pugh, "Service with a Smile: Emotional Contagion in the Service Encounter," *Academy of Management Journal* 44, no. 5 (2001): 1018–1027; S. Kopelman, A. S. Rosette, and L. Thompson, "The Three Faces of Eve: Strategic Displays of Positive, Negative, and Neutral Emotions in Negotiations," *Organizational Behavior and Human Decision Processes* 99, no. 1 (2006): 81–101.

CHAPTER ELEVEN

1. R. M. Emerson, "Power-Dependence Relations," *American Sociological Review* 27, (1962): 31–41.

2. D. Keltner, D. Gruenfeld, and C. Anderson, "Power, Approach and Inhibition," *Psychological Review* 10 (2003): 265–285.

3. J. C. Magee, A. D. Galinsky, and D. H. Gruenfeld, "Power, Propensity to Negotiate, and Moving First in Competitive Interactions," *Personality and Social Psychology Bulletin* 33, no. 2 (2007): 200–212.

4. B. Woodward, *State of Denial* (New York: Simon and Schuster, 2006).

5. D. H. Gruenfeld, M. E. Inesi, J. C. Magee, and A. D. Galinsky, "Power and the Objectification of Social Targets," *Journal of Personality and Social Psychology* 95, no. 1 (2008): 111.

6. E. A. Mannix and M. A. Neale, "Power Imbalance and the Pattern of Exchange in Dyadic Negotiation," *Group Decision and Negotiation* 2, no. 2 (1993): 119–133.

7. Just keep in mind as you read on that because something is simple to explain does not mean that it is easy to implement!

8. A. D. Galinsky, E. Chou, N. Halevy, and G. A. Van Kleef, "The Far Reaching Effects of Power: At the Individual, Dyadic, and Group Levels," in *Research on Managing Groups and Teams*, vol. 15: *Looking Back, Moving Forward*, ed. Margaret A. Neale and Elizabeth A. Mannix, 185–207 (Bringley, UK: Emerald Publishing, 2013).

9. P. Belmi and M. Neale, "Mirror, Mirror on the Wall, Who's the Fairest of Them All? Thinking That One Is Attractive Increases the Tendency to Support Inequality," *Organizational Behavior and Human Decision Processes* 124, no. 2 (2014): 133–149.

10. D. R. Carney, A. J. Cuddy, and A. J. Yap, "Power Posing Brief Nonverbal Displays Affect Neuroendocrine Levels and Risk Tolerance," *Psychological Science* 21, no. 10 (2010): 1363–1368. See also the TED talk by Amy Cuddy, www.ted.com/talks/amy_cuddy_your_body_language_shapes_who_you_are.html.

11. D. J. Kiesler, "The 1982 Interpersonal Circle: A Taxonomy for Complementarity in Human Transactions," *Psychological Review* 90, no. 3 (1983): 185; J. S. Wiggins, "A Psychological Taxonomy of Trait-Descriptive Terms: The Interpersonal Domain," *Journal of Personality and Social Psychology* 37, no. 3 (1979): 395; J. S. Wiggins, "Circumplex Models of Interpersonal Behavior in Clinical Psychology," in *Handbook of Research Methods in Clinical Psychology*, ed. P. S. Kendall and J. N. Butcher, 183–221 (New York: Wiley, 1982).

12. R. C. Carson, *Interaction Concepts of Personality* (Oxford, UK: Aldine, 1969); L. M. Horowitz, K. D. Locke, M. B. Morse, S. V. Waikar, D. C. Dryer, E. Tarnow, and J. Ghannam, "Self-Derogations and the Interpersonal Theory," *Journal of Personality and Social Psychology* 61, no. 1 (1991): 68; L. M. Horowitz, K. R. Wilson, B. Z. P. Turan, M. J. Constantino, and L. Henderson, "How Interpersonal Motives Clarify the Meaning of Interpersonal Behavior: A Revised Circumplex Model," *Personality and Social Psychology Review* 10 (2006): 67–86; D. J. Kiesler, "The 1982 Interpersonal Circle: A Taxonomy for Complementarity in Human Transactions," *Psychological Review* 90, no. 3 (1983): 185.

13. S. R. Blumberg and J. E. Hokanson, "The Effects of Another Person's Response Style on Interpersonal Behavior in Depression," *Journal of Abnormal Psychology* 92, no. 2 (1983): 196; L. M. Horowitz, K. R. Wilson, B. Z. P. Turan, M. J. Constantino, and L. Henderson, "How Interpersonal Motives Clarify the Meaning of Interpersonal Behavior: A Revised Circumplex Model," *Personality and Social Psychology Review* 10 (2006): 67–86; P. M. Markey, D. C. Funder, and D. J. Ozer, "Complementarity of Interper-

sonal Behaviors in Dyadic Interactions," *Personality and Social Psychology Bulletin* 29, no. 9 (2003): 1082–1090.

14. S. S. Wiltermuth, L. Z. Tiedens, and M. A. Neale, "The Benefits of Dominance Complementarity in Negotiations," *Negotiations and Conflict Management Research* (in press).

15. J. S. Carroll, M. H. Bazerman, and R. Maury, "Negotiator Cognitions: A Descriptive Approach to Negotiators' Understanding of Their Opponents," *Organizational Behavior and Human Decision Processes* 41, no. 3 (1988): 352–370; M. J. Prietula and L. R. Weingart, "Negotiation as Problem Solving," *Advances in Managerial Cognition and Organizational Information Processing* 5 (1994): 187–213.

16. L. Z. Tiedens, M. M. Unzueta, and M. J. Young, "An Unconscious Desire for Hierarchy? The Motivated Perception of Dominance Complementarity in Task Partners," *Journal of Personality and Social Psychology* 93, no. 3 (2007): 402.

17. S. D. Levitt, "Understanding Why Crime Fell in the 1990s: Four Factors That Explain the Decline and Six That Do Not," *Journal of Economic Perspectives* 18, no. 1 (2004): 163–190.

18. J. A. Hall, E. J. Coats, and L. S. LeBeau, "Nonverbal Behavior and the Vertical Dimension of Social Relations: A Meta-Analysis," *Psychological Bulletin* 131, no. 6 (2005): 898.

19. For a review, see T. L. Chartrand, W. W. Maddux, and J. L. Lakin, "Beyond the Perception-Behavior Link: The Ubiquitous Utility and Motivational Moderators of Nonconscious Mimicry," in *The New Unconscious* ed. R. R. Hassin, J. S. Uleman, and J. A. Bargh, 334–361 (New York: Oxford University Press, 2005).

20. F. J. Bernieri, "Coordinated Movement and Rapport in Teacher-Student Interactions," *Journal of Nonverbal Behavior* 12, no. 2 (1988): 120–138; see also M. LaFrance, "Nonverbal Synchrony and Rapport: Analysis by the Cross-Lag Panel Technique," *Social Psychology Quarterly* 42 (1979): 66–70; M. LaFrance, "Posture Mirroring and Rapport," in *Interaction Rhythms: Periodicity in Communicative Behavior,* ed. M. Davis, 279–298 (New York: Human Sciences Press, 1982).

21. R. B. Van Baaren, R. W. Holland, B. Steenaert, and A. van Knippenberg, "Mimicry for Money: Behavioral Consequences of Imitation," *Journal of Experimental Social Psychology* 39, no. 4 (2003): 393–398.

22. R. B. Van Baaren, R. W. Holland, K. Kawakami, and A. Van Knippenberg, "Mimicry and Prosocial Behavior," *Psychological Science* 15, no. 1 (2004): 71–74.

23. J. L. Lakin and T. L. Chartrand, "Using Nonconscious Behavioral Mimicry to Create Affiliation and Rapport," *Psychological Science* 14, no. 4 (2003): 334–339; R. B. van Baaren, W. W. Maddux, T. L. Chartrand, C. de Bouter, and A. van Knippenberg, "It Takes Two to Mimic: Behavioral Consequences of Self-Construals," *Journal of Personality and Social Psychology* 84, no. 5 (2003): 1093; T. L. Chartrand and J. A. Bargh, "The Chameleon Effect: The Perception–Behavior Link and Social Interaction," *Journal of Personality and Social Psychology* 76, no. 6 (1999): 893; C. M. Cheng and T. L. Chartrand, "Self-Monitoring without Awareness: Using Mimicry as a Nonconscious Affiliation Strategy," *Journal of Personality and Social Psychology* 85, no. 6 (2003): 1170.

24. N. Yee, J. N. Bailenson, M. Urbanek, F. Chang, and D. Merget, "The Unbearable Likeness of Being Digital: The Persistence of Nonverbal Social Norms in Online Virtual Environments," *CyberPsychology and Behavior* 10, no. 1 (2007): 115–121; J. Blascovich, J. Loomis, A. C. Beall, K. R. Swinth, C. L. Hoyt, and J. N. Bailenson, "Immersive Virtual Environment Technology as a Methodological Tool for Social Psychology," *Psychological Inquiry* 13, no. 2 (2002): 103–124.

25. W. Maddux, E. Mullen, and A. Galinksy, "Chameleons Bake Bigger Pies and Take Bigger Pieces: Strategic Behavioral Mimicry Facilitates Negotiation Outcomes," *Journal of Experimental Social Psychology* 44 (2008): 461–468.

26. S. S. Wiltermuth and M. A. Neale, "Master of the Universe versus the Chameleon: Comparing the Effects of Complementarity and Mimicry in Negotiation Behavior" (working paper, Stanford Graduate School of Business, Stanford, CA, 2008).

27. T. L. Chartrand, W. W. Maddux, and J. L. Lakin, "Beyond the Perception-Behavior Link: The Ubiquitous Utility and Motivational Moderators of Nonconscious Mimicry," in *Unintended Thought 2: The New Unconscious,* ed. R. Hassin, J. Uleman, and J. A. Bargh, 334–361 (New York: Oxford University Press, 2005).

28. M. LaFrance, "Nonverbal Synchrony and Rapport: Analysis by the Cross-Lag Panel Technique," *Social Psychology Quarterly* 42 (1979): 66–70.

29. Maddux, Mullen, and Galinksy, "Chameleons Bake Bigger Pies."

30. J. S. Lerner and L. Z. Tiedens, "Portrait of the Angry Decision Maker: How Appraisal Tendencies Shape Anger's Influence on Cognition," *Journal of Behavioral Decision Making* 19, no. 2 (2006): 115–137; N. H. Frijda, P. Kuipers, and E. Ter Schure, "Relations among Emotion, Appraisal, and Emotional Action Readiness," *Journal of Personality and Social Psychology* 57, no. 2 (1989): 212.

31. Remember our early discussion of the BAS (behavioral approach system) and the BIS (behavioral inhibition system). Clearly this approach perspective (the BAS) is the one most often found in individuals experiencing power or a powerful mindset. Eddie Harmon-Jones, "Clarifying the Emotive Functions of Asymmetrical Frontal Cortical Activity," *Psychophysiology* 40, no. 6 (2003): 838–848; E. Harmon-Jones and J. Segilman, "State Anger and Prefrontal Brain Activity: Evidence That Insult-Related Relative Left-Prefrontal Activation Is Associated with Experienced Anger and Aggression," *Journal of Personality and Social Psychology* 80 (2001): 797–803.

32. J. S. Lerner and D. Keltner, "Beyond Valence: Toward a Model of Emotion-Specific Influences on Judgment and Choice," *Cognition and Emotion* 14, no. 4 (2000): 473–493.

33. J. S. Lerner and D. Keltner, "Fear, Anger, and Risk," *Journal of Personality and Social Psychology* 81, no. 1 (2001): 146.

34. G. V. Bodenhausen, L. A. Sheppard, and G. P. Kramer, "Negative Affect and Social Judgment: The Differential Impact of Anger and Sadness," *European Journal of Social Psychology* 24, no. 1 (1994): 45–62; J. S. Lerner, J. H. Goldberg, and P. E. Tetlock, "Sober Second Thought: The Effects of Accountability, Anger, and Authoritarianism on Attributions of Responsibility," *Personality and Social Psychology Bulletin* 24, no. 6 (1998): 563–574; D. A. Small and J. S. Lerner, "Emotional Politics: Personal Sadness and Anger Shape Public Welfare Preferences" (paper presented at the Society for Personality and Social Psychology, New Orleans, 2005); L. Z. Tiedens, "Anger and Advancement versus Sadness and Subjugation: The Effect of Negative Emotion Expressions on Social Status Conferral," *Journal of Personality and Social Psychology* 80, no. 1 (2001): 86; L. Z. Tiedens and S. Linton, "Judgment under Emotional Certainty and Uncertainty: The Effects of Specific Emotions on Information Processing," *Journal of Personality and Social Psychology* 81, no. 6 (2001): 973.

35. A. W. Siegman and T. W. Smith, eds., *Anger, Hostility, and the Heart* (London: Psychology Press, 2013).

36. A. R. Fragale, "The Power of Powerless Speech: The Effects of Speech Style and Task Interdependence on Status Conferral," *Organizational Behavior and Human Decision Processes* 101, no. 2 (2006): 243–261.

37. V. L. Brescoll and E. L. Uhlmann, "Can an Angry Woman Get Ahead? Status Conferral, Gender, and Expression of Emotion in the Workplace," *Psychological Science* 19, no. 3 (2008): 268–275.

38. J. R. Overbeck, M. A. Neale, and C. L. Govan, "I Feel, Therefore You Act: Intrapersonal and Interpersonal Effects of Emotion on Negotiation as a

Function of Social Power," *Organizational Behavior and Human Decision Processes* 112, no. 2 (2010): 126–139.

CHAPTER TWELVE

1. Harris Sondak, Margaret A. Neale, and Elizabeth A. Mannix, "Managing Uncertainty in Multiparty Negotiations," in *Handbook on Negotiation*, ed. W. Adair and M. Olekalns, 283–310 (North Hampton, MA: Edward Elgar, 2013).

2. T. Wildschut, B. Pinter, J. L. Vevea, C. A. Insko, and J. Schopler, "Beyond the Group Mind: A Quantitative Review of the Interindividual Intergroup Discontinuity Effect," *Psychological Bulletin* 129 (2003): 698–722.

3. For a review, see Elizabeth A. Mannix and Margaret A. Neale, "What Differences Make a Difference? The Promise and Reality of Diverse Teams in Organizations," *Psychological Science in the Public Interest* 6 (2005): 31–55.

4. J. C. Turner, "The Analysis of Social Influence," in *Rediscovering the Social Group: A Self-Categorization Theory*, ed. J. C. Turner, M. A. Hogg, P. J. Oakes, S. D. Reicher, and M. S. Wetherell, 68–88 (Oxford: Blackwell, 1987); V. L. Allen and D. A. Wilder, "Group Categorization and Attribution of Belief Similarity," *Small Group Behavior* 10 (1979): 73–80.

5. I. Janis, *Groupthink: Psychological Studies of Policy Decisions and Fiascoes* (New York: Houghton-Mifflin, 1982).

6. K. W. Phillips, G. Northcraft, and M. Neale, "Surface-Level Diversity and Information Sharing: When Does Deep-Level Similarity Help?" *Group Processes and Intergroup Relations* 9 (2006): 467–482.

7. K. W. Phillips, "The Effects of Categorically Based Expectations on Minority Influence: The Importance of Congruence," *Society for Personality and Social Psychology* 29 (2003): 3–13; K. W. Phillips and D. L. Loyd, "When Surface and Deep Level Diversity Meet: The Effects of Dissenting Group Members," *Organizational Behavior and Human Decision Processes* 99 (2006): 143–160.

8. K. Y. Phillips and E. Apfelbaum, "Delusions of Homogeneity: Reinterpreting the Effects of Group Diversity, in *Research on Managing Groups and Teams*, vol. 16: *Looking Back, Moving Forward*, ed. M. A. Neale and E. A. Mannix, 185–207 (Bringley, UK: Emerald, 2012).

9. K. W. Phillips and D. L. Loyd, "When Surface and Deep Level Diversity Meet: The Effects of Dissenting Group Members," *Organizational Behavior and Human Decision Processes* 99 (2006): 143–160.

10. D. L. Loyd, C. S. Wang, K. W. Phillips, and R. L. Lount, "Social Category Diversity Promotes Pre-Meeting Elaboration: The Role of Relationship Focus," *Organization Science* (in press).

11. J. Cao and K. W. Phillips, "Team Diversity and Information Acquisition: How Homogeneous Teams Set Themselves Up to Have Less Conflict" (working paper, Columbia Business School, 2013).

12. N. Halevey, "Team Negotiation: Social, Epistemic, Economic, and Psychological Consequences of Subgroup Conflict," *Personality and Social Psychology Bulletin* 34 (2008): 1687–1702.

13. G. Borenstein, "Intergroup Conflict: Individual, Group, and Collective Interests," *Personality and Social Psychology Review* 7 (2003): 129–145.

14. M. B. Brewer, "In-Group Bias in the Minimal Intergroup Situation: A Cognitive-Motivational Analysis," *Psychological Bulletin* 86 (1979): 307–324.

15. H. R. Tajifel, R. Billig, C. Bundy, and C. Flament, "Social Categorization and Intergroup Behavior," *European Journal of Social Psychology* 1 (1971): 149–178; J. C. Turner, "The Experimental Social Psychology of Intergroup Behavior," in *Intergroup Behavior*, ed. J. C. Turner and H. Giles, 66–101 (Chicago: University of Chicago Press, 1981).

16. R. M. Kramer, "Intergroup Relations and Organizational Dilemmas: The Role of the Categorization Process," *Research in Organizational Behavior* 13 (1991): 191–228.

17. T. Wildschut, B. Pinter, J. L. Vevea, C. A. Insko, and J. Schopler, "Beyond the Group Mind: A Quantitative Review of the Interindividual Intergroup Discontinuity Effect," *Psychological Bulletin* 129 (2003): 698–722; B. Pinter, C. A. Insko, T. Wildschut, J. L. Kirchner, R. M. Montoya, and S. T. Wolf, "Reduction of Interindividual–Intergroup Discontinuity: The Role of Leader Accountability and Proneness to Guilt," *Journal of Personality and Social Psychology* 93 (2007): 250–265.

18. A. D. Galinsky, V. L. Seiden, P. H. Kim, and V. H. Medvec, "The Dissatisfaction of Having Your First Offer Accepted: The Role of Counterfactual Thinking in Negotiations," *Personality and Social Psychology Bulletin* 28, no. 2 (2002): 271–283.

19. S. Page, *The Difference* (Princeton, NJ: Princeton University Press, 2007); E. A. Mannix and M. A. Neale, "What Differences Make a Difference? The Promise and Reality of Diverse Teams in Organizations," *Psychological Science in the Public Interest* 6 (2005): 31–55.

20. J. P. Polzer, "Intergroup Negotiations: The Effect of Negotiating Teams," *Journal of Conflict Resolution* 40 (1996): 678–698.

21. R. Walton and R. McKersie, *A Behavioral Theory of Labor Negotiations* (New York: McGraw Hill, 1964).

22. R. Stout, J. Cannon-Bowers, E. Salas, and D. Milanovich, "Planning, Shared Mental Models, and Coordinated Performance: An Empirical Link Is Established," *Human Factors* 41 (1999): 61–71.

23. K. J. Behfar, R. S. Peterson, E. A. Mannix, and W. M. Trochim, "The Critical Role of Conflict Resolution in Teams: A Close Look at the Links between Conflict Type, Conflict Management Strategies, and Team Outcomes," *Journal of Applied Psychology* 93, no. 1 (2008): 170; J. M. Brett, R. Friedman, and K. Behfar, "How to Manage Your Negotiating Team," *Harvard Business Review* 87, no. 9 (2009): 105–109.

24. J. K. Murnighan, "Organizational Coalitions: Structural Contingencies and the Formation Process," *Research on Negotiation in Organizations* 1 (1986): 155–173; J. T. Polzer, E. A. Mannix, and M. A. Neale, "Interest Alignment and Coalitions in Multiparty Negotiation," *Academy of Management Journal* 41 (1998): 42–54.

25. J. K. Murnighan and D. Brass, "Intraorganizational Coalitions," in *Research in Negotiating in Organizations*, ed. R. Lewicki, B. Sheppard, and M. Bazerman, 283–306 (Greenwich, CT: JAI Press, 1991).

26. M. Watkins and S. Rosegrant, "Sources of Power in Coalition Building," *Negotiation Journal* 12 (1996): 47–68.

27. J. T. Polzer, E. A. Mannix, and M. A. Neale, "Interest Alignment and Coalitions in Multiparty Negotiation," *Academy of Management Journal* 41 (1998): 42–54.

28. J. K. Murnighan and D. Brass, "Intraorganizational Coalitions," in *Research in Negotiating in Organizations*, ed. R. Lewicki, B. Sheppard, and M. Bazerman, 283–306 (Greenwich, CT: JAI Press, 1991).

CHAPTER THIRTEEN

1. In the second century BC, Cato the Elder (*De Agri Cultura*, 2:7) recommends agricultural auctions for the harvest and for tools and, in *Orationum Reliquae* (53:303, Tusculum), for household goods. Plutarch (*Vitae Parallelae*, Poplikos 9:10) mentions auctions of prisoners of war in the sixth century BC.

2. J. Bulow and P. Klemperer, "Auctions vs. Negotiations" (NBER Working Paper No. w4608, National Bureau of Economic Research, 1994).

3. U. Malmendier and Y. H. Lee, "The Bidder's Curse," *American Economic Review* 101, no. 2 (2011): 749–787.

4. G. Ku, D. Malhotra, and J. K. Murnighan, "Towards a Competitive Arousal Model of Decision-Making: A Study of Auction Fever in Live and Internet Auctions," *Organizational Behavior and Human Decision Processes* 96, no. 2 (2005): 89–103.

5. D. Malhotra, G. Ku, and J. K. Murnighan, "When Winning Is Everything," *Harvard Business Review* 86, no. 5 (2008): 78.

6. G. Ku, D. Malhotra, and J. K. Murnighan, "Towards a Competitive Arousal Model of Decision-Making: A Study of Auction Fever in Live and Internet Auctions," *Organizational Behavior and Human Decision Processes* 96, no. 2 (2005): 89–103.

7. L. Ordonez and L. Benson III, "Decisions under Time Pressure: How Time Constraint Affects Risky Decision Making," *Organizational Behavior and Human Decision Processes* 71, no. 2 (1997): 121–140.

8. R. B. Zajonc, *Social Facilitation* (Ann Arbor, MI: Research Center for Group Dynamics, Institute for Social Research, University of Michigan: 1965); H. R. Markus, "The Effect of Mere Presence on Social Facilitation: An Unobtrusive Task," *Journal of Experimental Social Psychology* 14 (1978): 389–397.

9. Typically, we associate auctions in the form of one seller and multiple buyers. While this may be more common, there are examples of one buyer and multiple seller auctions. Governmental procurement processes often involve such a process. Recently General Motors announced that it was liquidating its internal parts suppliers and would, going forward, rely on an auction-like process for procuring its automobile parts. In contrast, exchanges (e.g., the New York Stock Exchange) bring together multiple potential buyers and multiple potential sellers.

10. Rafael Rogo, "Strategic Information and Selling Mechanism" (PhD diss., Kellogg School of Management, Northwestern University, Evanston, IL, 2009).

11. A distribution where all outcomes are equally likely is called a uniform distribution.

12. C. Glenday, ed., *Guinness World Records 2013* (New York: Random House LLC, 2013).

13. U. Malmendier, E. Moretti, and F. S. Peters, "Winning by Losing: Evidence on the Long-Run Effects of Mergers" (NBER Working Paper No. w18024, National Bureau of Economic Research, 2012).

14. G. Ku, A. D. Galinsky, and J. K. Murnighan, "Starting Low but Ending High: A Reversal of the Anchoring Effect in Auctions," *Journal of Personality and Social Psychology* 90, no. 6 (2006): 975.

15. R. Simonsohn and D. Ariely, "When Rational Sellers Face Non-Rational Consumers: Evidence from Herding on eBay" (working paper, Fuqua School of Management, Duke University, 2007).

CHAPTER FOURTEEN

1. J. R. Curhan, H. A. Elfenbein, and G. J. Kilduff, "Getting Off on the Right Foot: Subjective Value Versus Economic Value in Predicting Longitudinal Job Outcomes from Job Offer Negotiations," *Journal of Applied Psychology* 94, no. 2 (2009): 524–534.

2. A. L. Drolet and M. W. Morris, "Rapport in Conflict Resolution: Accounting for How Face-to-Face Contact Fosters Mutual Cooperation in Mixed-Motive Conflicts," *Journal of Experimental Social Psychology* 36, no. 1 (2000): 26–50.

3. J. R. Curhan, H. A. Elfenbein, and H. Xu, "What Do People Value When They Negotiate? Mapping the Domain of Subjective Value in Negotiation," *Journal of Personality and Social Psychology* 91 (2006): 493.

4. C. H. Tinsley, K. M. O'Connor, and B. A. Sullivan, "Tough Guys Finish Last: The Perils of a Distributive Relationship," *Organizational Behavior and Human Decision Processes* 88 (2002): 621.

5. J. R. Curhan, H. A. Elfenbein, and G. J. Kilduff, "Getting Off on the Right Foot: Subjective Value versus Economic Value in Predicting Longitudinal Job Outcomes from Job Offer Negotiations," *Journal of Applied Psychology* 94, no. 2 (2009): 524–534.

6. J. R. Curhan and H. A. Elfenbein, "What Do People Want When They Negotiate?" *The Subjective Value Inventory,* 2008, www.subjectivevalue .com.

7. As a reminder, a Pareto-optimal agreement is one that dominates all other potential agreements. There is no other settlement that all the negotiators would prefer over the one chosen.

8. B. O'Neil, "The Number of Outcomes in the Pareto-Optimal Set of Discrete Bargaining Games, *Mathematics of Operations Research* 6 (1981): 571.

9. H. Raiffa, "Post-Settlement Settlements," *Negotiation Journal* 1 (1985): 9.

10. S. Frederick, G. Loewenstein, and T. O'Donoghue, "Time Discounting and Time Preference: A Critical Review," *Journal of Economic Literature* 40 (2002): 351–401; G. Loewenstein, D. Read, and R. F. Baumeister, eds., *Time and Decision: Economic and Psychological Perspectives of Intertemporal Choice* (New York: Russell Sage Foundation, 2003); H. Movious and T. Wilson, "How We Feel about the Deal," *Negotiation Journal,* April 2011, 241–250.

11. D. Kahenman, "Reference Points, Anchors, Norms, and Mixed Feelings," *Organizational Behavior and Human Decision Processes* 51 (1992): 296–312.

12. N. Novemsky and M. Schweitzer, "What Makes Negotiators Happy? The Differential Effects of Internal and External Social Comparisons on Negotiator Satisfaction," *Organizational Behavior and Human Decision Processes* 95 (2004): 186–197.

INDEX